Forces of Labor

Recasting labor studies in a long-term and global framework, the book draws on a major new database on world labor unrest to show how local labor movements have been related to world-scale political, economic, and social processes since the late nineteenth century. Through an in-depth empirical analysis of select global industries, the book demonstrates how the main locations of labor unrest have shifted from country to country together with shifts in the geographical location of production. It shows how the main sites of labor unrest have shifted over time together with the rise or decline of new leading sectors of capitalist development and demonstrates that labor movements have been deeply embedded (as both cause and effect) in world political dynamics. Over the history of the modern labor movement, the book isolates what is truly novel about the contemporary global crisis of labor movements. Arguing against the view that this is a terminal crisis, the book concludes by exploring the likely forms that emergent labor movements will take in the twenty-first century.

Beverly J. Silver is Professor of Sociology at the Johns Hopkins University. She is coauthor (with Giovanni Arrighi) of *Chaos and Governance in the Modern World System* (1999). She has twice won the Distinguished Publication Award from the PEWS section of the American Sociological Association.

Advance Praise for *Forces of Labor*

"Beverly Silver's empirically rich and powerfully argued book provides the kind of historical and class analysis that has been so badly lacking in the globalization literature. Bravo!"

– Leo Panitch, York University

"By broadening the geography for understanding labor struggles, Silver shows us that these are going strong in many parts of the world even as they have weakened and fizzled in the North Atlantic. A great contribution to contemporary debates about the politics of contestation."

– Saskia Sassen , The University of Chicago

"Beverly Silver's new book is a challenge to political economists and economic sociologists and even to those historians who still care about capitalism's trajectories. Avoiding the deceptive poles of both 'race to the bottom' pessimism and liberal optimism, availing herself of both an immense database and of deep historical knowledge, Silver traces the recurring rises and declines of the world labor movement along two dimensions of capital mobility: its spatial displacement and its shift to new product lines – both in response to labor militancy. Sweeping and detailed, ponderous but readable, comparative and historical, this book takes the political economy of world systems to a new level."

– Sidney Tarrow, Cornell University

Cambridge Studies in Comparative Politics

General Editor

Margaret Levi *University of Washington, Seattle*

Assistant General Editor

Stephen Hanson *University of Washington, Seattle*

Associate Editors

Robert H. Bates *Harvard University*
Peter Hall *Harvard University*
Peter Lange *Duke University*
Helen Milner *Columbia University*
Frances Rosenbluth *Yale University*
Susan Stokes *University of Chicago*
Sidney Tarrow *Cornell University*

Other Books in the Series

Continued after index at back of book

Forces of Labor

WORKERS' MOVEMENTS AND GLOBALIZATION SINCE 1870

BEVERLY J. SILVER

The Johns Hopkins University

CAMBRIDGE
UNIVERSITY PRESS

CAMBRIDGE UNIVERSITY PRESS
Cambridge, New York, Melbourne, Madrid, Cape Town, Singapore, São Paulo

Cambridge University Press
40 West 20th Street, New York, NY 10011-4211, USA

www.cambridge.org
Information on this title: www.cambridge.org/9780521817516

First published 2003
Reprinted 2005

Printed in the United States of America

A catalog record for this publication is available from the British Library.

Library of Congress Cataloging in Publication Data

Silver, Beverly J.
Forces of labor : workers' movements and globalization since 1870 / Beverly J. Silver.
    p.   cm. – (Cambridge studies in comparative politics)
Includes bibliographical references and index.
ISBN 0-521-81751-X – ISBN 0-521-52077-0 (pbk.)
1. Labor movement – History.   2. Labor disputes – History.   3. Capitalism – History.
4. Globalization – Economic aspects – History.   5. Business relocation – History.
6. Manufacturing processes – History.   7. Automobile industry workers – History.
8. Textile workers – History.   I. Title.   II. Series.
HD4851 .S55   2003   2002031361

ISBN-13   978-0-521-81751-6 hardback
ISBN-10   0-521-81751-X hardback

ISBN-13   978-0-521-52077-5 paperback
ISBN-10   0-521-52077-0 paperback

To RS & RS

Contents

Polanyi - backlash resistance
         reactionary against capital from above
Marx - new class forming from /against historical
       capital forces

Figures

Tables

Preface and Acknowledgments

The origins of this book can be traced back to a conference paper presented almost twenty years ago with Giovanni Arrighi at the Seventh Political Economy of the World-System conference organized by Charles Bergquist at Duke University. The paper, entitled "Labor Movements and Capital Mobility: the United States and Western Europe in World-Historical Perspective," was a first attempt at understanding how outcomes for different national labor movements are linked to each other by world-economic processes, especially the transnational relocation of capital. Over the years, this first seed grew, fused with other seeds, and developed into the present book. Ongoing exchanges with Giovanni Arrighi over this entire time period have left an indelible mark on the final product, and I therefore start by acknowledging my intellectual debt to him.

Another debt is owed to the members of the World Labor Research Group – a group of faculty and graduate students who met regularly at the Fernand Braudel Center at Binghamton University in the 1980s. Apart from myself, the members of the research group were Giovanni Arrighi, Mark Beittel, John Casparis, Jamie Faricellia Dangler, Melvyn Dubofsky, Roberto Patricio Korzeniewicz, Donald Quataert, and Mark Selden. It was in the course of discussions within this group that it became clear that the serious study of labor movements from a global and historical perspective would require new types of data that were simply not available in existing compilations. In 1986 the group plunged into a massive data collection project, initiating the World Labor Group (WLG) database, on which this book stands.

It soon became clear that the creation of this database would require an enormous effort and that it risked never being completed. In order to be able to devote more time to the project, I abandoned the dissertation I had been working on and switched to a dissertation linked to the creation and analysis of the WLG database. It was in this context that Terence K. Hopkins (1928–1997), chair of my dissertation committee, left his profound imprint on what would eventually become this book. I also wish to thank Immanuel Wallerstein, another member of my dissertation committee, for his advice and support throughout this project.

Shortly after my arrival at Johns Hopkins University, I set up a small research group with three graduate students – Bruce Podobnik, Mahua Sarkar, and Nettie Legters. We met regularly in 1993 and, at the end of that year, presented the results of our work at the Social Science History Association meeting. I had come to believe that one of the most fruitful ways of proceeding with the project would be through a comparative analysis of global industries. It was in the context of discussions and research with this group that I took the first steps toward working out the comparative formulations that eventually became Chapter 3.

This comparative global industry research was partially supported by a grant from the sociology program of the National Science Foundation in 1993. This grant, together with a 1989 grant from the World Society Foundation (Zurich), provided important spurts of material and moral support at crucial moments in the project.

During the past ten years at Johns Hopkins, numerous graduate and undergraduate students have worked with me on the project in a variety of capacities that included helping to update and expand the WLG database. Sincere thanks are due to them all, along with my sincere apologies for not being able to acknowledge here by name each individual.

In the 1990s, I plunged into another major research project, which constituted both a significant detour from the road leading toward the speedy completion of this book, as well as an opportunity to think more deeply about the relationship between social unrest and the dynamics of world politics. The project originated in a Research Working Group at the Fernand Braudel Center on comparative world hegemonies and culminated in the book *Chaos and Governance in the Modern World System* (Minnesota 1999). This detour has, I hope, strengthened the analysis of the relationship among labor movements, war, and world politics in the present book.

I am grateful for the detailed comments, suggestions, and support that I received from numerous individuals who read the manuscript in the spring and summer of 2001: Giovanni Arrighi, John Markoff, Ravi Palat, Leo Panitch, Saskia Sassen, Alvin So, Sidney Tarrow, and Po-Keung Hui. I am also grateful for helpful comments received from the graduate students in the spring 2001 seminar on Comparative and World-Historical Sociology at Johns Hopkins University. In response to this feedback, I was able to clarify and develop (and I think significantly improve) the argument at various points in the book. I would also like to thank David Harvey, who suggested the title for the book.

The time span covered by the book is from the late-nineteenth century to the present. Any author who writes a book that deals with the present is faced with a strong temptation to continuously chase after the latest headlines. The first complete draft of the manuscript was finished in March 2001; that is, before September 11, 2001. The book went into production in the spring of 2002; that is, before the major wave of dockworker labor unrest on the West Coast of the United States in the fall of 2002. After September 11, I added a paragraph to Chapter 1 and a footnote to Chapter 5. Yet, while I will likely write more about the relationship between the dynamics of labor unrest and the "war on terrorism" in some other context, September 11 and its aftermath have served to underscore one of the central arguments of this book – that is, the trajectory of workers' movements is deeply embedded in the dynamics of war and world politics. Likewise, whereas it would be worthwhile to spend some energy on an analysis of the recent conflict on the docks, this event nevertheless has served to underscore another central argument of the book – that is, transportation workers have had, and continue to have, a strategic position within the world capitalist economy and within the world labor movement. No doubt, before this book is in print and read, fresh headlines will provide new temptations to further develop the arguments in this book; but hopefully they will also provide confirmation of the utility of the conceptual frameworks laid out herein for understanding the present and future of labor movements.

This book is dedicated to my parents – Robert and Rose Silver – who always believed that it would turn out well.

1

Introduction

I. Crisis of Labor Movements and Labor Studies

During the last two decades of the twentieth century, there was an almost complete consensus in the social science literature that labor movements were in a general and severe crisis. Declining strike activity and other overt expressions of labor militancy (Screpanti 1987; Shalev 1992), falling union densities (Western 1995; Griffin, McCammon, and Botsko 1990) and shrinking real wages and growing job insecurity (Bluestone and Harrison 1982; Uchitelle and Kleinfeld 1996) were among the trends documented. The bulk of the empirical literature focused on trends in wealthy countries (especially North America and Western Europe), yet many saw the crisis as world-scale, adversely affecting labor and labor movements around the globe.

This sense that labor movements are facing a general and severe crisis contributed to a crisis in the once vibrant field of labor studies. As William Sewell (1993: 15) noted: "Because the organized working class seems less and less likely to perform the liberating role assigned to it in both revolutionary and reformist discourses about labor, the study of working class history has lost some of its urgency" (see also Berlanstein 1993: 5).

For many, this double crisis of labor studies and labor movements is long term and structural – intimately tied to the momentous transformations that have characterized the last decades of the twentieth century going under the general rubric of "globalization." For some, the crisis is not just severe, it is *terminal*. Aristide Zolberg, for one, argued that late-twentieth-century transformations have brought about the virtual disappearance of "the distinctive social formation we term 'working class.'" With "post-industrial society," the "workers to whose struggles we owe the 'rights of labor' are

1

rapidly disappearing and today constitute a residual endangered species"
(1995: 28). Similarly, Manuel Castells argued that the dawn of the "Information Age" has transformed state sovereignty and the experience of work
in ways that undermine the labor movement's ability to act as "a major source
of social cohesion and workers' representation." It also has undermined any
possibility that workers might become emancipatory "subjects" in the future – the source of a new "project identity" aimed at rebuilding the social institutions of civil society. Non-class-based identity movements, for Castells,
are the only "potential subjects of the Information Age" (1997: 354, 360).

Nevertheless, beginning in the late 1990s, a growing number of observers
were suggesting that labor movements were on the upsurge, most visible
as a mounting popular backlash against the dislocations being provoked by
contemporary globalization. Among the events indicating a backlash was
the massive French general strike against austerity in 1995 – what *Le Monde*
rather Eurocentrically referred to as "the first revolt against globalization"[1]
(quoted in Krishnan 1996: 4). By the time of the World Trade Organization meeting in Seattle in November 1999, the force of the backlash was
sufficient to derail the launch of another round of trade liberalization and
to be front-page news around the world. Commentators began to suggest
that the Seattle demonstrations together with the new activist (organizing)
stance of the AFL-CIO (American Federation of Labor and Congress of
Industrial Organizations) were signs that a revitalized U.S. labor movement
was "rising out of the ashes" of the old (Woods et al. 1998; more broadly,
Panitch 2000). Inspired by the new activism, social scientists in the United
States, where the obituary of labor movements and labor studies had been
written most insistently, showed a resurgent interest in labor movements.
New journals were founded that sought to actively engage academics with
the labor movement (e.g., *Working USA*), large academic conferences on
the new labor movement were organized, and a new section of the American
Sociological Association on labor movements was founded in 2000.

For some, the new activism (while still scattered and weak) was potentially the first sign of an impending major earthquake of mass labor insurgency. For others, it was likely to remain too weak and scattered to affect
the much more powerful, disorganizing forces of globalization.

---

[1] Indeed, for those whose field of vision extended beyond the wealthy countries of the North,
an "unprecedented international wave of [mass] protests" against International Monetary
Fund (IMF)-imposed austerity politics could already be seen throughout the developing
world in the 1980s (Walton and Ragin 1990: 876–7, 888).

II. The Present and Future of Labor

Which of these divergent expectations about the future of labor movements is more plausible? This book starts from the premise that in order to answer this question adequately we need to recast labor studies in a longer historical and wider geographical frame of analysis than is normally done. Assessments about the future of labor movements are based – explicitly or implicitly – on a judgment about the historical novelty of the contemporary world. Those who see a terminal crisis of labor movements tend to see the contemporary era as one that is *fundamentally new and unprecedented*, in which global economic processes have completely reshaped the working class and the terrain on which labor movements must operate. In contrast, those who expect the reemergence of significant labor movements tend to perceive historical capitalism itself as being characterized by recurrent dynamics, including the continual re-creation of contradictions and conflict between labor and capital. This suggests that forecasts about the future of labor movements should be based on a comparison between contemporary dynamics and analogous past periods. For only through such a comparison can we distinguish historically recurrent phenomena from phenomena that are truly new and unprecedented.

Parts III and IV of this chapter lay out the theoretical, conceptual, and methodological issues raised by studying labor unrest as a world-historical phenomenon. But before moving on, the next section delves into some of the contemporary debates about the present and future of labor movements that underlay our study of the past. The first debate is around the question of whether contemporary processes of globalization have led to an unambiguous and unprecedented structural weakening of labor and labor movements on a world scale, bringing about a straightforward "race to the bottom" in wages and working conditions. The second debate is around the question of whether globalization is creating objective conditions favorable for the emergence of strong labor internationalism. The next section outlines these debates in turn.

II. Debates about the Present and Future of Labor and Labor Movements

A "Race to the Bottom"?

A common explanation of the crisis of labor movements is that the hypermobility of productive capital in the late twentieth century has created a single labor market in which all the world's workers are forced to

3

compete. By moving (or just threatening to move) production "halfway around the world," claimed Jay Mazur (2000: 89), multinational corporations have brought the competitive pressure of an "enormous mass of unorganized workers" to bear on "the international labor movement." As a result, labor's bargaining power has been weakened and a "race to the bottom" in wages and working conditions has been unleashed on a world scale (see also Bronfrenbrenner 1996; Brecher 1994/1995; Chossudovsky 1997; Godfrey 1986: 29; Fröbel, Heinrich, and Kreye 1980; Ross and Trachte 1990; Western 1995).

For others, the most important effect of the hypermobility of capital on labor movements is not so much its direct impact on workers, but its indirect impact. In this view, the hypermobility of capital has weakened de facto state sovereignty. And as states become incapable of effectively controlling flows of capital, their capacity to protect their citizens' livelihoods and other workers' rights, including the welfare state and substantive democracy, also declines (Tilly 1995; Castells 1997: 252–4, 354–5). States that insist on maintaining expensive social compacts with their citizens, including their working classes, risk being abandoned en masse by investors scouring the world for the highest possible returns. From this perspective, the most consequential aspect of the "race to the bottom" takes the form of pressure on states to repeal social welfare provisions and other fetters on profit maximization within their borders. The rocky debut of the new European currency (the Euro) has been taken as one example of this process, with European countries being "punished" for failing to dismantle social protection schemes at a sufficiently rapid pace to suit a hypermobile capital.

The pressures that can be brought to bear are even stronger in the South where more direct levers are available through debt rescheduling. The irony of the late-twentieth-century wave of global democratization, as John Markoff noted, is that while it brought formal democracy to a greater number of countries than ever before, the actual value of universal suffrage – historically a key demand of labor movements – is also more questionable than ever. Formally democratic states are forced to make key economic and social policy decisions with "an eye as much on pleasing the International Monetary Fund [and multinational capital] as appealing to an electorate" (1996: 132–5).

Another important explanation for the crisis of labor movements emphasizes recent transformations in the organization of production and labor process, rather than the impact of capital mobility. These transformations (or "process innovations") are widely seen as having undermined the traditional bases of workers' bargaining power. Thus, for example, Craig Jenkins and Kevin Leicht (1997: 378–9) argued that while the "traditional Fordist system of standardized mass production provided fertile ground for the development of labor and related movements . . . the development of a post-Fordist system . . . has transformed this organizing environment." Moreover, global competitive pressures have obliged employers across the globe to follow suit in implementing the new "flexible production" system or to perish in the competitive struggle. As a result of these transformations, once-stable working classes have been replaced by "networks of temporary and cursory relationships with subcontractors and temporary help agencies." The result is a structurally disaggregated and disorganized working class, prone more to "a politics of resentment" than to "traditional working-class unions and leftist politics" (see also Hyman 1992).

While the race-to-the-bottom thesis and its variations are widespread in the literature, we should be cautious about concluding that world-economic forces are producing a general downward convergence of conditions for workers and workers' movements worldwide. There are, that is, alternative interpretations of each of the dynamics emphasized in the "race to the bottom" literature discussed above. With regard to capital mobility, the race-to-the-bottom thesis emphasizes the movement of capital from high-wage to low-wage areas in search of cheap labor. Contrary to this view, however, a recent United Nations Conference on Trade and Development (UNCTAD) report shows that the majority of foreign direct investment (FDI) flows continue to be intra-North (between high-wage countries). Thus, in 1999 more than 75 percent of total FDI flows went to high-income countries. The $276 billion of inflows to the United States alone surpassed the *combined* total of $226 billion going to Latin America, Asia, Africa, and Central and Eastern Europe (UNCTAD 2000: 2–3).

To be sure, relocation of industrial capital to low-wage areas has indeed taken place – and for some industries and regions, it has taken place on a massive scale. Nevertheless, as will be argued in Chapter 2, the impact of this relocation has been far less unidirectional than the race-to-the-bottom thesis suggests. While labor has been weakened in the locations from which productive capital emigrated, new working classes have been created and strengthened in the favored new sites of investment. Thus, the cheap labor economic "miracles" of the 1970s and 1980s – ranging from Spain and Brazil to South Africa and South Korea – each created new, strategically located working classes, which in turn produced powerful new labor movements rooted in expanding mass production industries. These labor movements were not only successful in improving wages and working conditions; they were also key "subjects" behind the spread of democracy in the late twentieth century. According to Ruth Collier, "the comparative and theoretical literature [on democratization] has largely missed the importance of the working class and the labor movement in the democratization process of the 1970s and 1980s.... In the overwhelming majority of cases, the roles of unions and labor-affiliated parties were important to a degree that is at most hinted at in the literature" (1999: 110).[2]

Moreover, as Chapters 2 and 3 argue, the impact of transformations in the organization of production on labor is less unidirectional than normally thought. Indeed, as we shall see in Chapter 2, in some situations just-in-time (JIT) production actually *increases* the vulnerability of capital to disruptions in the flow of production, and thus can *enhance* workers' bargaining power based on direct action at the point of production. This is true not only of industries using JIT methods but also for workers in the transport and communications industries whose reliability this production method is dependent upon. And there is reason to think that the more globalized the networks of production, the wider the potential geographical ramifications of disruptions, including by workers.

Indeed, there is some irony in the fact that early-twentieth-century observers of the transformations associated with Fordism were certain that these changes spelled the death of labor movements. Fordism not only made the skills of most unionized (craft) workers obsolete but also allowed employers to tap new sources of labor, resulting in a working class that was seen as hopelessly divided by ethnicity and other ascriptive differences, as well as isolated from each other by "an awesome array of fragmenting and alienating technologies" (Torigan 1999: 336–7). It was only post facto – with the success of mass production unionization – that Fordism came to be seen as inherently labor strengthening rather than inherently labor weakening. Is there a chance that we are on the eve of another such post-facto shift in perspective?

Finally, there is an intense debate about whether and to what degree there has been a genuine erosion of de facto state sovereignty. Indeed, many

---

[2] On South Africa and Brazil, see Seidman (1994); for the United States and Mexico, see Cowie (1999); and for South Korea, see Koo (1993, 2001). See also Evans (1995: 227–9), Beneria (1995), Markoff (1996: 20–31), Moody (1997), Arrighi and Silver (1984: 183–216), and Silver (1995b, 1997).

see the race-to-the-bottom as the outcome of political conflict rather than the outcome of inexorable global economic processes undermining state sovereignty. Seen from this perspective, the rhetoric surrounding globalization (especially TINA – Margaret Thatcher's "there is no alternative") is a purposefully created shield guarding governments and corporations from political responsibility for policies that favor the massive redistribution of benefits from labor to capital. Assertive political struggles by labor movements, they argue, have the potential to expose the TINA rhetoric, transform the ideological environment, and force a shift toward more labor-friendly national political and economic policies (see Block 1990: 16–18, 1996; Gordon 1996: 200–3; Tabb 1997; Piven 1995).

This is the point William Greider (2001) made with regard to what he sees as the new political environment in the United States and worldwide in the aftermath of the September 11 attacks. For Greider, the new crisis "upends the fictitious premises used to sell the supposed inevitability of corporate-led globalization." States, "at least the largest and strongest ones," had never "lost their power to tax and regulate commerce," they had "simply retreated from exerting those powers." The September 11 crisis, however, has required "leading governments, especially that of the United States, to do an abrupt about-face and begin to employ their neglected sovereign powers, that is, to intrude purposefully in the marketplace and impose some rules on behalf of society." Government efforts to regulate the international flow of capital as a way of policing terrorist money inevitably raises doubts about why analogous efforts are deemed impossible for states seeking to achieve other social and political goals. For Greider, the "patriotic tensions generated by war and recession can spawn a rare clarifying moment" and new political opportunities "to educate and agitate."

Whether the final months of 2001 will be seen in retrospect as having spawned a "rare clarifying moment" or some other kind of turning point remains to be seen.[3] In any event, as Chapter 4 makes clear, the historical trajectory of labor movements throughout the twentieth century has shaped and been shaped by global politics – especially the dynamics of hegemony, rivalry, interstate conflict, and war. Our conclusions about the future of

---

[3] Indeed, with the cancellation of planned strikes and demonstrations worldwide in the immediate aftermath of the September 11 attacks, the closing down of political opportunities was at least as much in evidence as any opening (Labor Notes 2001: 3; Reyes 2001: 1–2; Slaughter and Moody 2001: 3).

world labor in Chapter 5 will thus be based on two iterations of world-historical analysis – an analysis of global economic dynamics (the focus of Chapters 2 and 3) embedded in an analysis of global political dynamics (the focus of Chapter 4).

To be sure, the nature of this double embeddedness is more complex than suggested so far. For one thing, the "globalization versus state sovereignty" debate as presented earlier is framed in overly dichotomous terms, as a "zero-sum" game between the global and the national. As Saskia Sassen pointed out, states themselves are key participants "in setting up the new frameworks through which globalization is furthered" (1999a: 158; 1999b). Moreover, not *all* states are key participants in constructing these new frameworks. Thus, to talk about general trends in state sovereignty, as is common in the literature, makes little sense. For some states, globalization *is* an exercise in state sovereignty;[4] for others, it marks a new twist in a long-running situation of weak or nonexistent sovereignty (from colonialism to neocolonialism to globalization). This, in turn, has important implications for the debate around labor internationalism – to which we now turn.

A New Labor Internationalism?

Many of the same themes discussed in the previous section come back into play in the debates about whether conditions favorable to a robust labor internationalism are emerging in the early-twenty-first century. Indeed, one strand of the debate argues that the seeds of a new labor internationalism are to be found in the very same processes that have brought about the crisis of old labor movements. With the "globalization of production," according to this view, polarizing tendencies now operate primarily *within* countries rather than between them, and as a result, the North–South divide is becoming increasingly irrelevant (Harris 1987; Hoogvelt 1997; Burbach and Robinson 1999; Held et al. 1999; Hardt and Negri 2000). A single homogeneous world working class with similar (and unpalatable) conditions

---

[4] Powerful states have exercised this sovereignty under multiple pressures, including pressures from struggles by workers and other subordinate groups around the globe. Indeed, a central argument of Chapter 4 is that the global social-economic regime constructed after the Second World War (itself *an exercise of U.S. state sovereignty*) had relatively "labor-friendly" elements embedded in it precisely because of these types of pressures. Likewise, the powerful states now "setting up the new frameworks through which globalization is furthered" are likely to introduce labor-friendly elements in the new structures only to the extent that they feel similarly challenged from below.

of work and life is in the process of formation. In the words of William Robinson and Jerry Harris (2000: 16–17, 22–3), current transnational processes are "resulting in the accelerated division of the world into a global bourgeoisie [or transnational capitalist class] and a global proletariat." This transnational capitalist class is increasingly both "a class-in-itself and for-itself . . . pursuing a class project of capitalist globalization." The "transnational working class" (while "not yet a class-for-itself") is increasingly "a class-in-itself," thus providing the objective basis for labor internationalism.

Indeed, many observers of (and participants in) the mass protests against globalization, beginning with the anti-WTO (World Trade Organization) demonstrations in Seattle in November 1999, saw these demonstrations as the first signs of just such an emerging new labor internationalism. According to an editorial in *The Nation* (1999: 3), Seattle marked "a milestone for a new kind of politics" in which the U.S. labor movement "shed its nationalism for a new rhetoric of internationalism and solidarity." In the wake of Seattle, Jay Mazur (Chair of the ALF-CIO International Affairs Committee) maintained that "[t]he divide is not between North and South, it is between workers everywhere and the great concentrations of capital and governments they dominate" (2000: 92).

Moreover, globalized production, it is argued, not only creates a world working class that increasingly shares common conditions of life and work but also creates a world-scale labor force that often faces the same multinational corporate employer. The threat of whipsawing workers in one corner of a corporate empire against workers in another corner has led labor movement activists and observers to argue that workers must build organizations equal in geographical scope to that of their multinational corporate employers (Mazur 2000; Cowie 1999; Moody 1997). Declining state sovereignty would further justify such a call. For if states are suffering a major de facto decline in sovereignty vis-à-vis supranational actors, it is clear that workers can find little or no satisfaction by targeting their demands at their own national governments. If the real arena of power is now at the supranational level (whether in the form of private multinational corporations or international institutions of global governance such as the International Monetary Fund [IMF] and the WTO), then labor politics must also move to the supranational level.

Despite these arguments, caution is nonetheless required before concluding that we are moving toward a world context favorable to labor internationalism. For one thing, recent empirical research on world income inequality is not easy to square with the image of an emergent homogeneous

9

global working class-in-itself. This research shows that *between* country inequalities rather than *within* country inequalities still account for an overwhelming proportion of total world income inequality – a proportion ranging between 74 percent and 86 percent (Milanovic 1999: 34; Korzeniewicz and Moran 1997: 1017). Likewise, a more straightforward calculation based on World Bank data reveals that the average gross national product (GNP) per capita of Third World countries has remained a tiny fraction of the average GNP per capita of First World countries – 4.5 percent in 1960, 4.3 percent in 1980, and 4.6 percent in 1999 (calculated from World Bank 1984, 2001; see Arrighi, Silver, and Brewer 2003). Such extreme income inequality does not in itself undermine the arguments made in favor of the tactical benefits to be derived from the international coordination of actions by workers with the same multinational corporate employer. Nevertheless, it does make "documenting the existence of an actual community of fate" in which harm to another is understood as harm to one's self (Levi and Olson 2000: 313) a challenge to labor internationalism that should not be underestimated.

Part of the argument for promoting labor internationalism is based on the sense that only a global labor movement is up to the task of effectively challenging global organizations and institutions. But for those who see the decline of state sovereignty as a myth, and believe that states (or at least some states) still have the power to protect their working classes, investing in international labor solidarity is not the only, or indeed the best, political choice available to labor movements. Rather, from this perspective, the most efficient strategy for labor movements is to pressure their own governments to implement policies favorable to workers.[5]

Alternatively, if one takes the position that certain powerful states are the key actors determining the parameters of globalization (while other states are effectively powerless), then a handful of powerful states are the most strategic targets for labor movements. Seen from this point of view, the worker-citizens of these powerful states would appear to be positioned differently than worker-citizens of less powerful states. That is, they are better positioned to engage in political struggles designed to pressure the most "strategic target," the national governments that actually have the power

---

[5] This does not preclude trying to mobilize international solidarity to help pressure one's own government, as would be the case, for example, in the "boomerang" strategy discussed by Keck and Sikkink (1998: 12–13). In teasing out different possible national–international combinations, Doug Imig and Sidney Tarrow's (2000: 78) distinction between the level of mobilization of protests and the level of the target of protests is quite useful.

to reform the supranational institutions and organizations. The worker-citizens of these powerful states might use their privileged position in a way that is in the interests of all the world's workers, being vanguards of labor internationalism. The extent and persistence of the North–South income divide, however, raises the question as to whether struggles by Northern workers aimed at reforming supranational institutions are more likely to be steps toward the formation of a global working class "for itself" or signs of an emergent new form of national protectionism.

Indeed, Third World delegates to the WTO meeting in Seattle interpreted the demonstrations, not as evidence of a new labor internationalism, but rather as the expression of a national-protectionist agenda on the part of Northern labor in alliance with Northern governments.[6] In the weeks leading up to the WTO meetings, Third World countries passed a unanimous resolution opposing the insertion into trade agreements of social clauses demanding higher labor and environmental standards. These social clauses, they argued, were not the expression of internationalist concern for the well being of Third World workers but rather a new way of erecting barriers to the entry of Third World exports into the wealthy countries – "protectionism in the guise of idealism" (Dugger 1999). There was also "unexpected resistance" from Southern trade unionists to a proposal for basic labor standards to be observed worldwide, with delegates to the April 2000 International Confederation of Free Trade Unions (ICFTU) Congress arguing that sanctions for the violation of labor standards were potential national-protectionist weapons (Agence France-Presse 2000).

In short, present trends and events in international labor politics are subject to radically different interpretations. We will intervene in this debate at various points. Chapters 2 and 3, for example, will show how the globalization of industrial production has been a contradictory process that simultaneously produced elements of both *convergence* and *divergence* in the material conditions of geographically dispersed working classes – a contradictory process that has similarly contradictory implications for the past and future of labor internationalism.[7] Chapter 4 will recast this process within a century-long view of the relationship between labor movements, state

---

[6] The fact that, a month before the November 30 demonstration, AFL-CIO President John Sweeney joined a group of business leaders in signing a letter endorsing the Clinton administration's trade agenda for the WTO negotiations (Moody 1999: 1) no doubt bolstered this view. On North–South tensions leading up to Seattle, see O'Brien (2000: 82–92).

[7] Section III of this chapter will address the question of whether a tendency toward the homogenization of workers' conditions is actually favorable to the development of labor

sovereignty, and world politics. It will show that the bargaining power of worker-citizens vis-à-vis their states increased with the escalation of inter-imperialist rivalries and warfare in the late nineteenth and early twentieth centuries, as workers became increasingly important (industrial and battle-front) cogs in the war machines. Over the course of the first half of the twentieth century, as workers used this enhanced bargaining power in militant struggles, states sought to guarantee their loyalty by expanding their rights as citizens and workers.

Writing at the close of the Second World War, E. H. Carr suggested that this incorporation of workers into national-state projects was at the root of the collapse of nineteenth-century labor internationalism. In the nineteenth century, "when the nation belonged to the middle class and the worker had no fatherland, socialism had been international." However, for Carr, the "crisis of 1914 showed in a flash that . . . the mass of workers knew instinctively on which side their bread was buttered [that is, on the side of their own state's power]." Thus with the outbreak of the First World War, "[i]nternational socialism ignominiously collapsed" (1945: 20–1).

Are global political conditions once again favorable for the flourishing of a new phase of labor internationalism? From what we have said so far, this depends in part on how we judge the nature of contemporary sovereignty, the nature of workers' bargaining power, and the nature of the North–South divide. For even if (some) states have the power to implement "labor-friendly" policies, do workers have the strength to make their governments use that power on their behalf? And if some workers do have the necessary strength, will they use it (and will governments respond) in ways that consolidate or break down the North–South divide? Alternatively, if workers no longer have the bargaining power necessary to influence their governments, will they once again find themselves without a "fatherland" and will labor politics turn "instinctively" internationalist once again?

We return to all these questions in Chapter 5. Their answer, however, depends on an assessment of the long-term dynamics of workers' bargaining power vis-à-vis their states, vis-à-vis their employers, and vis-à-vis "the powers that be," at whatever level they might be found. Thus, before we go on, we must lay out some tools for the analysis of transformations over time in the sources and nature of workers' bargaining power.

solidarity among workers of different nations, races, genders, and the like – something assumed to be the case in much of the "optimistic" labor internationalism literature.

III. Labor Unrest in World-Historical Perspective: A Conceptual and Theoretical Framework

Sources of Workers' Power

Contentions about the state of world labor are based on assumptions about the impact of contemporary globalization on workers' bargaining power. A useful starting point for differentiating types of workers' bargaining power is Erik Olin Wright's (2000: 962) distinction between associational and structural power. *Associational power* consists of "the various forms of power that result from the formation of collective organization of workers" (most importantly, trade unions and political parties). *Structural power*, in contrast, consists of the power that accrues to workers "simply from their location . . . in the economic system." Wright further divides "structural" power into two subtypes. The first subtype of structural power (which we shall call *marketplace bargaining power*) is the power that "results directly from tight labor markets." The second subtype of structural power (which we shall call *workplace bargaining power*) is the power that results "from the strategic location of a particular group of workers within a key industrial sector."

Marketplace bargaining power can take several forms including (1) the possession of scarce skills that are in demand by employers, (2) low levels of general unemployment, and (3) the ability of workers to pull out of the labor market entirely and survive on nonwage sources of income.[8] Workplace bargaining power, on the other hand, accrues to workers who are enmeshed in tightly integrated production processes, where a localized work stoppage in a key node can cause disruptions on a much wider scale than the stoppage itself. Such bargaining power has been in evidence when entire assembly lines have been shut down by a stoppage in one segment of the line, and when entire corporations relying on the just-in-time delivery of parts have been brought to a standstill by railway workers' strikes.[9]

Those who credit globalization with bringing about a severe and/or terminal crisis of labor movements see globalization's various manifestations as

---

[8] On this latter type of marketplace bargaining power, see Erik O. Wright's discussion of "the parable of the shmoo" (1997: 4–9); see also Arrighi and Silver (1984: 193–200).

[9] On workplace bargaining power, see Arrighi and Silver (1984: 193–5). For analogous concepts, see Edwards' (1979) "the limits of technical control" and Perrone's (1984) "positional power," which was also used by Wallace, Griffin, and Rubin (1989). See also Tronti (1971). On the workplace bargaining power of Third World export workers, see Bergquist (1986).

13

undermining all these forms of workers' bargaining power (see Section II). Seen from this perspective, labor's marketplace bargaining power has been undermined by the mobilization of a world-scale reserve army of labor, creating a global glut on labor markets. Moreover, to the extent that the global spread of capitalist agriculture and manufacturing is undermining nonwage sources of income and forcing more and more individuals into the proletariat, marketplace bargaining power is undermined further. Finally, by weakening state sovereignty, globalization has undermined the associational bargaining power of labor. Historically, associational power has been embedded in state legal frameworks that guaranteed such things as the right to form trade unions as well as the obligation of employers to bargain collectively with trade unions. This weakening of state sovereignty, in turn, has also led to a further weakening of marketplace bargaining power, which had been bolstered by state welfare policies forming a "social safety net" and curbing labor market competition.

Indeed, globalization is widely seen as having created a vicious circle in which weakening marketplace bargaining power undermines associational power and vice versa. Thus, the mobilization of global labor reserves has not only directly undermined workers' marketplace bargaining power but also helped de-legitimize existing trade union organizations and labor parties in the eyes of many workers by making it increasingly difficult for these organizations to deliver benefits to their members. Moreover, direct attacks by employers and states on workers' organizations (with the collapse of the postwar social contracts) directly undermined workers' associational power. They also contributed to the further erosion of workers' marketplace power by making it increasingly difficult for workers' organizations to successfully defend/extend state "social safety net" policies.

If the hypermobility of capital is widely seen as having undermined marketplace and associational bargaining power, related "post-Fordist" transformations in the organization of production and labor process are widely seen as having undermined labor's workplace bargaining power. Thus, subcontracting and other forms of vertical disintegration are seen as having reversed the historical trend toward increased workplace bargaining power that was brought about through the spread of Fordist systems of mass production. Fordism tended to dramatically increase workplace bargaining power by increasing the vulnerability of capital to workers' direct action at the point of production. To be sure, continuous flow production (including the assembly line) tended to decrease labor's marketplace bargaining power by homogenizing and deskilling industrial work and by making it possible (indeed preferable) to draw on latent reserve armies of labor with little or no industrial experience. Moreover, continuous flow production tended to weaken associational power by bringing into the proletariat "a mass of unorganized workers" who could not be easily absorbed into the existing artisanal unions or left political parties.

Nevertheless, labor's workplace bargaining power grew at multiple levels. First, as was to become clear in the United States in the 1930s and to be demonstrated repeatedly in far-flung locations in subsequent decades, the assembly line has allowed a relatively small number of strategically placed activists to disrupt the output of an entire plant (see Chapter 2). Second, with the increasing integration of production among plants within a corporation, a strike in a plant producing a key input part could bring all downstream plants, and even an entire corporation, to a standstill. Finally, with the increasing concentration and centralization of production, the disruption caused to a country's economy by a strike in a key corporation or key industry (including transportation industries linking plants to each other and to markets) also grew. This has been the case especially where workers are located in an industry on which a country overwhelmingly depends for foreign exchange. As Charles Bergquist (1986) argued, relatively small groups of workers linked to major export industries and allied transport industries (e.g., docks, railways, airports) in the Third World have had the capacity to disrupt an entire economy as well as industry or company. [10]

Whether and to what degree marketplace, workplace and associational bargaining power have been undermined by post-Fordist transformations in the organization of production – as the bulk of contemporary analyses suggest – is one of the central themes to be taken up in Chapters 2 and 3. In Chapters 3 and 4, we also explore the possibility that there is not a strict correspondence between workers' bargaining power and the actual use by workers of that power to struggle for better working and living conditions. Indeed, one strand in the globalization and labor literature discussed earlier

---

[10] Workplace bargaining power points to a different relationship between the concentration/centralization of production and labor's bargaining power than that more commonly emphasized in the Marxist literature (e.g., Wright 1997). The latter tends to emphasize the effect of the concentration and centralization of capital on the associational bargaining power of workers. That is, by "bringing masses of workers into contact and interdependency with one another," the advance of capitalism promotes the conditions for the development of workers' collective consciousness and organization. In either case, post-Fordist transformations that promote a vertical disintegration and fragmentation of production are widely seen as weakening labor.

argues that the crisis of labor movements has been brought about, not so much by any transformations in the structural conditions facing workers' movements but by transformations in the discursive environment. In particular, the belief that there is no alternative has had a powerful demobilizing impact on labor movements. As Frances Piven and Richard Cloward (2000: 413–14) put it, the "idea of power" itself has been an important source of workers' power. Mobilizations over the past century have been fueled by the belief that workers do indeed have power and, moreover, that their power can be used to effectively transform their conditions of work and life for the better. What globalization has done more than anything else, they argued, is to "puncture this century-old belief in worker power" and to create a discursive environment that has dramatically deflated popular political morale and the willingness to struggle for change. Such shifts in workers' beliefs partly mirror shifts in structural and associational bargaining power but, no doubt, also play a role of their own in dynamics of labor movements.

In disentangling how transformations in these various forms of workers' bargaining power have changed over time and space, our analysis will be guided by two sets of hypotheses concerning the relationship between labor unrest and processes of capital accumulation on a world scale. Both sets focus on the social contradictions involved in the transformation of labor into a commodity. But while the first set focuses on the temporal unevenness of the transformation, the second set focuses on its spatial unevenness. Let us briefly examine each set in turn.

Labor as Fictitious Commodity

Karl Marx and Karl Polanyi provide different but related theoretical lenses through which to view the world-historical development of labor movements. In different ways, both contended that labor is a "fictitious commodity" and any attempt to treat human beings as a commodity "like any other" would necessarily lead to deeply felt grievances and resistance. Nevertheless, as discussed later, our reading of Marx leads to an emphasis on the stage-like nature of transformations in the labor resistance that has characterized historical capitalism, while our reading of Polanyi leads to an emphasis on the pendulum-like nature of that resistance.

For Marx, the fictitious nature of the commodity labor power reveals itself in the "hidden abode of production." In Volume I of *Capital*, Marx assumed (for the sake of argument) that, in the labor market, "Freedom, Equality, Property, and Bentham" rule; thus, labor power is freely exchanged for a wage representing its full value (i.e., the cost of its re-production). However, the purchaser of labor power soon finds out that it is not a commodity like any other. Rather, it is embodied in human beings who complain and resist if they are driven too long, too hard, or too fast. Struggle thus becomes endemic to, and in theory defines, the labor-capital relation at the point of production.

If for Marx labor reveals its fictitious nature at the point of production, for Polanyi its fictitious (and hence inflexible) nature is already visible with the creation and operation of a market for labor. Labor, land, and money are all essential factors of production, but they are *not* real commodities because either they are not produced at all (land) or they are produced for reasons other than sale on the market (labor and money). "Labor and land are no other than the human beings themselves of which every society consists and the natural surroundings in which it exists. To include them in the market mechanism means to subordinate the substance of society itself to the laws of the market" (Polanyi 1944: 71).

Thus, for Polanyi, the extension/deepening of unregulated markets for labor and other fictitious commodities inevitably provokes a corresponding countermovement for the "protection of society," what Polanyi called the "double movement" (1944: 130). Each extension or deepening of the labor market is countered by mobilization to regulate and constrain "the market for that factor of production known as labor power" through a variety of mechanisms including social legislation, factory laws, unemployment insurance, and trade unions (1944: 176–7). But such a relative decommodification of labor can only become a stable solution in a society that subordinates the pursuit of profits to the provision of livelihood.

Polanyi's analysis provides a useful lens through which to view the trajectory of labor movements in the twentieth century. With this lens, we can detect a pendulum-like motion. When the pendulum swings toward the commodification of labor, it provokes strong countermovements demanding protection. Thus, the late-nineteenth- and early-twentieth-century globalization of markets produced a strong countermovement from workers and other social groups (see Chapter 4). In response to rising labor militancy, and in the wake of the two world wars and depression, the pendulum swung toward the decommodification of labor after the Second World War. The establishment of national and international social compacts binding labor, capital, and states partially protected labor from the vagaries of an unregulated global market. But these compacts protecting livelihood came to be perceived as a growing fetter on profitability – a fetter

17

that was broken with the late-twentieth-century wave of globalization (see Chapter 4). If we observe contemporary processes of globalization through this Polanyian lens, we would expect a new swing of the pendulum. And indeed, numerous contemporary analysts have drawn on Polanyi's (1944) analysis of the nineteenth and early twentieth centuries as a theoretical foundation for both explaining contemporary backlashes against globalization and for predicting future (and growing) backlashes (or countermovements). (See Kapstein 1996: 16–28; 1999: 38–9; Rodrik 1997; Mittleman 1996; Gill and Mittleman 1997; Block 2001; Stiglitz 2001; Smith and Korzeniewicz 1997.)

In Polanyi's analysis, the extension of the self-regulating market provokes resistance in part because it overturns established and widely accepted social compacts on the right to livelihood – in other words, it is in part fueled by a sense of "injustice." But the concept of "power" is largely missing from Polanyi. For in Polanyi's analysis, an unregulated world market would eventually be overturned "from above" even if those below lacked effective bargaining power. This is because the project of a self-regulating global market is simply "utopian" and unsustainable on its own terms – it is one that is bound to wreak such havoc as to be replaced from above regardless of the effectiveness of protest from below.[11]

Marx's analysis, in contrast, emphasized power as well as injustice in identifying the limits of capital. Capitalism is seen as simultaneously producing growing mass misery and growing proletarian power. In Marx's analysis, capital is nothing without labor, and capitalist development itself leads to a long-term structural strengthening of the possessors of labor power. Toward the end of Volume I of *Capital*, for example, Marx described how the advance of capitalism leads not only to misery, degradation, and exploitation of the working class but also to a strengthening of its capacity and disposition to resist exploitation. It is "a class always increasing in numbers and *disciplined, united, organised by the very mechanism of the process of capitalist production itself*" (1959: 763, emphasis added). This position was stated even more clearly in *The Manifesto*: "The advance of industry, whose involuntary promoter is the bourgeoisie, replaces the isolation of the labourers due to competition, by their revolutionary combination, due to association. The

---

[11] This conclusion is somewhat muted by Polanyi's analysis of the 1930s, which also suggests that the nature and strength of popular movements from below may be important in determining the *form* that the inevitable shift away from self-regulating markets takes (e.g., fascism, communism, or New Deal).

development of Modern Industry, therefore, cuts from under its feet the very foundation on which the bourgeoisie produces and appropriates products" (1967: 93–4). Marx's formulation suggests that although "the advance of industry" may weaken the *marketplace bargaining power of labor*, it tends to increase both *workplace bargaining power* and *associational power*.

Marx's formulation has been the just target of extensive criticism in the labor studies literature, especially insofar as it has formed the basis of the so-called master narrative – a generalized linear narrative in which proletarianization necessarily leads to class consciousness and (successful) revolutionary action. (See Katznelson and Zolberg 1986 for an elaboration of this critique.) Yet, a reading of Volume I of *Capital* as a whole suggests a much less linear progression of working class power, and one that resonates strongly with contemporary dynamics. The core of Volume I can be read as a history of the dialectic between workers' resistance to exploitation at the point of production and the efforts of capital to overcome that resistance by constantly revolutionizing production and social relations. In each move – from handicraft industry to the factory system to machinofacture – old forms of workers' bargaining power are undermined only to create new forms on a larger and more disruptive scale.

This reading of Marx leads us to expect a constant transformation of the working class and the form of labor–capital conflict. Revolutions in the organization of production and social relations may disorganize some elements of the working class, even turning some into "endangered species" – as the transformations associated with contemporary globalization have doubtless done (see Section I). But new agencies and sites of conflict emerge along with new demands and forms of struggle, reflecting the shifting terrain on which labor–capital relations develop. Thus, while our reading of Polanyi suggests a pendular movement (or repetition), our reading of Marx suggests a succession of stages in which the organization of production (and hence the working class and the terrain on which it struggles) is continually and fundamentally transformed.

The insight that labor and labor movements are continually made and remade provides an important antidote against the common tendency to be overly rigid in specifying who the working class is (be it the nineteenth-century craftworkers or the twentieth-century mass production workers). Thus, rather than seeing an "historically superseded" movement (Castells 1997) or a "residual endangered species" (Zolberg 1995), our eyes are open to the early signs of new working class formation as well as "backlash" resistance from those working classes that are being "unmade." A key task becomes the identification of emerging responses from below to both the creative and destructive sides of capitalist development.

Our investigation into the long-term dynamics of world labor will thus be on the lookout for a combination of Marx-type and Polanyi-type labor unrest. By Polanyi-type labor unrest, we mean the backlash resistances to the spread of a global self-regulating market, particularly by working classes that are being unmade by global economic transformations as well as by those workers who had benefited from established social compacts that are being abandoned from above. And by Marx-type labor unrest, we mean the struggles of newly emerging working classes that are successively made and strengthened as an unintended outcome of the development of historical capitalism, even as old working classes are being unmade.

Boundary Drawing and the Spatial Contradictions of Historical Capitalism

The preceding discussion suggests a fundamental contradiction of historical capitalism. On the one hand, the expansion of capitalist production tends to strengthen labor and, therefore, brings capital (and states) recurrently face to face with strong labor movements. The concessions made to bring labor movements under control, in turn, tend to drive the system toward crises of profitability. On the other hand, efforts by capital (and states) to restore profits invariably involve breaking established social compacts and intensifying the commodification of labor, thereby producing crises of legitimacy and backlash resistance.

These two tendencies – crisis of profitability and crisis of legitimacy – define an ongoing tension within historical capitalism. One type of crisis can be resolved only by measures that eventually bring about the other type of crisis. This alternation creates a tendency for a periodic oscillation between historical phases characterized by a move toward the de-commodification of labor and the establishment of new social compacts and phases characterized by the re-commodification of labor and the breaking of old social compacts.

This temporal dynamic is deeply intertwined with a spatial dynamic. In other words, the periodic oscillation over time between phases tending toward the commodification and de-commodification of labor is intertwined with an ongoing process of spatial differentiation among geographical areas with regard to the level/intensity of labor commodification. As a first approximation in understanding this intertwining of temporal and spatial dynamics, we can draw on Immanuel Wallerstein's notion that historical capitalism is characterized by a "system-level problem." That is, profits can be made – even with the partial de-commodification of labor and the establishment of expensive social contracts – as long as those concessions are made to only a small percentage of the world's workers. As Wallerstein put it, with reference to the post–Second World War social contracts: "One could cut in several-hundred-million western workers and still make the system profitable. But if one cut in several billion Third World workers, there would be nothing left for further capital accumulation" (1995: 25).

Indeed, as we shall argue in Chapter 4, it was the split between the discursive promises that were made to globalize mass consumption American-style and the inability to do so profitably that would become a central limit of U.S. hegemony as instituted after the Second World War. Moreover, the explosion of this contradiction in the 1970s provided the context in which a new swing of the pendulum back toward global self-regulating markets (the contemporary phase of globalization) would take place.

More generally, there is a continual struggle not only over defining the content of working-class "rights" but also over the types and numbers of workers with access to those rights. How – and how quickly – a new crisis of legitimacy/profitability is reached is determined in large part by "spatial strategies" – efforts to draw "boundaries" delineating who will be "cut in" and who will be "left out."

Indeed, a key feminist critique of mainstream labor studies is its failure to recognize the pervasiveness and importance of boundary-drawing strategies. Traditionally, labor studies has told a story of working-class formation that focuses on artisanal and skilled workers in Western Europe and the United States, who facing proletarianization and deskilling, organized politically and resisted threats to their livelihoods and work traditions. But as feminist scholars have emphasized, by implicitly defining certain actors as the prototypical or universal subject of class formation, the race (white) and gender (male) of these historically specific actors is made to seem irrelevant. As a result, the ways in which "both gender and race . . . have been *constitutive* of class identities" are ignored. Moreover, the way in which workers themselves have actively constructed identities that have excluded other workers from the community of rights becomes invisible[12] (Rose 1997: 138–9, emphasis in original).

---

[12] Thus, with regard to the "quintessential worker" of the late nineteenth century, these skilled artisans did more than exclude unskilled laborers from their political organizations; they constructed "skill itself" through "exclusive apprenticeships." Moreover, it was

In ignoring or downplaying the centrality of race, ethnicity, gender, and nationality to class formation, traditional labor studies followed in the footsteps of Marx. Marx expected that proletarianization processes would produce an increasingly homogeneous working class over time, with converging experience, interests, and consciousness, thus laying the basis for unified national (and international) labor movements. Famously, Marx and Engels argued that modern "subjection to capital, the same in England as in France, in America as in Germany, has stripped [the proletarian] of every trace of national character," and that differences "of age and sex have no longer any distinctive social validity for the working class. All are instruments of labor, more or less expensive to use according to their age and sex" (1967: 88, 92, 102).

These conclusions were based on a conflation of two perspectives: that of labor and that of capital. As Giovanni Arrighi (1990a: 63) pointed out, the cost-cutting race of the late twentieth century provided "new and compelling evidence in support of the observation that *for capital* all the members of the proletariat are [interchangeable] instruments of labor" (regardless of age, sex, color, nationality). But Marx was incorrect to infer that just because capitalists treat workers as interchangeable, *workers themselves* would willingly relinquish nonclass bases of identity. Indeed, precisely because the ongoing unmaking and remaking of working classes creates dislocations and competitive pressures on workers, there is also an endemic tendency for workers to draw nonclass borders and boundaries as a basis for claims for protection from the maelstrom.[13]

Whenever faced with the predisposition of capital to treat labor as an undifferentiated mass with no individuality other than a differential capability to augment the value of capital, proletarians have rebelled. Almost invariably they have seized upon or created anew whatever combination of distinctive traits (age, sex, color, and assorted geographical specificities) they could use to impose on capital some kind of special treatment. As, a consequence, patriarchalism, racism,

---

"historically constructed as a [white and] masculine attribute" (Rose 1997: 147; see also Barton 1989; Somers 1995; Phillips and Taylor 1980; Cockburn 1983; Elson and Pearson 1981; Rose 1992; Tabili 1994; Roediger 1991).

[13] This discussion is clearly relevant to the debates on labor internationalism reviewed earlier. Some of those who take the "optimistic" position on labor internationalism are operating from an underlying logic that sees capital's tendency to homogenize labor across national borders as increasing the chances that workers will actively break down divisions among themselves and cooperate across previously existing divides.

and national-chauvinism have been integral to the making of the world labor movement ... and live on in one form or another in most proletarian ideologies and organizations. (Arrighi 1990a: 63)

While the preceding discussion suggests that it is in the interest of workers to draw boundaries and in the interest of capital to break down those boundaries, it would be wrong to maintain that this is the only dynamic by which exclusionary boundary drawing takes place. Indeed, there is an extensive literature that focuses on the benefits that capital and states gain from exclusionary boundary drawing. Frederick Cooper's (1996) analysis of the experience of African trade unions in the immediate postwar years provides an effective example of workers actively seeking to break down exclusionary boundaries. Drawing on the universalistic discourse of the colonial powers, African trade unionists called for an extension of the notion of "workers' rights" to include all workers in the Empire – metropolitan and colonial, black and white, equally. These efforts by African workers to establish the legitimacy of empire-wide workers' rights (i.e., to break down existing boundaries separating metropolitan from colonial domains) were met by the efforts of capitalists and states to draw new boundaries and reaffirm old ones. The colonial powers' decision to move toward decolonization and national sovereignty resulted in clear new boundaries that limited the obligations of the metropolitan countries by excluding the workers and citizens of their former colonies. Workers' universalistic demands had brought the colonial state and capital face to face with a "system-level problem" (see earlier), and a redefinition of "citizenship rights" (and hence workers' rights) helped defuse the explosive potential of the clear gap between universalistic discourse and actual practice.

Another example is to be found in the reactions by colonial and postcolonial states to the enduring strong ties of African urban workers with rural communities. Indigenous working-class culture was producing and reproducing fuzzy boundaries, and thereby raising the specter of mass labor movements expanding beyond the urban workplace and engulfing whole regions. Fearing the potential for uncontrollable unrest that these fuzzy boundaries opened up, capitalists and governments sought to draw new boundaries – creating and enforcing rigid urban/rural and primary/secondary sector divides. Their goal was to produce a "compact, stable, reasonably well paid labor force – set apart from the rest of African society" (Cooper 1996: 457). By demarcating a visible but relatively small primary sector of urban workers with special workers' rights, it was hoped that legitimacy, control, and profits might be made to coexist.

For Mahmood Mamdani (1996: 218–84), the case of Apartheid South Africa provided a variation on the same theme. In 1948, with the victory of the Nationalist Party, South Africa abruptly shifted away from labor stabilization policies toward "the massive expulsions of Africans from cities and the vigorous policing of influx and residence" (Cooper 1996: 6). As a result, South African migrant workers, writes Mamdani, became "the conveyer belts between urban activism and rural discontent." They "carried forms of urban militancy from the towns to the reserves in the 1950s" and then carried "the flame of revolt from the rural to the urban" in the 1960s, culminating in the 1976 Soweto uprising. In the decade after Soweto, the South African state was forced to move back to labor stabilization policies. It sought to "set up a Chinese wall between migrant and township populations" and to limit union organizing rights to resident urban labor while "tightening the screw of 'influx control' on migrants." This boundary-drawing strategy, in turn, helped turn a "difference" between migrant and resident urban workers into a tension-ridden "divide" (Mamdani 1996: 220–1).[14]

In sum, boundary-drawing strategies have taken three main interconnected forms: segmenting labor markets (pursued mainly by capital), bounding citizenship (pursued mainly by states), and constructing exclusionary class identities on nonclass bases (pursued mainly by workers themselves). Rather than suggest that exclusionary boundary drawing is invariably the act of a specific group, this book works with the premise that historical capitalism is indeed characterized by a system-level problem that gives great salience to the practice of boundary drawing. Who uses boundary drawing (and how) in an attempt to resolve/exploit this system-level problem cannot be determined a priori from theoretical considerations. It is instead a question to be answered on the basis of historical-empirical analysis. It does seem plausible to suggest that workers facing intense competition from differently located workers will be more likely to take up a strategy of exclusion, while emerging new working classes excluded from existing social contracts are most likely to attempt to contest and break down existing

---

[14] For analogous but different stories of state boundary-drawing strategies that have created and divided two classes of workers – established urban and migrant-rural – with different citizenship and workers' rights, see Solinger (1999) for China and Roberts (1995) for Latin America.

boundaries. But the interaction of these tendencies with the exclusion-ary/inclusive propensities of states and capitalists complicates considerably the actual dynamic of boundary drawing and boundary breakdown.

IV. Research Strategies

The Time and Space of Labor Unrest

As mentioned at the outset of this chapter, a central premise of this book is that a full understanding of the dynamics of contemporary labor move-ments requires that we cast our analysis in a longer historical and wider geographical frame than is normally done. Assessments about the future of labor movements are based – explicitly or implicitly – on a judgment about the historical novelty of the contemporary world. Those who see a terminal crisis of labor movements tend to see the contemporary era as one that is *fundamentally new and unprecedented*, in which global economic processes have completely reshaped the working class and/or the terrain on which labor movements must operate. In contrast, those who expect the reemer-gence of significant labor movements tend to perceive historical capitalism itself as being characterized by recurrent dynamics, including the continual creation of contradictions and conflict between labor and capital. To the extent that this latter perspective is plausible, it suggests that forecasts about the future of labor movements must be based on a comparison of contem-porary dynamics with analogous dynamics of past historical periods. Thus, the book reaches back in time in search of patterns of recurrence and evo-lution, so as to be able to isolate what, if anything, is truly novel about the situation currently facing labor movements.

The justification for widening the geographical scope of the analysis be-yond that which is typical in labor studies is, in part, related to the same issue of *newness*. It is by now fairly commonplace to assume that the fate of workers and labor movements in one locale can crucially affect the outcome of labor–capital conflict in another locale (especially as mediated through processes of trade and capital mobility). Nevertheless, this assumption is widely regarded as relevant only for the study of late-twentieth-century la-bor movements and beyond, not for earlier periods, because contemporary globalization is seen as a fundamental historical divide.

Yet, if globalization is taken to mean "an increase in the geographi-cal range of locally consequential social interactions" (Tilly 1995), then, as many argue, the current period of globalization is not the first such period. Among those who see globalization as a recurrent phenomenon, there is some debate about how far back in history globalization processes can reasonably be identified.[15] Nevertheless, there is widespread agreement among these same individuals that strong analogies exist between the current phase of globalization and the late nineteenth century. Indeed, some argue that the interconnectedness of national economies and societies is no greater today than it was at the end of the nineteenth century – that is, the period widely taken to mark the birth of the modern labor movement.

One clear example of late-nineteenth-century interconnectedness (and one with a significant impact on labor and labor movements) is the massive global labor migration of that period.[16] This migration played a major role both in transmitting styles of labor unrest and in precipitating Polanyi-esque movements of "self-protection" (i.e., campaigns to restrict immigration). This example simultaneously demonstrates the strong interconnectedness of late-nineteenth-century economies and societies and the relevance of this interconnectedness for labor movement behavior and outcomes, while also suggesting that late-twentieth-century globalization (with its tighter restrictions on labor mobility) is not a simple repeat of the past.

In broad terms, then, a central methodological premise of the book is that workers and workers' movements located in different states/regions are linked to each other by the world-scale division of labor and global political processes. An understanding of *relational processes among "cases" on a world scale across both time and space* is fundamental to understanding the dynamics of labor movements since at least the late nineteenth century.

Throughout the book, special attention will be paid to both "direct" and "indirect" relational processes. In the case of direct relational processes, the actors are aware of and consciously promoting the links among the cases. These direct relational processes can take two different forms: diffusion and solidarity. In the case of diffusion, actors located in "cases" that are separated in time and space are influenced by the spread of information about the behavior of others and its consequences (Pitcher, Hamblin, and

---

[15] For a sample of the debate, see Tilly (1995), Wallerstein (1979), Gills and Frank (1992), Chase-Dunn (1989), and O'Rourke and Williamson (1999).

[16] As David Held and his co-authors have shown, migration flows in the late nineteenth and early twentieth century, relative to world population, were more significant than migration flows in the late twentieth century (Held et al. 1999: Chapter 6; see also O'Rourke and Williamson 1999: Chapters 7–8).

Miller 1978). "Social contagion" is a common image used in the method-ological literature on diffusion. The contagion of a language of workers' rights "caught" by African trade unionists (discussed earlier) would be one example of diffusion. This type of diffusion can take place without active cooperation between the source site and recipient site of the "social dis-ease" (e.g., cooperation between European and African trade unionists). In contrast, the second form of direct relational processes singled out earlier – that is, solidarity – involves personal contact and the development of social networks – transnational social networks in the case of labor internation-alism (Tarrow 1998; McAdam and Rucht 1993: 69–71; Keck and Sikkink 1998).

In the case of indirect relational processes, the affected actors are often not fully conscious of the relational links. Rather, actors are linked behind their back by systemic processes including the unintended consequences of a series of actions and reactions to what we have been calling the system-level problem. If a strong labor movement leads capitalists to re-spond by relocating production to a new site (thus weakening labor in the de-industrializing site but strengthening labor in the industrializing site), then we can say that the fates of these two labor movements are linked by indirect relational processes. Indeed, the implicit argument underlying the "new international division of labor" literature is that industrializa-tion in low-wage areas and de-industrialization in high-wage areas have been two sides of the same coin. (See, among others, Fröbel et al. 1980; Bluestone and Harrison 1982; Sassen 1988; MacEwan and Tabb 1989; Dicken 1998.)

In the example of late-nineteenth-century migration, we can detect both indirect and direct relational processes linking labor movements across time and space. The spread of labor movement ideologies and practices as work-ers moved across the globe (referred to earlier) is an example of diffusion. But, we can also detect critical indirect relational processes. The U.S. labor movement's success in having open immigration outlawed in the 1920s set the stage for the stabilization of the U.S. working class and contributed to the subsequent CIO (Congress of Industrial Organizations) victories in the 1930s. At the same time, however, this U.S. labor movement "success" shut off what had been an essential social safety valve for Europe in the nineteenth century. It thereby transformed the terrain on which workers' movements operated in Europe and, according to E. H. Carr (1945), helped set the stage for the defeat of European labor movements and the rise of fascism.

Lumping and Splitting the World Labor Movement

By making the relationship among cases across time and space a central part of the explanatory framework, this book departs in strategy from the comparative-historical approach to labor studies. The comparative-historical perspective, like the approach outlined here, criticizes the strategy of making generalizations from one or a limited number of cases, and thus calls for a widening of the geographical scope of the analysis. In particular, comparative-historical scholars have criticized the tendency in traditional labor studies to set up a single model of working-class formation (the so-called master narrative) as the standard against which all actual historical experiences are judged as "exceptional" or "deviant" (Katznelson and Zolberg 1986: 12, 401, 433). Instead, the approach involves a "variation finding" strategy that analyzes how the *same* experience of proletarianization has led to *different* outcomes. Put differently, much of the comparative-historical literature follows the strategy of "splitting" in search of distinctiveness, in contrast to the strategy of "lumping" cases in search of commonalties and generalizations (Hexter 1979: 241–3; Collier and Collier 1991: 13–15). These differences in outcome are then generally traced to preexisting and independently produced differences in the *internal* characteristics of the various cases.[17]

While some of the most interesting recent scholarship in labor studies comes out of the comparative historical approach, a total reliance on the comparative-historical strategy impedes full access to what we take to be a key explanatory variable of labor movement behavior and outcomes (i.e., the relationships among the cases themselves). As Charles Tilly (1984: 146)

---

[17] Examples of this strategy abound. Richard Biernacki (1995: 1–3) argued that divergent shop-floor practices and labor movement strategies developed in German and British textile industries despite their technical uniformity (same kinds of machines, same markets) because of differing cultural conceptions of the meaning of buying and selling labor. As a result of these different cultural understandings, Germany and Britain took "opposite journeys among an array of developmental pathways to wage labor in western Europe." Likewise, among the conclusions that Katznelson and Zolberg (1986: 450) reached – on the basis of essays on France, Germany, and the United States in their edited volume – is the crucial role played by the nature of the state at the time of initial working-class formation. The "single most important determinant of the variation in the patterns of working class politics . . . is simply whether, at the time this class was being brought into being by the development of capitalism . . . it faced an absolutist state or liberal state." In other words, they trace the divergent outcome among labor movements in terms of the degree to which they were heavily involved in politics to preexisting and independent differences in the character of the individual cases (states).

among others has pointed out, the results of a strict cross-national analysis may be misleading. A social unit's connection to the whole system of social relationships in which it is embedded "frequently produces effects [that] seem to be autonomous properties of the social unit itself." As a result, the patterned diversity among social units *appears* to be consistent with cross-national variation-finding explanations. This has been referred to as Galton's problem in the anthropology literature: that is, in a situation in which cases are *presumed* to be independent – but are actually linked relationally – the relations among the cases become a lurking (unexamined) variable. In the examples given earlier, and throughout the book, similarity/variation is not merely the outcome of the cases' similar/different independent and preexisting internal characteristics. Rather, relationships among the cases, and relationships between the cases and the totality, are key parts of the explanation of similar/different outcomes.[18]

In sum, the perspective adopted in this book requires an analytical strategy that is sensitive to the relational processes among key actors (labor, capital, states) in the system as a whole, as well as the systemic constraints affecting those actors. Needless to say, such an approach presents enormous problems of complexity, and a strategy for reducing complexity and making research feasible is needed.

The most well-known strategy for reducing the complexity of world-historical analysis is what Tilly (1984) labeled "encompassing comparison" and is best illustrated by Immanuel Wallerstein's approach to the study of the "modern world-system" and John Meyer's approach to the study of "world society" (see, e.g., Wallerstein 1974; Meyer et al. 1997). Encompassing comparisons reduce complexity by starting "with a mental map of the whole system and a theory of its operation." Similarities/differences in the attributes and behavior of the units are then traced to their similar/different position within the overarching totality (Tilly 1984: 124). Meyer's "mental map" of the system leads him to emphasize a growing convergence among national cases as a result of a world-scale process of "rationalization." Wallerstein's mental map, in contrast, leads him to emphasize a process of recurrent geographical differentiation among core and periphery resulting from the unequal distribution of rewards in a capitalist world economy. Yet for both, local attributes and behavior are seen as the product of a unit's

---

[18] On Galton's problem, see Naroll (1970) and Hammel (1980). For a methodological critique of the comparative-national approach from a world-systems perspective, see Hopkins (1982b).

location in the system. The larger system has a steamroller-like quality, transforming social relations at the local level along a theoretically expected path.[19]

The strength of this perspective is that it emphasizes the very real constraints that the totality imposes on the range of possible action open to local actors. But its weakness is that it excludes a priori a situation in which local action (agency) significantly impacts local outcomes, much less a situation in which local agency impacts the operation of the system as a whole. Moreover, as should be clear from the preceding discussion of borders and boundary drawing, the units of the system cannot be part of an initial mental map because they themselves are constructed, and this process of construction is itself a critical part of the story of working-class formation.

Thus, while keeping in focus the real systemic constraints that the totality imposes on local actors, this study cannot adopt the "encompassing comparison" approach as a strategy for reducing complexity. Instead, the research strategy followed in this book most closely resembles what Phillip McMichael (1990) called "incorporating comparison" – a strategy in which the interactions among a multiplicity of subunits of the system are seen as *creating* the system itself over time. The resultant conceptualization is one in which relational processes in space unfold in and through time.

The most appropriate type of causal analysis for the strategy adopted here – and the primary one used in this book – is a modified version of the narrative mode advocated by most comparative-historical sociologists. The narrative strategy, Larry Griffin (1992: 405) argued, allows us to understand social phenomena "as temporally ordered, sequential, unfolding, and open-ended 'stories' fraught with conjunctures and contingency." As a strategy for *explanation*, "descriptively accurate narratives, which depict a sequence of events in chronological order ... do more than tell a story," according to Jill Quadagno and Stan Knapp (1992: 486, 502). Such narratives can "serve, among other purposes, to identify causal mechanisms" because "when things happen ... affects how they happen."[20]

---

[19] This approach has led to complaints from otherwise sympathetic scholars that "world-systems theory," in "assuming the systematicity and functionality of the capitalist world system," has produced a "mechanical picture of different labor forms in different parts of the world" (Cooper 2000: 62).

[20] As will become evident, statistical elaboration abounds in this book. Its purpose is not "explanation" but the identification of patterns of labor unrest across time and space that

IV. Research Strategies

~~But while historical sociologists~~ have stressed the importance of treating *time* as dynamic, they have generally continued to treat *space* as static (e.g., conceptualizing national cases as fixed, independent units). This may be seen as a reasonable strategy for reducing the complexity of the analysis. However, as should be clear by now, it is not a strategy that can be followed here. In contrast, this book attempts to create a narrative of working-class formation in which events unfold in *dynamic time-space*.

Having rejected the two most common strategies for reducing complexity in the study of macro-historical social change (i.e., encompassing comparison and cross-national comparative research), the problem of managing the complexity of the analysis remains. A first complexity-reduction strategy used here is to place limits on the number of levels at which the analysis simultaneously proceeds. In an attempt to unpack the class-in-itself/class-for-itself "master narrative," Katznelson and Zolberg (1986: 14–21) distinguish four levels at which the study of working-class formation should proceed. These are (1) the structure of capitalist economic development, (2) ways of life, (3) dispositions, and (4) collective action. This book is primarily an analysis of the interrelationship between the first and the fourth level (i.e., the interrelationship between the political-economic dynamics of world capitalist development and the world-historical patterning of labor unrest). Levels 2 and 3 are touched upon at various points, but no attempt is made to integrate these levels systematically into the analyses presented here.

In leaving aside Katznelson's second and third levels, we are also sidestepping a whole range of issues that have been the subject of ongoing trench

---

then become the explicandum of a multidimensional causal "story" (see Hopkins 1982a: 32; Danto 1965: 237).

[21] McAdam, Tarrow, and Tilly's (2001: 26) emphasis on "relational mechanisms" that operate at the level of "webs of interactions among social sites" moves in this direction. But their approach assigns priority to what they call "cognitive mechanisms" over "environmental mechanisms" (e.g., processes of capitalist development). As a result, to the extent that they trace relational processes beyond the local or national level, they tend to emphasize only what we have called direct relational processes. Their approach abstracts from crucial indirect relational processes that operate behind the backs, and independently of the cognitive awareness of affected groups and individuals (see previous subsection). Put differently, they do not operate with a conceptualization of capitalism as a historical social system. The approach adopted in this study, in contrast, concurs with Don Kalb's (2000: 38) point that "[t]o get at class ... we need to recapture capitalism." Or as Frederick Cooper put it, in rejecting the "meta"(of meta-theory), it would be too bad if scholars shy away from the "mega," for "capitalism remains a megaquestion" (1996: 14; 2000: 67).

warfare in labor studies.[22] In some cases, our intention *is* to abstain from the debate. For example, no particular assumption is being made here about the relationship between intense phases of labor militancy and the presence or absence of working-class consciousness (or the exact nature of that consciousness). As E. P. Thompson suggested, it is possible, even likely, that class consciousness emerges out of struggles; that is, "in the process of struggling" the protagonists "discover themselves as classes" (Thompson 1978: 149; see also Fantasia 1988; McAdam et al. 2001: 26). Or, it is possible that important transformations in cognition must take place before collective action can emerge.[23] It is also possible that major waves of labor militancy are neither preceded by, nor lead to the development of something we might meaningfully call working-class consciousness. While it would no doubt be important to uncover patterned relationships between collective action and consciousness, to do so for the macro-historical sweep of cases included here, *in a way that is methodologically relational and dynamic*, is simply unfeasible in the context of this book.

Moreover, our choice of levels would seem to imply a favoring of structural processes over cultural processes in explaining global and historical patterns of labor militancy. This is not strictly the case. It is true that at various points the book makes a strong claim that the patterns of labor unrest being described *cannot* be attributed to cultural factors. Most notably, a central argument of Chapter 2 is that *strikingly similar* labor movements emerged among mass production autoworkers in *vastly different* cultural and political settings over the course of the twentieth century. Moreover, the anomalous (and least conflict-prone) case in the chapter – Japan[24] – shares a cultural tradition of Confucianism with one of the most conflict-prone cases analyzed in the chapter (Korea). If, as in Chapter 2, we treat different national movements, not as independent fixed entities, but as interrelated parts of an unfolding systemic totality, then cultural explanations of cross-national *differences* often prove less than compelling.

---

[22] See for example, the articles collected under the title of "Scholarly Controversy: Farewell to the Working Class?" in the Spring 2000 issue of *International Labor and Working-Class History*.

[23] Thus, Doug McAdam, John McCarthy, and Mayer Zald (1996: 6–8) argued that protest action presupposes "shared understandings of the world . . . that legitimate and motivate collective action."

[24] It is anomalous in the sense that it is the one case where a rapid expansion of mass production in the automobile industry did not lead to a mass wave of labor unrest within a generation. As Chapter 2 points out, that expansion was *preceded* by a major wave of labor unrest.

IV. Research Strategies

All this is not to say that there are no differences between the kind of language and symbols that labor movements use to mobilize in, say, Brazil, South Africa, Japan, or South Korea. Moreover, it is not to say that these different symbols and rituals of mobilization are not attributable to distinct cultural heritages. Nevertheless, for a book such as this, whose main focus is on explaining the long-term, world-scale patterning of labor movements, such cultural *differences between* national labor movements are less relevant than the *relationships among* these movements.

It is also true that most of the relationships among workers and workers' movements emphasized in this book are classically "structural" in nature (e.g., the impact of the geographical location and relocation of productive capital on the world-scale distribution of employment and workers' bargaining power). Nevertheless, some are "cultural" in nature. Section III pointed to some ways in which labor movements are linked to each other through what we might call macro-cultural relational processes – or the culture of world capitalism. For example, we have already referred to the transnational diffusion of a discourse about workers' and citizens' rights carried by migrating workers. This might be conceptualized as a form of transnational cultural diffusion *from below*. But we have also referred to the role of empires (e.g., the British and French empires in Africa) in spreading discourses about universal rights that were later picked up and transformed into a basis for legitimating claims made by local labor movements. This second type might be labeled a form of transnational cultural diffusion *from above*. This type of diffusion plays a central role in the story told in Chapter 4, where a Gramscian concept of world hegemony is employed in the analysis of the post–Second World War period. U.S. world hegemony is seen, among other things, as a transnational cultural construct that attempted to formulate a response at the cultural level to the worldwide waves of labor unrest and revolutionary upheavals of the first half of the twentieth century. In so doing, it also inadvertently provided universal cultural elements for framing and legitimating challenges by workers' movements well beyond the borders of the United States.

A final note of clarification is needed with regard to our approach to Katznelson and Zolberg's fourth level – collective action. This book does not attempt to analyze all forms of workers' collective action.[25] Our focus

---

[25] For Katznelson and Zolberg (1986: 20), working-class "collective action" refers to "classes that are organized through movements and organizations to affect society and the position of the class within it."

is rather on periods of particularly intense labor unrest – what Piven and Cloward (1992: 301–5) labeled episodes of nonnormative conflict, or what McAdam et al. (2001: 7–8) call "transgressive action."[26] These major waves of labor unrest, rather than more institutionalized forms of protest, provoke capitalists/states to implement innovations and are thus the most relevant form of labor unrest for understanding periods of dramatic transformation in the world capitalist system (e.g., the contemporary phase of globalization). Put differently, by focusing on these major waves of labor unrest, we expect to be able to analyze both the Polanyi-esque pendulum swings and the Marxian stages conceptualized in Section III, and hence better understand the shifting grounds on which contemporary world labor movements unfold.[27]

This brings us to our final strategy for reducing the complexity of the analysis. This book would have been impossible to write without an empirical map of the time-space patterning of labor unrest. This map allows us to identify the times/places of major waves of labor unrest and thus has provided a way to navigate a path through the bewildering totality of potentially relevant episodes of labor unrest in the world over the past century. In other words, it allows us to identify patterns across time/space and thus make informed decisions about what (where/when) to study more closely. The empirical map allows us to "lump" and "split" cases as a tactic for uncovering patterns; the latter will be explained through the construction of relational narratives. The empirical map, successively drawn in the following chapters, is based on a new data source on labor unrest that covers the world for the entire twentieth century – the World Labor Group (WLG) database – to which we now turn.

---

[26] McAdam et al. (2001: 7–8) distinguish between "contained contention" and "transgressive contention." Transgressive contention differs from contained contention in that "at least some of the parties to the conflict are newly self-identified political actors, and/or . . . at least some of the parties employ innovative collective action."

[27] In terms of the protagonists of collective action, our focus is on the "proletariat" (i.e., those who must sell their labor power in order to survive). The proletarian condition encompasses a range of concrete situations, from those who possess scarce skills that are in demand (and hence have relatively strong marketplace bargaining power) to those who are unemployed. It includes those who are employed by private entrepreneurs and those who are employed by the state, for the latter are ultimately no more insulated from the pressures of being treated as a commodity than, say, workers in the internal labor market of a large firm. In both cases, when push comes to shove, the demands of profitability (and their links with tax receipts) can wipe away in short order whatever insulation from the labor market had existed.

IV. Research Strategies

Mapping World-Scale Patterns of Labor Unrest: The World Labor Group Database

In order to pursue the research strategy set out here, we need a picture of the overall patterning of labor militancy. The picture must be of sufficient historical and geographical scope to allow for an examination of the potential feedbacks among local level actions as they unfold over time. Given our emphasis on the totality of relationships among local actions, we need this information for all the potentially related cases (i.e., for the social whole), in this case, for the world from the beginnings of the modern labor movement in the late nineteenth century to the present.

Until recently, information on labor unrest of such historical and geographical scope simply did not exist. Long-term time series of strike activity – the most commonly used indicator of labor unrest – exist only for a handful of core countries. For most countries, either there are no strike statistics at all, or they begin only after the Second World War. Furthermore, with the exception of the United Kingdom, all countries' series contain major gaps (e.g., during the period of fascism and world wars in Germany, France, and Italy and for a period in the early twentieth century when the U.S. government decided to discontinue strike data collection). Moreover, the strike statistics that do exist are often collected according to criteria that exclude what may be very relevant strikes from the point of view of measuring "labor unrest." For example, most countries at one time or another have excluded "political strikes" from the official count of strike activity. Yet, workers' demands directed at their states (e.g., through political strikes) rather than at their employers have been a critical dimension of world-scale labor unrest throughout the twentieth century.

Data collections covering nonstrike forms of labor unrest are even more rare, yet they are important to the overall construction of a map of labor unrest. The strike is not the only significant form in which labor unrest is expressed. Labor unrest frequently manifests itself in nonstrike forms of struggle ranging from slowdowns, absenteeism, and sabotage to demonstrations, riots, and factory occupations. Anonymous or hidden forms of struggle such as undeclared slowdowns, absenteeism, and sabotage are especially significant in situations where strikes are illegal and open confrontation difficult or impossible.

This book relies on a new database specifically designed to overcome the geographical (core-centric), temporal (short-term), and action-type (strike-oriented) limitations of previously existing data sources on labor unrest.

The World Labor Group database was specifically designed for the kind of dynamic global analyses of labor unrest carried out in this book.[28] Building on a well-established tradition within the social sciences, the WLG constructed the database by using information from newspaper reports of labor unrest (strikes, demonstrations, factory occupations, food riots, etc.) throughout the world beginning in 1870. The result is a database with over 91,947 "mentions" of labor unrest for 168 "countries" covering the 1870–1996 period. The remainder of this section will provide a brief overview of issues related to the construction and use of the WLG database. (For a far more in-depth and precise discussion, the reader is referred to Appendices A and B.)

Tapping major newspapers as a source to construct indexes of social protest (including labor unrest) has become a fairly widespread and developed practice in the social sciences. Existing studies have used information gleaned from local/national newspapers to measure occurrences of local/national protest. The WLG's goal, however, was to construct reliable indicators of *world* labor unrest. Recording all reports of labor unrest from a major national newspaper for *each* country in the world over the past century would have been an unfeasible project. Moreover, even if the data collection effort were feasible, intractable problems of comparability of data sources would arise in attempting to combine the information retrieved from different national sources into a single world indicator. The WLG's solution was to rely, at least initially, on the major newspapers of the world's two hegemonic powers – *The Times* (London) and the *New York Times*.

There were several reasons behind the choice of sources. First, *The Times* (London) and the *New York Times* have had world-level information-collecting capabilities throughout the twentieth century. As a result, geographical bias rooted in the technological limits of newspaper reporting is not a major problem (especially with respect to *The Times*). Second, as the major newspapers of the two world-hegemonic powers of the twentieth century, the two sources' coverage is more likely to be global than alternative sources. Third, while the reporting of both newspapers can be expected to be global, both are also likely to show regional biases in favor of areas that have been historically considered special spheres of influence or interest (e.g., South Asia and Australia for *The Times* [London]

---

[28] The results of the first phase of the project were published in Silver, Arrighi, and Dubofsky (1995).

and Latin America for the *New York Times*). Combining the two sources into a single indicator of world labor unrest helps to counterbalance the regional biases of each source taken separately. (Because of the overwhelming bias of each source in favor of domestic events, we excluded reports of labor unrest in the United Kingdom from our search of *The Times* [London] and reports of labor unrest in the United States from the *New York Times*.)

Individual members of the research group read through the Indexes of *The Times* (London) and the *New York Times* from 1870 to 1996 and recorded each incident of labor unrest identified onto a standard data collection sheet. Working from a conceptualization of labor as a "fictitious commodity" (see discussion of Marx and Polanyi), the goal was to identify all reported acts of resistance by human beings to being treated as a commodity, either at the workplace or in the labor market. This would include all consciously intended open acts of resistance (but also "hidden" forms of resistance when these were widespread, collective practices). Labor unrest generally targets either the employer directly or the state as an intermediary or as an agent of capital. Nevertheless, given the importance of boundary drawing in workers' efforts to protect themselves from being treated as a commodity (see Section III), mobilization by one group of workers against competition from another group of workers was also conceptualized as labor unrest, and any reports of such actions were recorded.

It is necessary to emphasize that the data collection project was *not* designed to produce a count of *all or even most incidents* of labor unrest that have taken place in the world over the last century. Newspapers report on only a small fraction of the labor unrest that occurs. Instead, the procedure is intended to produce a measure that reliably indicates *the changing levels* of labor unrest – when the incidence of labor unrest is rising or falling, when it is high or low – *relative to* other points in time and locations in space. And given the underlying theoretical perspective emphasizing the role of major waves of labor unrest in provoking periods of transformation/restructuring, we were particularly interested in being able to identify major *waves* of labor unrest.

Extensive reliability studies of the database have been carried out in which the temporal profile of labor unrest derived from the WLG database was compared to that derived from other existing sources (the labor history literature and any existing statistical sources). Based on these reliability studies, we have concluded that the WLG database is an effective and reliable tool for identifying years of exceptionally high or intense levels of labor unrest within individual countries.[29] More specifically, we found that the central strength of the WLG database is its fairly consistent ability to identify those waves of labor unrest that represent turning points in the history of labor–capital relations.[30]

In sum, then, the WLG database provides a reliable map of the world-scale patterns of major waves of labor unrest over the century. We use this map to navigate our way through the story of world-scale labor unrest told in the central chapters of the book. Appendix A contains a significantly more in-depth discussion of conceptualization, measurement, and data collection issues related to the construction and use of the WLG database than that which has been offered here. Appendix B reproduces the data collection instructions used by coders. Readers interested in a more detailed treatment of methodological issues related to the database may wish to consult these appendices before moving on to the next chapters of the book.

V. Workers of the World in the Twentieth Century: An Outline of the Book

Chapter 2 focuses on the world-scale dynamics of labor unrest and capital mobility in what is widely taken to be the leading industry of twentieth-century capitalism – the world automobile industry. It traces the global spread of automobile mass production from its origins in Detroit to the present. Drawing on the WLG database, the chapter shows how in virtually every site where the mass production of automobiles expanded rapidly, strong labor movements – what we have referred to above as Marx-type waves of labor unrest – also emerged and won major gains in wages and working conditions. The chapter identifies a recurrent pattern in which automobile corporations responded to each successive wave of labor unrest by shifting production to new sites with relatively cheap and controllable labor. This strategy of capital mobility had a significant weakening effect on labor movements in the sites from which capital was relocated, but created

---

[29] For extensive reliability studies on the World Labor Group database, see Silver et al. (1995).

[30] This reliability in identifying turning-point waves of unrest is tied to the particular characteristics of newspapers as a source for sociohistorical data. That is, newspapers tend to be biased against reporting routine events (such as institutionalized strike activity) and biased in favor of reporting labor unrest that is not routine (episodes that either quantitatively or qualitatively depart from the norm). Given our focus on nonnormative or transgressive episodes of labor unrest (see earlier in this section), this bias is actually beneficial for this study.

and strengthened new labor movements in each successive site of industry expansion.

Elaborating on the concept of spatial fixes introduced by David Harvey (1989: 196; 1999: 390, 415, 431–45), Chapter 2 argues that the successive geographical relocation of capital constitutes an attempted spatial fix for crises of profitability and control that only succeeds in rescheduling crises in time and space. Chapter 2 also focuses on the automobile corporations' efforts to deal with crises of profitability and labor control by introducing major changes in the organization of production and labor process. To capture this dynamic, we introduce the concept of the technological fix. Post-Fordist transformations in the organization of production, we argue, constituted an effort to implement a technological fix to problems of profitability and control. Nevertheless, as we also shall argue, such technological fixes have not provided a solution that is any more long-term and stable than that provided by the successive spatial fixes.

Chapter 3 introduces the concept of the product fix: for capitalists attempt to increase profits and control not only by moving to new geographical sites or transforming the labor process, they also move into new industries and product lines less subject to intense competition and other woes. Chapter 3 focuses on the internal and interrelated dynamics of three macro-product cycles: the world textile industry (the quintessential industry of the nineteenth century), the world automobile industry, and the newly emerging leading sectors of the late twentieth and early twenty-first centuries. We find that, just as labor unrest has shifted geographically with the relocation of production *within* industries, so it has shifted *intersectorally* over time with the rise and decline of new leading industries.

Chapters 2 and 3 purposely keep the angle of vision focused on the labor–capital dynamic in relation to the recurrent spatial and technological/organizational restructuring of processes of capitalist accumulation. Chapter 4 widens the angle of vision, arguing that the overall trajectory of world labor unrest (and of capitalist restructuring) has been deeply embedded in the dynamics of state formation, interstate conflict, and world war. Indeed, the most striking feature of the overall time series of twentieth-century labor unrest derived from the WLG database is the strong interrelationship between waves of labor unrest and world wars – and relatedly, the interrelationship between labor unrest and world hegemonies. Chapter 4 retells the story of twentieth-century world labor unrest with world politics at center stage, and in so doing introduces one final fix – the financial fix. For just as capital shifts to new industries and product lines to escape intense competitive pressures in established spheres of production (our product fix), so, in periods of widespread, intense competition, capital has tended to shift out of trade and production entirely and into finance and speculation. Drawing on Giovanni Arrighi's (1994) concept of "financial expansions," we call this strategy the financial fix.

As we shall see in Chapter 4, the financial fix was a key mechanism in the development of the late-nineteenth-century crisis of overaccumulation and had a profound impact on the trajectory of world labor unrest in the first half of the twentieth century. Likewise, an even more massive financial fix has been a key mechanism in the development of the late-twentieth-century crisis of overaccumulation and, as we will argue, has also had a profound impact on the trajectory of world labor unrest in the last decades of the twentieth century. We turn to these and other similarities between the past and present in the fifth and final chapter in an effort to assess the nature and likely future development of the contemporary crisis of labor movements. In the process, we also return in Chapter 5 to the debates with which we began this chapter.

2

Labor Movements and Capital Mobility

This chapter analyzes the world-scale dynamics of labor unrest in what is widely regarded as the leading industry of twentieth-century capitalism – the world automobile industry. The first section of the chapter presents a picture of the temporal and spatial patterning of labor unrest in the world automobile industry from 1930 to the present based on indexes derived from the World Labor Group database. We identify a series of spatial shifts in the distribution of labor unrest – with the epicenter of militancy moving from North America through Western Europe to a group of newly industrializing countries over the course of the twentieth century.

The second section then narrates the dynamics of these spatial shifts and their interrelationship with successive rounds of capital relocation. We argue that mass production in the automobile industry has tended to re-create similar social contradictions wherever it has grown, and, as a result, strong and effective labor movements have emerged in virtually every site where Fordist mass production expanded rapidly. Yet each time a strong labor movement emerged, capitalists relocated production to sites with cheaper and presumably more docile labor, weakening labor movements in the sites of disinvestment *but* strengthening labor in the new sites of expansion.

Our story of the interrelationship between labor movements and capital relocation thus paints a far more ambiguous picture than that suggested by the race-to-the-bottom thesis (see Chapter 1). To put it in a sentence, the trajectory for the world automobile industry suggests that where capital goes, conflict goes. Or to paraphrase David Harvey (1989: 196; 1999: 390, 442), the geographical relocation of production is a "spatial fix" that only "reschedules crises"; it does not permanently resolve them.

The analysis presented in the first two sections of the chapter emphasizes the similarities and connections among waves of labor unrest in key
sites of automobile industry expansion. The Japanese automobile industry
is conspicuously absent from the discussion – its great postwar expansion
did not culminate in a major wave of labor militancy. Yet, as we argue in
the fourth section, a major wave of labor unrest is critical to explaining
this "Japanese exceptionalism." Japan experienced a mass upsurge of labor militancy at the end of the Second World War (i.e., just *prior* to the
take-off of the Japanese automobile industry). To cope with the constraints
imposed by this wave of labor militancy, the automobile companies chose to
depart in significant ways from the Fordist style of mass production. Discarding their early attempts at vertical integration, Japanese automobile
producers established a multilayered subcontracting system that simultaneously allowed them to guarantee employment to (and establish cooperative relations with) a core labor force, while obtaining low-cost inputs
and flexibility from the lower rungs of the supply network. This combination not only allowed Japan to escape the kind of labor unrest experienced by all the other major producers but also allowed Japanese corporations to introduce a series of cost-cutting measures in the 1970s (so-called
lean production) and, hence, to triumph in the global competition of the
1980s.

In the 1980s and 1990s, lean production methods spread globally as
Fordist-style producers around the world sought to imitate Japanese producers *selectively* and as Japanese automobile companies themselves became
major transnational corporations. These combined processes are widely
seen as having created a fundamentally different post-Fordist "beast" in
which the traditional bases of workers' bargaining power have been undermined (see Chapter 1). Yet, as we argue in the third section of this chapter,
this post-Fordist reorganization of production departed in a critical way
from the Japanese model. The cost-cutting measures of lean production
were adopted, but the employment security provisions were not; thus, the
motivational basis for workers' active cooperation with employers was absent. Moreover, the impact of these transformations on workers' bargaining
power has not been unambiguously negative. Indeed, in some situations,
lean production methods have actually increased the vulnerability of capital to disruptions in the flow of production and increased labor's workplace
bargaining power.

Thus, we find that neither the post-Fordist technological fix nor the
successive spatial fixes have provided a stable solution to problems of labor

control in the world automobile industry. Recent efforts by major automobile corporations to gain the active cooperation of their workers while simultaneously cutting costs, we argue in the final section, are creating an intensified geographical stratification of the auto labor force along the core–periphery divide as well as along gender, ethnic, and citizenship lines. Moreover, the contradictions and limits of these efforts, in turn, reveal at the firm- and industry-level how labor–capital conflict is embedded in an inherent tension (discussed in Chapter 1) between crises of legitimacy and crises of profitability.

I. World-Historical Patterns of Labor Militancy in the Automobile Industry

The picture of world-scale autoworker labor unrest derived from the World Labor Group database is summarized in Figure 2.1 and Table 2.1. Figure 2.1 shows the distribution of mentions of autoworker labor unrest by decade and region. A series of geographical shifts over time in the epicenter of autoworker militancy are visible – from North America in the 1930s and 1940s to northwestern (and then southern) Europe in the 1960s and 1970s

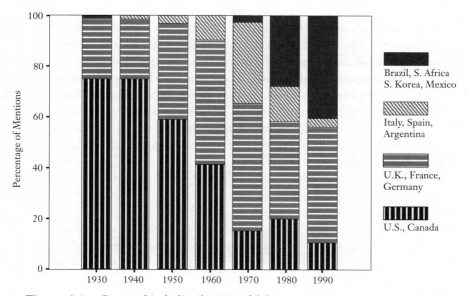

Figure 2.1. Geographical distribution of labor unrest mentions, automobile industry, 1930–1996.

Table 2.1 *High Points of Labor Unrest in the World Automobile Industry, 1930–1996*

	1930–34	1935–39	1940–44	1945–49	1950–54	1955–59	1960–64	1965–69	1970–74	1975–79	1980–84	1985–89	1990–96
United States		X											
Canada		X											
United Kingdom						X							
France								X					
Italy								X			X		
Germany									X				
Spain									X				
Argentina										X			
South Africa											X		
Brazil											X		
South Korea												X	

Note: The countries included in the chart are those that contribute at least 1% to the total mentions of automobile labor unrest in the WLG database. "X" indicates the peak and/or periods in which at least 20% of auto labor unrest mentions for that country take place.

to a group of rapidly industrializing countries in the 1980s and 1990s.[1] Whereas North America accounts for an overwhelming majority of the total reports of labor unrest in the 1930s and 1940s (75% in both decades), by the 1970s and 1980s North America accounts for a distinct minority of the total reports (15% and 20%, respectively). In contrast, the northwestern European share of total labor unrest reports rises from 23% in the 1930s and 1940s to 39% in the 1950s and almost 50% in the 1960s and 1970s, before dropping off in the 1980s and 1990s. The large increase in the southern European share[2] takes place in the 1970s, rising from 2% in the 1950s to 10% in the 1960s to 32% in the 1970s. The last major shift is the increase in the aggregate for the rapidly industrializing South, whose share jumps from 3% in the 1970s to 28% in the 1980s and 40% in the 1990s.

Table 2.1 reinforces this picture of successive spatial shifts in au- toworker militancy, identifying "high points" of autoworker labor unrest for eleven countries where autoworker militancy has been a significant social phenomenon.[3]

The next section of this chapter briefly describes the "high-point waves" identified in Table 2.1.[4] As will become clear in the course of the narra- tive, these labor unrest waves – taking place in vastly different cultural– political settings and world-historical periods – share amazingly similar characteristics. They burst on the scene with a suddenness and strength

---

[1] The eleven countries included in Figure 2.1 and Table 2.1 met a threshold criterion: the number of mentions of auto industry labor unrest for the country had to be greater than 1 percent of the total number of mentions in the WLG database for the auto industry worldwide. See Appendix A for a definition of "mentions" and related measurement issues.

[2] Argentina is included in the southern European aggregate for reasons explained in Footnote 5.

[3] High points (indicated in Table 2.1 with an "X" mark) are defined as the peak year of labor unrest for a given country and/or the year(s) in which the mentions of labor unrest are greater than 20 percent of the total mentions for that country. (See Footnote 1 for this chapter for the threshold criteria met by the eleven countries included in the table.)

[4] Japan does not make it into the list of countries with autoworker unrest waves singled out for analysis in Table 2.1. The rapid expansion of the automobile industry in Japan did not culminate in a major wave of labor unrest – an anomaly that is the focus of Section III. Nevertheless, as will also be discussed in Section III, Japan did experience a major wave of labor unrest in the immediate postwar years, which is picked up by the World Labor Group database. This wave of unrest affected all industries, including automobiles. However, because the automobile industry was not one of the key industries in Japan in the immediate aftermath of the war, the newspaper indexes did not single out the automobile industry when reporting on the strike wave. Thus, Japan also does not make it into Table 2.1 even for the immediate postwar wave of labor unrest in the automobile industry (Farley 1950; Levine 1958).

that was unexpected by contemporaries. They rapidly achieved major victories, despite being confronted by hostile anti-union employers (and, in some cases, hostile governments). All relied on unconventional forms of protest – most notably the sit-down strike – which, in each case, paralyzed the production of huge industrial complexes, effectively exposing the vulnerability of the industry's complex technical division of labor to workers' direct action at the point of production. In all cases, the workforces were predominantly first- and second-generation (international and interregional) migrants, and strong community support was an essential component of the struggles. Finally, the autoworkers' struggles took on a broad political significance for the nation beyond the particular industry and its workers. As such, these waves also represented "turning points" in labor–capital relations for each country.

The automobile industry also seems to produce a characteristic form of direct action. Strategic strikes, especially sit-down strikes targeted at a sensitive point in the automotive corporation's overall technical division of labor, were the weapons of choice in each of these high-point waves. The recurrence of this form (and its success) can be tied to autoworkers' strong workplace bargaining power. The complex technical division of labor characteristic of mass production in the automobile industry increases the vulnerability of capital to workers' direct action at the point of production.

The high-point waves, as we shall see, not only were similar in their characteristic form and style of militancy but also followed similar paths of containment, with victories inspiring a series of managerial strategies that structurally weakened the workers' movements. In the short run, the promotion of "responsible unionism" and the institutionalization of collective bargaining were used to elicit the cooperation of trade union leaders in restraining rank-and-file disruptions. In the short and medium run, work was increasingly automated, and new investments were targeted away from union strongholds. This capital restructuring undermined both the bargaining power of workers at the point of production and the resources on which resistance was based.

The recurrent corporate efforts to find a spatial fix for the problem of labor control means that these high-point waves are not just a series of independent instances of a general process. Rather, they are also *linked relationally* by the successive relocation of production away from militant labor forces. Thus the next section's narrative is also the story of a single historical process of labor militancy and capital mobility. As capital migrated from

46

established sites of production, workers' bargaining power was contained, yet new working classes were created in the locations favored for industrial expansion. The upshot has been a trajectory from the 1930s through the 1990s during which automobile mass-production techniques and a characteristic form of militancy spread across the globe, from the United States through Western Europe to a group of rapidly industrializing countries.

II. *From Flint to Ulsan:* **Déjà Vu** *in Major Auto Strike Waves*

The United States

On December 30, 1936, workers occupied General Motors' Fisher Body Plants No. 1 and No. 2 in Flint, Michigan. By March 12, 1937, General Motors (GM; the United States' largest industrial corporation with vast financial resources and a network of anti-union spies) was forced to capitulate and sign a contract with the United Auto Workers (UAW). This was the beginning of a flood of strikes that brought unionization to the mass-production industries of the United States, at a time of both high unemployment (i.e., weak market-based bargaining power) and feeble labor organization (i.e., weak associational power).

A key to the UAW's success was labor's workplace bargaining power: the ability of the workers to exploit their position within the complex division of labor characteristic of mass production. The Flint sit-down strike that paralyzed GM's Fisher Body plant was planned and executed by a "militant minority" of autoworkers who by "unexpectedly stopping the assembly line and sitting down inside the plant . . . catalyzed pro-union sentiment among the vast majority of apathetic workers" (Dubofsky and Van Tine 1977: 255). The strike wave demonstrated the limits of the assembly lines' technical control of the workforce: a relatively small number of activists could bring an entire plant's production to a halt. As Edwards (1979: 128) put it, "[technical] control linked the entire plant's workforce, and when the line stopped, every worker necessarily joined the strike."

Moreover, just as a militant minority could stop production in an entire plant, so if the plant was a key link in an integrated corporate empire, its occupation could paralyze the corporation. With the occupation of the Fisher Body plants and the Flint plant that produced the bulk of Chevrolet's engines, autoworkers succeeded in crippling General Motors' car production. The corporation's rate of output decreased from 50,000 cars per month in December to only 125 for the first week of February. GM was forced to abandon its uncompromisingly anti-union stance and negotiate a contract with the UAW covering workers in twenty plants in order to end the strike and resume production (see Dubofsky and Van Tine 1977: 268–9; Arrighi and Silver 1984: 184–5, 194–5; Rubenstein 1992: 235–7).

The early experience of the automobile industry shows that the strategy of capital mobility is not a novelty introduced in the most recent (late-twentieth-century) phase of globalization. Indeed, "avoiding concentrations of militant workers influenced locational decisions even in the early days of the automotive industry." Among the many reasons why the automobile industry had concentrated in the Detroit area in the early twentieth century was the anti-union environment successfully imposed through an "open shop" campaign carried out by the Employers' Association of Detroit. "By 1914, when Ford's moving assembly line transformed automotive production from a skilled to an unskilled occupation, the open shop concept... had become strongly entrenched in Detroit and the automotive industry in particular" (Rubenstein 1992: 234–5).

With the success of the UAW, relocation of production away from UAW strongholds became one of the consistent strategies followed by the auto companies over the next half century. Immediately in 1937, GM acquired an engine plant in Buffalo to reduce its dependence on Flint, and shortly thereafter it began to diffuse production sites to rural areas and the U.S. South (Rubenstein 1992: 119, 240–1).

But the geographical relocation of the automobile industry was not, in the post–world-war period, primarily an intra-U.S. phenomenon. The breakup of the world market – from the crash of 1929 until the return to currency convertibility in Europe in 1958 – closed off capital's international escape route. But as soon as postwar Europe stabilized, in particular with the establishment of the Common Market and the restoration of currency convertibility, U.S. multinationals (including U.S. automakers) flooded Europe with investments.

For several decades following the CIO victories, three employer responses – relocation of production (disinvestment in union strongholds), process innovations (mainly automation), and "political exchange" (the promotion of "responsible" unionism and the repression of "irresponsible" unionism) – progressively undermined the structural strength of U.S. labor in general, and autoworkers in particular. When a new upsurge in rank-and-file unrest at the end of the 1960s (symbolized by the "Lordstown Blues") pushed the UAW back toward confrontational tactics with "Operation Apache" (a campaign of short, small, but highly disruptive strikes), the automakers abandoned the promotion of "responsible unionism" and pursued geographical relocation and automation of production with a new-found zeal.

During the 1970s, GM built or planned fourteen plants in the U.S. South, primarily in rural areas or small towns. But GM's "Southern Strategy" to avoid militant workers was made obsolete by a 1979 showdown with the UAW in which the latter succeeded in getting the union's national agreement with GM extended to all the Southern plants. In this confrontation, the UAW once again exploited the autoworkers' position within a complex division of labor: by striking at seven strategically located plants, the UAW could credibly threaten to shut down production of the company's two best-selling models. With the extension of UAW contracts to all Southern plants, the U.S. South lost its main appeal (Rubenstein 1992: 240–1). The automobile corporations responded by intensifying their *ongoing* strategy of moving production to regions with greater labor reserves outside the United States. The bargaining power of U.S. autoworkers, already weakened by decades of restructuring, collapsed in the 1980s. The political assault on organized labor associated with the "Reagan Revolution" was just the icing on the cake.

Western Europe

In the interwar period, Western Europe lagged far behind the United States in extending Fordist mass production techniques to automobile production. In the 1920s, the European industry was characterized by many small firms involved in the custom-manufacture of cars; none had the resources or sufficient market-share to make the huge investments in fixed plant and special-purpose machinery necessary to "catch up" with the United States. In the 1930s, centralization of capital proceeded quickly with the support of governments, but the ability to take advantage of the economies of scale inherent in Fordist methods simply was lacking. The barriers to intra-European trade combined with generally low wages for workers meant than no true mass market existed. U.S. autoworkers could afford to buy the product they were making (even in the 1920s); European workers could not (Landes 1969: 445–51; see also Tolliday 1987: 32–7).

Given the limited extension of mass production techniques, the workplace bargaining power of European workers was relatively weak in the interwar period. Associational power, in contrast, was relatively strong in the years immediately following the First World War. But, although militant

49

labor movements and left political parties surged, and in some cases obtained major workplace and electoral victories, by the mid-1920s, most of these victories had been overturned. (The Italian *Biennio Rosso* of 1919–20, in which Fiat workers played a major role, was one such example.) By the early 1930s, fascist governments were in power in Italy and Germany, and the Labour Party was turned out of power in the United Kingdom in favor of the Conservatives. Even the gains from the stunning workers' victories in France during the French Popular Front – which most closely parallel (and perhaps to some extent inspired) the CIO struggles in the United States – were short-lived. Soon after the Matignon agreement of 1936, a reinvigorated employer offensive successfully blocked the implementation of national collective bargaining agreements. Within two years, the substantial wage gains achieved through Matignon were wiped out by inflation; and within three years Confédération Générale du Travail (CGT) membership fell to around a quarter of the 5 million members claimed in 1936. By 1940, with France at war, "serf-like regulations . . . surrounded workers in the war production industries," and in W. Kendall's words, fascism was prepared "in the guise of resistance to Hitler" long before the Vichy regime assumed power (Kendall 1975: 43–8; Arrighi and Silver 1984: 186–90).

Apart from the far more successful medium-term results of the U.S. strike waves, the basis of whatever success the two movements had was clearly different. Both strike waves were notable for the use of the sit-down strike and factory occupation tactic. But the power of the Paris strikes was based on an enormous and politicized mass movement, with the factory occupations "enthusiastically supported by the worker inhabitants of Paris' red suburbs," including those associated with anti-Communist unions. In contrast, "the GM strike was a minority movement" that had to struggle against a serious "back to work" countermovement. In sum, whereas the relatively weak workplace bargaining power of the Parisian factory workers was partly compensated for by strong associational power, the opposite dynamic obtained in the case of the U.S. strikes. The relatively weak associational power of the Flint strikers was more than compensated for by their ability to "cripple the highly integrated circuit of auto production" (Torigian 1999: 329–30).

Nevertheless, by the 1950s and 1960s, the levels of workplace bargaining power on both sides of the Atlantic began to converge. The center of growth in the world automobile industry shifted to Western Europe following the 1930s and 1940s upsurge of labor militancy among U.S. autoworkers. For Altshuler et al. (1984: Chapter 2) the first major wave of expansion of the auto industry lasted from 1910 to 1950 and was centered in the United States. The second major wave of expansion occurred in the 1950s and 1960s and was centered in Western Europe. The production of automobiles in Western Europe increased fivefold during the 1950s, from 1.1 million in 1950 to 5.1 million in 1960; it doubled in the 1960s to reach 10.4 million in 1970 (Altshuler et al. 1984: 19).

The dynamic behind this expansion was a combined "American challenge" and European response. U.S. direct investment in the European automobile industry had begun in the 1920s as a way to avoid tariff barriers and save on transport and labor costs. But investment soared in the 1950s and 1960s. GM invested over DM 100 million in a major expansion of Opel (Germany) between 1950 and 1955 and afterwards continued adding to its facilities every year. GM also invested 36 million pounds in Vauxhall between 1952 and 1956 to enlarge its Luton plant and build a new factory at Dunstable. Likewise, in the 1950s, Ford rapidly expanded its Dagenham facility in the United Kingdom and its Cologne factory in Germany (Dassbach 1988: 254–5, 296–300). A combined corporate–government response in Europe resulted in the rapid growth of European automobile corporations through consolidation and the introduction of the latest mass-production techniques. Thus, for example, the automobile industry in Italy (which experienced little direct investment by foreign car manufacturers) more than tripled its output during the 1950s and then doubled it in the 1960s. By 1970 motor-vehicle production in Italy had reached almost 2 million with Fiat accounting for the vast majority of the output (Laux 1992: 178, 200).

The rapid extension of mass-production techniques in Western Europe had contradictory effects on the labor force, similar to those experienced by U.S. autoworkers in the early twentieth century. On the one hand, labor's market-based bargaining power declined as craftworkers (and their unions) were marginalized from production and new reserves of labor were tapped. On the other hand, the expansion and transformation of the industry created a new semiskilled working class composed of recently proletarianized migrant workers. In the case of the early-twentieth-century United States, the migrants had been from Eastern and Southern Europe (and the U.S. South). In the case of Western Europe in the 1950s and 1960s, the migrants came from the peripheral regions of Europe (southern Italy, Spain, Portugal, Turkey, and Yugoslavia). In both cases, the first generation of migrant workers generally did not protest against the harsh conditions of work and life. Unions were weak and the arbitrary power of management over issues such as hiring, firing, promotion, and job assignments was unchallenged in the automobile factories. But in both cases, the second generation became the backbone of militant struggles that succeeded in radically transforming relationships within the factory and within society.

The late-1960s Western European strike waves caught unions, management, and states by surprise. In these strikes, mass-production workers, like their U.S. counterparts in the 1930s, were able to exploit the bargaining power that accrued to them as a result of their location within a complex division of labor. Autoworkers in plants across Western Europe came to realize that strategically located and timed strikes could do great damage to a corporation, while minimizing the sacrifice made by the workers themselves. Perhaps the most dramatic example was the "hot autumn" of 1969 at Fiat:

> For Italian strikers, coordinated dispute activity within a large-scale production unit [was] undertaken with a view to paralysing production at the least cost to the workers. A judicious application of strike action *a singhiozzo* (shop-floor strikes) and *a scacchiera* (coordinated in-plant stoppages) soon leads to production chaos. (Dubois 1978: 9)

Spot strikes, rolling strikes, and lightning strikes were designed to create the maximum disruption to the flow of production by targeting the most sensitive links in the productive chain. Similar tactics were employed by autoworkers throughout Western Europe in the late 1960s and early 1970s (see, e.g., Crouch and Pizzorno 1978).

The successful exploitation of such tactics resulted in a rapid expansion of the role of unions and workers' control on the shopfloor and an unprecedented explosion of wages in the 1970s. Major limits on management prerogatives were imposed. For example, at Fiat *consigli dei delegati* (workers' delegates councils) were set up at the factory level, with the goal of providing workers (through their delegates) with some direct control over the organization of production and with a say in the day-to-day exercise of what had heretofore been fundamental managerial prerogatives: for example, assigning work tasks, loads, and speed; changing the organization of production; and introducing new technology. Management was required to inform, consult, and negotiate with workers' delegates on all decisions relating to the organization of the shopfloor (Silver 1992: 29–30; Rollier 1986). Here, however, it is important to distinguish between northwestern Europe, on the one hand, and southwestern Europe, on the other hand. In southwestern Europe, the autoworkers' struggles were far

[handwritten: fighting for more than just labor rights]

more explosive than the northwestern European pattern. Moreover, the autoworkers' struggles in Spain and Italy were far more central (including symbolically) to the broader national-level social and political struggles of the time. *[handwritten circled: A]*

Both these differences can be linked to the nature of the migrant labor pool. The northwestern European industries relied on noncitizen immigrant labor (including Italian and Spanish workers), while the southwestern European industries relied on migrant, but citizen, labor forces. This difference had both labor-market and social–political implications. While northwestern European countries had multiple sources of immigrant labor, Italy and Spain only relied on internal sources – and other countries were also tapping these internal sources. This combined situation in the labor market made the Italian and Spanish reactions to the initial upsurges far less flexible, and thus contributed to their greater explosiveness. *[handwritten circled: A]*

Moreover, the fact that the workers in Italy and Spain were citizens opened the space for other social movements to harness the autoworkers' struggles as part of broader struggles for economic and political democratization. In both cases, as in the case of the so-called NICs (newly industrializing countries), which are discussed later, the labor movement strengthened (and was strengthened by) other movements aimed at broad social, economic, and political transformations. (Foweraker 1989; Tarrow 1989; Martin 1990: 417–26; Perlmutter 1991; cf. Fishman 1990).

The response of automakers producing in Western Europe to the startling successes of the workers' movements was analogous to the U.S. corporate response to the CIO victories of the 1930s and 1940s. "Process innovations" (including the rapid robotization of labor-intensive tasks), attempts to promote "responsible unionism," and the relocation of production were all vigorously pursued. For Volkswagen, a strategy of geographical relocation – shifting investments to more peripheral locations, especially Brazil and Mexico – took precedence. Overall, foreign direct investment from Germany increased fivefold between 1967 and 1975 (OECD 1981; Ross 1982; Silver 1992: 80). At Fiat, on the other hand, massive robotization projects were emphasized, including the complete automation of engine assembly (Volpato 1987: 218).

The effect on the bargaining power of workers was also analogous to the U.S. case. By the early 1980s, labor movements in Western Europe (including autoworkers) were generally on the defensive, and the promotion of "responsible unionism" was abandoned. By 1980, Fiat was able to bypass the workers' councils and unilaterally implement a policy of aggressive automation and rationalization that reduced the number of employees from 140,000 to 90,000 (Rollier 1986: 117, 129). The gains of the late 1960s had been largely overturned. The other side of this process, however, was the creation (and strengthening) of new automobile proletariats in the favored sites of industry expansion in the 1970s and 1980s.[5]

Brazil and EOI Fordism

The Brazilian "economic miracle" from 1968 to 1974 corresponded precisely to the period in which core capitalists increasingly sought to escape militant workers' struggles at home. Brazil provided a seemingly perfect site for investment: the 1964 military coup installed an extremely repressive regime, which succeeded in smashing the old corporatist trade-union movement and effectively eliminating any working-class opposition at both the plant level and national political level.[6]

The Brazilian automobile industry experienced very rapid expansion in the 1970s. By 1974 Brazil was among the world's top ten vehicle producers. From 1969 to 1974, vehicle output increased by an average annual rate of 20.7%; from 1974 to 1979 (while vehicle output collapsed throughout the core in response to the oil crisis and labor militancy), the Brazilian industry continued to grow at 4.5% per year (Humphrey 1982: 48–50). While retrenching their operations in core countries, multinationals invested heavily in Brazil in the 1970s: Ford, for example, invested over U.S.$300 million and increased plant capacity by 100% (Humphrey 1987: 129).

[5] The Argentine case adds another variation to the same basic story being told here. It is a case of early, rapid growth of the mass-production automobile industry through ISI (import-substitution-industrialization) in the 1950s and 1960s. The timing and patterning of both the expansion of the industry and the outbreak of a major wave of labor unrest is similar to that described for Western Europe, except that the lower relative level of wealth in Argentina made a stable social contract solution more difficult to fund. (This contrast between the options open to high-income and middle-income countries in accommodating labor unrest through reforms is elaborated at length in Chapter 3.) For Argentina, as for Japan, labor unrest was a problem from the early days. Yet in contrast to Japan, labor unrest did not provoke a major departure from Fordism (see our discussion of Japan later in this chapter). In Argentina, the growth in automobile manufacturing, although fitful, further strengthened the working class, culminating in the major uprising in the late 1960s known as the *Cordobazo*, followed by a military coup and a period of brutal deindustrialization (Jelin 1979; James 1981; Brennan 1994).

[6] Moreover, ISI efforts elsewhere in Latin America (especially Argentina) were producing major labor unrest waves (see Footnote 5 in this chapter), further enhancing Brazil's attractiveness as an alternative site for investment.

The rapid expansion of manufacturing in general, and the automobile industry in particular, created a new working class: new in size and in experience. From 1970 to 1980, employment in manufacturing doubled (Humphrey 1987: 120). In the industrial suburb of Sao Bernardo do Campo where the automobile industry concentrated, the number of workers employed in manufacturing increased from 4,030 in 1950 to 20,039 in 1960 to 75,118 in 1970 (Humphrey 1982: 128–9). This new working class tended to be concentrated in plants of enormous size. Three plants in Sao Bernardo – Volkswagen, Mercedes, and Ford – employed over 60,000 people (Humphrey 1982: 137).

Like the protagonists of the CIO struggles of the 1930s and the strike waves in Western Europe of the late 1960s, Brazil's autoworkers were strategically located within a complex technical division of labor inside the Brazilian factories. But this new working class was also strategically situated in what was now the key export sector of the Brazilian economy: transportation equipment was Brazil's largest export, worth $3.9 billion in 1988 (Economist Intelligence Unit 1990: 3). Strikes and militancy in the automobile industry would affect not only the profitability of the specific firms involved but also the ability of the Brazilian government to service its enormous debt to foreign banks.

In the closing years of the 1970s, as labor movements were experiencing decisive defeats throughout the core, a new trade union movement burst onto the scene in Brazil, bringing to an end almost one and a half decades of worker quiescence. An intense strike wave in 1978 inaugurated a period of activism that survived (even flourished) through a decade of repression and recession in the 1980s. Brazil's autoworkers formed the central core of this new labor movement with auto- and metalworkers accounting for almost half of all strikes in the 1978 to 1986 period (Seidman 1994: 36).

On May 12, 1978, the day shift workers entered the Saab-Scania plant's tool room in Sao Bernardo but refused to start up their machines. The strike quickly spread to the whole plant with thousands of workers standing by their machines in silence with their arms crossed. From Scania, the stoppages spread to other auto plants – Mercedes, Ford, Volkswagen, and Chrysler. Within a few days, workers were crossing their arms and refusing to work in all the major plants. Reminiscent of the U.S. strikes of the 1930s and the Western European strike waves of the late 1960s, these were mainly conducted as sit-down strikes, with workers reporting to work each day, eating in the canteen, but refusing to work (Moreira Alves 1989: 51–2; Humphrey 1982: 166). The strikes resulted in major worker victories, including substantial wage increases and the recognition of new, independent trade unions (not linked to the official state-sponsored trade unions). Implacably anti-union employers had been forced to negotiate with new independent unions and to sign collective contracts.

The automobile multinationals did not accept this defeat and carried on a battle to repress strikes and eliminate the unions from the plants. They believed that the victory of the workers in 1978 resulted from their own lack of preparation, rather than from any inherent strength of the workers. But repression only resulted in a change of tactics from large-scale confrontations to smaller-scale (but very disruptive) protests on the shopfloor (slowdowns, spot strikes, and general non-cooperation with management). These tactics were reminiscent of those used in the Western European strike wave of the late 1960s and early 1970s to maximize the disruption while minimizing the costs to the workforce.

By 1982, the major employers had accepted the inevitability of unionization, union involvement in shopfloor management, and rising wages. Ford was the first to come to believe that the maintenance of discipline on the shopfloor required the promotion of "responsible unionism." In 1981, Ford recognized plant-level committees made up of workers elected at the shopfloor level and linked to the independent unions as having the right to negotiate with management over workers' concerns and grievances (Humphrey 1987: 125; Humphrey 1993: 103, 111–12). Volkswagen (VW) held out longer, but by 1982 VW was forced to recognize the independent unions and accept factory committees similar to those that had been introduced at Ford.

Strike activity in Brazil reached a peak of 9 million workers involved in 1987 (Moreira Alves 1989: 67). During the four years from 1985 to 1988, *real* industrial wages in Greater Sao Paulo grew by an average of 10 percent per year (Economist Intelligence Unit 1990). The strike movement thus effectively nullified the IMF-inspired government anti-inflation plan (Moreira-Alves 1989: 67). The new union movement also took an active role in pushing for a broader democratization, especially with regard to the provisions to be included in the new constitution. The latter (adopted in 1989) gave workers the right to strike, to form independent trade unions, and to manage their affairs without state interference. It also guaranteed the right to shopfloor representation. As Margaret Keck (1989: 284) pointed out, the amount of "attention paid to labor issues in the Constituent Assembly . . . speak[s] to the change in labor's political clout in Brazil."

II. *Déjà Vu* in Major Auto Strike Waves

Tellingly, however, the labor movement failed to win one of the provisions they had fought hard for: job security guarantees incorporated into the Constitution itself. And indeed, workers' movements in the industrial suburbs of Sao Paolo where the auto industry had concentrated have been progressively undermined as new investment has gone elsewhere and existing jobs have been eliminated. For at least a decade – from the mid 1980s to the mid 1990s – Brazil was no longer a favored site of investment as new investments by the auto multinationals dried up (Gwynne 1991: 75–8). In the mid and late 1990s – especially after Cardoso's 1994 presidential election victory – foreign investment once again began flowing into the Brazilian automobile industry. But the expansions being carried out by foreign automobile companies are *outside* the traditional Sao Paolo/Sao Bernardo stronghold of the metalworkers' union. In the mid 1990s, reports of major new investments in Rio State, Minas Gerais, and the northeast were interspersed with reports of massive layoffs at factories located in the strongholds of the Brazilian labor movement (Brooke 1994; New York Times 1995; Rodrídguez-Pose and Arbix 2001). At VW's Sao Bernardo plant, for example, the number of workers dropped from 40,000 in 1978 to 26,000 in 1996, and the number was expected to continue to drop further as VW simultaneously built new plants in greenfield sites in Resende (Rio State) and Sao Carlos. Likewise, Fiat built its new factory in Minas Gerais where workers are unorganized and wages are 40 percent lower than at its Sao Bernardo plant. As a result of these trends, membership in the metalworkers' union in the ABC+ (suburban Sao Paolo) region dropped from 202,000 in 1987 to 150,000 in 1992 and 130,000 in 1996 (DIEESE 1995: 44; Bradsher 1997: D1; Sedgwick 1997: 3; Automotive News 1996: 9; author interviews with Human Resources Manager, VW Sao Bernardo and director of Sindicato dos Metalurgicos do ABC, June 13, 1996).

South Africa

Like Brazil, although on a less spectacular scale, South Africa became a favored site for investment by the automobile multinational corporations in the late 1960s and 1970s. During the late 1950s and early 1960s, foreign capital had shied away from South Africa. The strength of national liberation movements was peaking across the continent, and mass protests against the implementation of apartheid laws within South Africa were spreading – including nationwide "stayaways" organized in 1957, 1958, 1960, and 1961 by the South African Congress of Trade Unions (SACTU). However, foreign investment boomed in the late sixties, after the Nationalist government showed that it could successfully smash the opposition and, moreover, institute repressive and racist legislation that ensured a steady flow of cheap labor. As a 1972 article published by *Fortune* observed, South Africa was considered to be a "gold mine" by foreign investors:

[O]ne of those rare and refreshing places where profits are great, and problems are small. Capital is not threatened by political instability or nationalization. Labour is cheap, the market is booming, the currency hard and convertible. (Blashill 1972: 49; quoted by Seidman and Seidman 1977: 76)

From 1965 to 1969, the average annual net inflow of foreign capital was $308 million per year; and between 1970 and 1976 the inflow mushroomed to an average of $1 billion per year (Litvak et al. 1978: 40). The motor vehicle industry was one of the main targets of these inflows of capital. From 1967 to 1975 the motor vehicle industry grew by 10.3 percent annually (Litvak et al. 1978: 24; Myers 1980: 256).

A large, urban, Black proletariat was formed, concentrated in semiskilled positions in mass-production industries. The number of Blacks employed in manufacturing doubled between 1950 and 1975. And while apartheid laws reserved skilled and salaried positions for white workers, the strategic semiskilled jobs within manufacturing were almost entirely performed by Blacks.

As in Brazil, this new proletariat became the backbone of a wave of labor militancy in the 1970s and early 1980s. The first sign of the changing balance of class power was the 1973 wave of strikes centered in the factories of Durban that shattered over a decade of labor quiescence. Most of these strikes ended in victory with workers winning large wage increases; membership in the newly formed (illegal) Black trade unions mushroomed. Yet neither the state nor employers resigned themselves to these victories.

Indeed, throughout the 1970s, employers, backed by the state, fiercely resisted union recognition. The metal industry's employers association advised its members to call in the police "if at any time it appears that law and order are in danger" (Seidman 1994: 179). And in virtually all disputes, the police were indeed called in, strikers were arrested, union leaders banned, workers fired and forced to leave the urban areas. Yet repression, which "had proven in the past to be highly effective in suppressing Black unionization drives," did not succeed in undermining the independent unions in the 1970s (Beittel 1989: 3). Given the "hostile political environment," the fact that the new unions managed to survive the 1970s was, argued Maree (1985: 294), in itself "a major achievement."

Not only did the labor movement survive, but it also forced the government to rethink its repressive labor policy. Indeed, Gay Seidman (1994: 185) suggested that "the 1979 strikes in the automobile industry in the Eastern Cape were the final straw prompting the state to legalize nonracial unions." These strikes "seemed to herald a new and uncontrollable wave of industrial action, which could only be prevented by allowing unions some legal channels for expressing workers' demands."

The legalization of Black trade unions in 1979 was followed by the largest and longest strike wave in South African history. The number of signed union-recognition agreements rose from 5 in 1979 to no less than 403 in 1983 (Maree 1985: 297). In 1985, the independent trade unions federated to form the Congress of South African Trade Unions (COSATU), which by the end of the 1980s was dubbed "the fastest growing trade union movement in the world" (Obrery 1989: 34).

As in Brazil, the South African strike wave demonstrated the strong workplace bargaining power of this new working class, which effectively exploited its position within a complex technical division of labor. This bargaining power was most visible in the automobile industry, whose workers formed the frontline of the industrial class battle in the early 1980s.[7] Indeed, between 1979 and early 1986, strikes in the South African metal and automobile sectors accounted for 30 percent of person-days lost to industrial action (Seidman 1994: 37). While some strikes were large-scale conflicts involving thousands of workers (e.g., in 1980 at Ford, VW, Datsun, and BMW; in 1981 at Leyland; and in 1982 at Ford and GM), others involved the use of disruptive but low-key tactics such as slowdowns and small strikes limited to key departments within plants. For example, in an August 1984 strike at Volkswagen, the workers limited their stoppage to the paint shop, but because of the latter's strategic location within the factory's division of labor, the entire plant was forced to shut down for five days. The plant reopened when management agreed to union demands (Southall 1985: 321, 329).[8]

---

[7] Strong workplace bargaining power was also visible among mineworkers who labored in an increasingly mechanized industry and who, by the mid 1980s, had taken the lead in the continuing wave of labor unrest.

[8] The South African autoworkers derived power not only from their strategic location within the technical division of labor within the South African automobile industry but also from

The strike movement was all the more impressive because it took place within the context of a deep recession within the auto industry and in the economy in general. As in Brazil, mass layoffs did not dampen labor militancy. Instead, they refocused strike demands on questions of job security; strikes protesting retrenchments became common. Moreover, as in Brazil, the new South African unions made headway in achieving agreements that recognized shop stewards' rights to be consulted about key decisions in the running of the plants including decisions about hiring and firing (Lewis and Randall 1986: 71–3; Maree 1985: 12).

The 1980s experience in South Africa and Brazil contrasts sharply with that of the 1950s and 1960s. In the earlier period in both countries, a militant labor movement (without a strong shopfloor base) succumbed to state repression, while in the 1980s, arrests and other forms of repression tended only to fan the flames of militancy rather than to drown them. In a summary of the year 1988, Obrery and Singh (1988: 37) catalogued massive repression of workers by the South African state and then concluded: "rank and file ... militancy and anger seem largely untouched by years of union-bashing and emergency rule." Indeed, the workers' movement was able to withstand the crackdown on anti-apartheid activities in the second half of the 1980s better than the community and political groups with which they were allied. COSATU found itself catapulted to playing the leading role in the anti-apartheid movement, bringing "a distinctively working class perspective" to the question of national liberation (Obrery 1989: 34–5; see also Adler and Webster 2000).

With repression failing to maintain labor control, capital began to shift out of the South African automobile industry. Sales of locally produced automobiles peaked in 1981 (Hirschsohn 1997: 233). By the end of the 1980s, automobile multinationals had largely divested from South Africa. As Gwynne (1991: 50) noted: "While political factors [anti-apartheid campaign] have been emphasized, the ... withdrawal of Ford and General Motors from South Africa [had] a significant economic basis." In the place

their position within the world-scale organization of labor of their corporate employers. Workers in South Africa were often able to bring pressure to bear on management by enlisting support from autoworkers' unions in the country where the corporation headquarters were located. Thus, for example, in the 1979–80 strike at its Port Elizabeth plant, Ford was forced to retract the mass dismissal of strikers and to reinstate its employees "after coming under pressure from Ford (Detroit), which had been assailed by US auto unions and Black American politicians" (Southall 1985: 317). In this case, associational power grew out of the concentration/centralization of production on a world-scale (see Chapter 1, Footnote 10, on this form as contrasted with workplace bargaining power).

of local production, more and more CBUs (completely built-up motor vehicles) flooded the South African market from around the world in the 1990s (Cargo Info 1997).

usually moving to areas of political repression

| South Korea |

The South Korean "economic miracle" overlapped with the fading of the Brazilian and South African "economic miracles." In 1973 the South Korean government targeted automobiles as one of the priority industries for development. While output and employment in light industries grew rapidly in the 1970s, the take-off of the South Korean automobile industry only took place in the early 1980s (i.e., during the years in which labor militancy, unionization, and rising wages had come to characterize the Brazilian and South African industries). Like Brazil and South Africa at the time of their big spurts in automobile production, an authoritarian regime in South Korea banned independent trade unions and strike activity, arrested and blacklisted labor activists, and helped keep wages low and working conditions harsh and despotic. In the early 1980s, "organized labor found no legitimate space in which to operate, and the labor movement was forced into a state of apparent quiescence" (Koo 1993: 149, 161; also Rodgers 1996: 105–10; Vogel and Lindauer 1997: 98–9; Koo 2001).

This environment proved attractive for the three domestic conglomerates that had been given governmental permission to produce automobiles (Hyundai, Kia, and Daewoo), as well as for their multinational corporate partners (Mitsubishi, Ford/Mazda, and GM/Isuzu, respectively). South Korean motor vehicle output increased eightfold in just seven years, from 123,135 units in 1980 to 980,000 units in 1987 (Wade 1990: 309–12; AAMA 1995: 60; Bloomfield 1991: 29).

Both U.S. and Japanese multinationals moved into Korea through joint ventures. In 1981, GM obtained a 50 percent stake in Daewoo. Through this joint venture, GM began selling a cheap Korean-made car in North America as the Pontiac Le Mans. A 1985 agreement between GM and Daewoo called for the latter to supply starter motors and alternators for GM's worldwide operations. In 1986, Ford paid U.S.$30 million for a 10 percent shareholding in Kia and opened a Korean branch office of Ford International Business Development in order to develop sources of automotive components in South Korea (Gwynne 1991: 73–4). By the 1980s, "an industrial belt of heavy industry" including steel, shipbuilding, and automobiles "stretched forty miles along the Ulsan coast, with hundreds of thousands of new workers recruited from all over the country" (Vogel and Lindauer 1997: 106).

As South Korean production reached one million automobiles annually (and surpassed Brazilian output), the *New York Times* filed the following report on August 12, 1987: "A wave of labor unrest is sweeping through this country. . . . The unrest has shut plants in the nation's largest conglomerates, including Hyundai, Daewoo, Samsung, Lucky-Goldstar. Hyundai Motors, which manufactures the popular Excel, settled a dispute that had shut its factory but said labor troubles at its suppliers had forced the company to suspend car exports for now."

On August 18, 1987, the *New York Times* headline read "Workers Seize Hyundai Plants in South Korea." And it was reported that:

> More than 20,000 workers climbed over a barricade and occupied factory buildings and a shipyard operated by the Hyundai Group. . . . Hyundai has been the most badly hit of the large conglomerates. At the heart of the struggle is the demand by Hyundai's workers to form their own unions. Hyundai has long taken a tough anti-union stance, and until the recent turmoil, Hyundai employees had no union.

Then, on August 20, 1987, only eight days after the initial report, the *Times* carried a photograph with the caption: "Chung Ju Yung, in white suit, founder and honorary chairman of the Hyundai Group, toasting the agreement with leaders of the newly formed labor union in Seoul yesterday." The accompanying article was entitled "South Korean Company Agrees to Recognize Union."

The initial workers' victories were rapid and dramatic, leading to the establishment of new democratic unions independent of the government and employers. Ulsan heavy industry workers received wage increases ranging from 45 percent to 60 percent or more over the next two years "as management tried to buy peace and keep control" (Vogel and Lindauer 1997: 108). Nevertheless, as with the initial strike waves and labor victories in Brazil and South Africa, Korea's automobile producers were not reconciled to the changing balance in labor–capital relations. "Management . . . could not get over the conviction that excising the trouble-makers would get rid of the cancer." Employers tended to ascribe the wave of labor militancy to the work of outside agitators, especially radical students. The South Korean government, which initially refrained from repressing strike activity in 1987, cracked down on labor unrest in 1989–90. Unions were resisted through "bad faith" collective bargaining, repression of labor activists (firings, arrests, kidnappings), and the use of paramilitary troops to break up strikes (Kirk 1994: 228; Koo 1993: 158–9; Vogel and Lindauer 1997: 93, 110).

However, as in the Brazilian case, the labor movement could not be successfully repressed. According to Ezra Vogel and David Lindauer (1997: 110), even though strike activities were partially contained, "large masses of workers and ordinary citizens who opposed the crackdown were further alienated." Moreover, the Korean experience showed mass production's vulnerability, not only to disruptions by workers' direct action, but also to repressive countermeasures by employers and states. During a 1990 strike at the Hyundai Group, auto assembly-line workers described the following incidents:

> "Only a small number of [Hyundai Motor] workers were blocking the road at first [in solidarity with striking Hyundai shipyard workers]", said Roh Sang Soo, a young assembly line worker. . . . "Then the police threw teargas into the compound while we were working. We could not work. . . . I was on the Excel line at the time. I smelled the teargas. I came out of the plant and joined the demonstration". . . . Those who came to work the next day again got teargassed. "We couldn't work because of the gas", said assembly line worker Lee Sang Hui. "*If one person cannot work, the whole line stops*. I just joined the demonstration and sang songs and clapped." (Kirk 1994: 246; emphasis added)

Workers also responded to repression by turning toward smaller-scale, less-open, but highly disruptive forms of protest. Slowdowns, sabotage, and refusals to work overtime all caused major losses in output at Hyundai in the early 1990s, the latter having invested heavily in advanced capital equipment. Hyundai Motors' hardline position was aggravating "other subjective or less easily quantifiable problems" (Rodgers 1996: 116, see also Kirk 1994: 257, 262).

One recurrent employer response to major waves of labor unrest has been automation. Significantly, exactly one year after the outbreak of the 1987 strikes in Ulsan, the Hyundai Group added a new company to the conglomerate – Hyundai Robot Industry (Kirk 1994: 344–5). Moreover, Korean automobile producers moved to turn themselves into multinational corporations at breakneck speed. After surveying Korean plans to build automobile plants in northeast Brazil, the Ukraine, and Poland (Daewoo); China (Hyundai); and Indonesia (Kia), *Automotive News* concluded that Korean-owned companies are on "the cutting-edge of international expansion" (Johnson 1997: 14).

Despite rising wages and endemic labor unrest, the Korean conglomerates (although *not* their multinational partners) continued to expand automobile production *in* Korea. While capacity utilization was hurt by strikes and slowdowns, actual output climbed on a yearly basis from about 1 million in 1987 (the year of the first major strike) to almost 1.5 million in 1991 and over 2 million in 1993 (AAMA 1995: 60). By 1996, total Korean capacity had reached well over 3 million and expansion plans foresaw an output capacity of over 6 million by the year 2002 (Treece 1997b: 4).

The overambitious nature of these plans was revealed by the Asian financial crisis of 1997. While it lasted, however, this expansion only further heightened the intensity and effectiveness of labor militancy – especially in the context of continued employer hostility toward independent unions. A new peak of labor militancy was reached with the twenty-day general strike in December 1996–January 1997 in which autoworkers played a central role. Prompted by government passage of a new law that further undermined both labor and democratic rights, the mass general strike resulted in "a de facto surrender to the working class" by the government. The labor law was reamended in ways that have greatly strengthened the juridical status of the independent trade union federation. And there are growing indications that employers are finally reconciling themselves to institutionalizing trade unions and collective bargaining. Moreover, because of the undemocratic way in which the government passed the original laws – secretly, at dawn, without notifying opposition parties – the general strike drew broad support beyond the working class. Workers were seen as fighting for "the interests of the people in general," taking the leadership role in the broader struggle for democracy (Sonn 1997: 125–8).

Another Round of Relocation and Militancy?

In sum, it appears that corporations in the automobile industry have been chasing the mirage of cheap and disciplined labor around the world, only to find themselves continuously recreating militant labor movements in the new locations. Rather than providing a permanent spatial fix to the problems of profitability and labor control, relocation has only succeeded in geographically relocating the contradictions from one site of production to another (see also Silver 1995b: 173–85).[9]

---

[9] The time required to bring each wave of militancy under control has decreased over the course of the half century, a point to which we will return in Chapter 3 when we reformulate this process within a modified product cycle framework.

II. *Déjà Vu* in Major Auto Strike Waves

Recent trends might be interpreted as the beginnings of yet another new cycle of spatial relocation and militancy. The world's major automobile producers have singled out at least two new low-wage sites for rapid expansion: northern Mexico and China. If past dynamics are a guide to future trends, then we have good reasons to expect the emergence of strong, independent autoworkers' movements in Mexico and China during the coming decade.

The automobile industries in both countries have expanded rapidly. Mexican motor vehicle production tripled from 357,998 units in 1984 to 1,122,109 units in 1994 and 1,755,000 units in 2001 (AAMA 1995: 28, 257; Standard & Poor's 2002).

China's output almost doubled in just three years, increasing from 708,820 in 1991 to 1,353,368 in 1994 and to 1,995,000 in 2001 (China Automotive Technology and Research Center 1998: 11; Standard & Poor's 2002). The Chinese government has chosen the automobile industry as one of the seven "pillar industries" of economic development, and the industry is expected to continue to grow rapidly as multinationals rush in to establish production of parts and vehicles (Treece 1997a). By 1996, eighteen out of the twenty-eight automobile firms ranked in the Fortune 500 list had already invested in automobile production in China (Zhang 1999: Table 1). The trend since the 1980s has been toward the creation of larger production units as well as the concentration of production in specific geographical areas, a reversal of the previous policy emphasis on geographical dispersion and regional self-sufficiency in production (Harwit 1995: 26–37). The proportion of the total number of automobiles produced in China by the top ten firms increased from 66 percent in 1987 to 78 percent in 1996. This proportion was expected to increase further once new investments by major automobile multinationals (including GM, Citroën, VW, and Toyota) come on line in the late 1990s and 2000s (Zhang 1999).[10]

Another trend that emerged in the late 1980s and 1990s might also, perversely, be interpreted as a continuation of the same dynamic of militancy

---

[10] Yet, it should also be pointed out that the 1990s growth in production and employment by automobile multinational corporations in China has gone hand in hand with massive layoffs from state-owned industrial enterprises, including automobile industrial enterprises. These layoffs (and the breaking of the "iron rice bowl" social contract more generally) sparked significant Polanyi-type waves of labor unrest in China in the late 1990s and early 2000s (see, e.g., Pan 2002) – a point to which we return in subsequent chapters. Whether these unrest waves are also a prelude to the emergence of Marx-type waves of labor unrest in the expanding multinational corporate-controlled automobile industry in China, as our analysis here would predict, remains to be seen.

and capital relocation. The automobile multinationals came full-circle and began to concentrate production in the core regions from which they had fled in the 1950s, 1960s, and 1970s (particularly the United States and the United Kingdom). In the case of the United States, the southern Great Lakes states are once again a favored site for both automotive assembly and automotive components production; however, former union strongholds are avoided, and small towns with no automotive production history are preferred (Rubenstein 1992: 171–82). This reconcentration in the core can be interpreted, at least in part, as a continuation of the long trajectory of militancy and relocation – that is, as mass-production unions have been undermined in the core by the disinvestment of the previous decades, producers are once again choosing to relocate to an area of weak labor movements.[11]

Moreover, this reconcentration in the core has been accompanied by major transformations in the organization of production and labor process over the past two decades that raise questions about whether we are witnessing a repeat of the cycle of relocation and militancy. It is to the character and impact of these transformations that we now turn.

III. A Post-Fordist Technological Fix?

By the 1980s, with the emergence of militant labor movements in the Brazilian and South Korean automobile industries, it was no doubt clear to the automobile corporations that geographical relocation would not provide a long-run stable solution to the problems of profitability and labor control. This awareness, combined with the competitive threat posed by the phenomenal success of Japanese automobile firms in the 1980s, led U.S. and Western European corporations to focus on the implementation of major process innovations – technological fixes to the problems of profitability and labor control. The result, it is widely argued, has been a fundamental transformation of the nature of labor–capital relations within the automobile industry.

The post-Fordist organizational transformations were spearheaded by the rapid overseas expansion of Japanese multinationals in the 1980s. In response to rising wages at home, Japanese automakers moved into lower-wage areas in East and Southeast Asia (see discussion that follows). And in

---

[11] It should be noted that protectionist measures, especially targeting Japanese auto imports, were also a key motivation underlying this reconcentration of production in the United States and the United Kingdom (a point to which we return in Chapter 3).

III. A Post-Fordist Technological Fix?

response to rising protectionist measures in the West (most notably the open or tacit imposition of "voluntary" export restrictions), they expanded rapidly in North America and Western Europe. By the mid 1990s, production by Japanese multinationals accounted for approximately 25 percent of total U.S. and 20 percent of total U.K. passenger car output, and these shares were projected to grow further (AAMA 1995: 199, 272).

The Japanese automakers brought to these sites many of the organizational practices of automobile production in Japan. These practices spread still further as U.S. and Western European automobile firms responded to the Japanese competitive threat by *selectively* emulating Japanese organizational practices.[12] Thus, in the 1980s, flexible work rules, just-in-time delivery systems, teamwork, quality circles, and a move away from vertical integration toward the extensive use of subcontracted inputs (outsourcing) were widely adopted. There was, however, a crucial difference between the original Japanese model and that adopted by the U.S. and Western European multinationals. That is, the latter *did not* promise job security to their core labor force. In other words, the cost-cutting measures of Japanese lean production were adopted without the related employment policies. This model might thus be labeled "lean and mean" (cf. Harrison 1997). In contrast, the original "Toyotist" model – which offers employment security to a core labor force in exchange for cooperation, but at the same time creates a large buffer of less privileged workers without the same rights and benefits – might be labeled "lean and dual." The difference between these two models, we will argue, is crucial to understanding the dynamics of contemporary labor unrest in the world automobile industry.

Through the 1990s, the lean-and-mean version predominated. Whereas Japanese multinationals operating in core countries tended to implement the homegrown model (Florida and Kenney 1991: 390–1), U.S. corporations have generally taken the lean-and-mean road, as have Japanese producers operating in Southeast Asia and Latin America. Deyo (1996a: 9) argued that "authoritarian politics and repressive labor regimes" are characteristic of the main sites of industry expansion in low-wage countries. In Thailand, Mitsubishi has not extended employment guarantees to its core workforce (Deyo 1996b: 145–6). In Korea, the domestic auto producers (except Kia) continue to pursue a low-wage, high-turnover strategy of mass production and an anti-union and autocratic managerial style (Rodgers

---

[12] On the U.S. automobile industry's emulation of Japanese production methods, see among others Abo (1994).

67

1996: 115–19). And in China, "layoffs are becoming a painful reality" as the central government promotes a "leaning-out of the industry" in an effort to bring labor productivity in Chinese automobile factories in line with the standards set by international "market rule" (Treece 1997c). Likewise, Japanese transnationals in Mexico are employing traditional Fordist techniques; they have found it "economically rational to place a heavier emphasis on low wages, even if the consequent high turnover disrupts quality circles and other lean production techniques" (Shaiken 1995: 248–9, 254).

Nevertheless, it also has become clear that, as was the case with the spatial fixes discussed earlier, the technological fix of lean-and-mean production has not provided a stable solution to labor unrest. Indeed, without employment guarantees, automakers have found that it is very difficult to elicit the active cooperation of the workforce; thus, the dynamic of labor–capital conflict has remained largely the same as in the traditional Fordist model. Thus, where quality circles have been implemented without concomitant employment security guarantees, they have failed to succeed in eliciting workers' cooperation. Mitsubishi's Thai plant has been plagued by high quit rates and has been forced to abandon quality control circles due to a lack of worker cooperation (Deyo 1996b: 145–6). Ford's Hermosillo plant – hailed as a leader in lean production techniques – implemented JIT and teamwork, but without measures to develop worker commitment and loyalty to the firm. That plant has experienced high turnover rates, several major strikes, and mass firings of workers (Shaiken 1995: 248–9, 254).

Moreover, it is clear that subcontracting systems based on JIT production have not weakened the workplace bargaining power of autoworkers. To the contrary, JIT production is even more vulnerable than Fordist mass production to strikes at component factories as well as in transportation. As an October 8, 1992, *New York Times* article (p. 5) noted regarding the U.S. experience:

Because the automobile industry has largely adopted the Japanese system of keeping production inventories low, strikes at part plants have a much broader impact than in the past. . . . The ability of the union to cripple production by putting only a few thousand workers on strike is a way of imposing costs on the company that may outweigh the savings from job cuts [through automation, outsourcing, etc.]. (See also Rubenstein 1992: 198; Schoenberger 1997: 57–61)

This vulnerability of JIT production was demonstrated in a series of strikes at General Motors. For example, in July 1997, workers went on strike at a GM transmission factory in suburban Detroit that supplies parts to all of GM's North American assembly plants except Saturn. Workers were protesting outsourcing and demanding greater employment levels and security. By the third day of the strike by the factory's 2,800 workers, GM had been forced to shut down four assembly plants, idling a total of 19,300 workers. If the strike had lasted two or three weeks, it would have "virtually paralyze[d] the North American assembly operations of the General Motors Corporation." The strike was settled in three days with the union declaring victory (New York Times 1997).

Thus, employment practices in many of the main sites of automobile industry expansion still retain the characteristics that both provoked and facilitated the historic waves of autoworker militancy, from the CIO struggles of the 1930s to the more recent labor upheavals in Brazil, South Africa, and South Korea. To the extent that lean-and-mean practices continue to be predominant in the future, the dynamic whereby the automobile corporations produce new militant labor movements at each new site of rapid expansion is likely to continue.

IV. Boundary Drawing and the Contradictions of Lean-and-Dual Production

By the late 1990s, some industry analysts began to note the limits of lean production in the form in which it had been widely adopted. The failure of some automakers to turn lean production techniques into successful performance, suggested Thomas Kochan, Russell Lansbury, and John MacDuffie (1997: 307–9), is rooted in the failure to adopt employment policies that elicit active worker cooperation. Success requires "an organization characterized by flexibility, problem solving, and motivation, which lean practices have been designed to encourage." Yet, in firms and plants where lean production practices were introduced together with considerable downsizing and/or layoffs, the "behavioral and motivational benefits" of lean practices were undermined. They suggest that the employment relationships that lie "beyond lean production" will have to pay more attention to "achieving improved wages, security, and working conditions" (see also Camuffo and Volpato 1997 for this argument with special reference to Fiat). Indeed, as already suggested above, employment security for a core labor force is what separates the "Toyotist" lean-and-dual model from the more widely adopted lean-and-mean model.

The strong managerial commitment in Japan to employment security for a core labor force is rooted in experiences from both the immediate postwar

69

period and the 1970s. The attempted postwar take-off of the Japanese automobile industry took place in the midst of a massive nationwide wave of labor unrest in which layoffs frequently triggered strike action and protest (Cusumano 1985; Farley 1950; Okayama 1987). In order to cope with the constraints imposed by this wave of labor militancy as well as financial constraints, the automobile companies chose to depart in significant ways from the Fordist style of mass production. Discarding their earlier attempts at vertical integration, Japanese automobile producers established a multilayered subcontracting system that simultaneously allowed them to guarantee employment to (and establish cooperative relations with) a core labor force, while obtaining low-cost inputs and flexibility from the lower rungs of the supply network. The subcontracting system allowed Toyota to increase its output fivefold while only increasing its workforce by 15 percent between 1952 and 1957. More importantly, it allowed Toyota and the other auto assemblers to avoid layoffs (and the confrontations with militant workers that layoffs provoked) (Smitka 1991: 2–7).[13]

Japanese managers' commitment to a policy of employment security was reinforced by the experience of the 1970s. The organizational innovations of the 1970s (lean production), which helped the Japanese automobile industry survive the oil crisis and emerge as the world's giant in the 1980s, would not have been possible without guarantees of employment security for the core labor force. Worker cooperation with cost-cutting measures and continuous improvements in productivity and quality could only happen in the context of an "understanding between management and labour that workers' cooperation over productivity and quality" would not cost workers their jobs (Sako 1997: 8; Chalmers 1989: 132). Employment security is thus key to explaining the fact that the great postwar expansion of the Japanese automobile industry – unlike all other cases of rapid expansion – did not *lead to* a major wave of labor militancy.

In the 1990s, under the impact of extreme recessionary pressures, the large automobile assemblers introduced a modification in the "lifetime employment" system: core workers were to be guaranteed employment within an extended enterprise grouping (assemblers and primary suppliers) rather than within a single firm. But, despite repeated predictions to the contrary,

---

[13] The long-term impact of the immediate postwar strike wave on Japanese managers can even be seen in the "no-layoffs" policy followed by small- and medium-sized Japanese-owned firms in California. Ruth Milkman (1991: 85–6) found few signs of lean production techniques at these companies, but she did find a firm managerial belief that "layoffs . . . invite unionism" and thus should be avoided at all cost.

managerial commitment to the central principle of "lifetime employment" remained strong through the 1990s. Management understood that "without it, the motivational basis of workers' and unions' cooperation would falter" (Sako 1997: 11; cf. Pollack 1993).

In the late 1990s, faced with the limits of the lean-and-mean model, U.S. and Western European producers appeared to be moving towards a lean-and-dual strategy (Kochan et al. 1997). Nevertheless, this strategy has its own contradictions and limits. The strategy's success depends on the establishment of a large "buffer" made up of insecure workers in the lower-tiers of the subcontracting system and of "part-time" and "temporary" workers in the upper-tier firms. In the case of Japan, the bottom rungs of the multilayered subcontracting system were filled in the 1950s and 1960s by a large reserve army of labor from the rural areas and by women. Women – who tended to work prior to marriage, withdraw from the labor force, and return on a part-time basis once the children reached school age – were especially important in filling the part-time and temporary positions in the large firms and in affiliated supplier firms. Often, they were the wives and daughters of permanent male workers; hence, labor–capital contradictions (between women workers and their employers) were mediated (and moderated) through the power relations within the family. Indeed, the incentive to be "cooperative workers" extended to the whole family, as wives and daughters would be held responsible for risking the "lifetime employment security" of the family's main (male) breadwinner (Sachiko 1986; Sumiko 1986; Muto 1997: 152–4).

As Japan's rural reserves of labor dried up and the bargaining power of the workers in the lower rungs of the subcontracting system increased in the late 1960s, two responses by employers helped contain the inherent contradictions. On the one hand, Japan's growing wealth allowed for a general upgrading of the labor force. Primary (and some secondary) suppliers began to resemble the main automotive assembly firms in terms of employment security and wage levels (Smitka 1991). On the other hand, Japanese producers moved the lower tiers of the subcontracting pyramid to low-wage countries in east and southeast Asia in order to contain costs and remain internationally competitive. The rapid rise of the yen in the late 1980s provided a further incentive to move production to lower-cost sites in Asia (Ozawa 1979: 76–110; Machado 1992: 174–8, Arrighi, Ikeda, and Irwan 1993: 48–65; Steven 1997: 215).

This relocation of the lower tiers of the Japanese subcontracting system to low-income countries endowed with large reserves of cheap labor has enabled Japanese automakers to reproduce their compeitiveness in global markets, while retaining the loyalty of their core labor force. Indeed, according to Mitsuo Ishida, in the mid 1990s, Toyota embarked on a program of worker-friendly technological innovations designed to humanize auto work and thereby attract and retain the loyalty of a highly skilled primary sector workforce (1997).

Nevertheless, to the extent that labor-market dualism has taken on a new spatial form – with the lower and higher rungs of the multilayered subcontracting system in separate countries – the likelihood that the lower strata will remain quiescent decreases. For one thing, the patriarchal family (with male "labor aristocrats" helping to discipline women and youth) can no longer function as a prop of the system. And once dualism is no longer a "family matter," its other markers – gender, nationality, citizenship, ethnicity – are likely to come to the forefront as mobilizing (rather than demobilizing) facets of labor unrest.

Thus, both versions of lean production have contradictions and limits. These contradictions provide an illustration at the firm and industry level of the ongoing tension that exists between crises of profitability and crises of legitimacy (see Chapter 1). Labor unrest pressures are pushing automakers toward protecting a segment of their labor force from the harshest verdicts of an unregulated world market economy in an effort to strengthen the legitimacy of the labor–capital hierarchy. But intense competitive pressures are creating crises of profitability that push the automakers toward cost-cutting measures that continuously threaten the depth and breadth of those protections. Given these contradictory pressures, it is difficult to predict the relative weight of lean-and-mean and lean-and-dual strategies in the future. It may very well appear, in retrospect, that the lean-and-mean model has performed the historical function of "downsizing" traditional mass producers (ranging from the U.S. Big Three to China's state-owned enterprises) to the point where the lean-and-dual model could be profitably deployed.

Where the lean-and-mean model continues to predominate, we have already suggested that the dynamic of labor militancy and capital relocation described in Section II is likely to repeat itself. In these sites of production (such as China and Mexico) strong workplace bargaining power and major grievances will continue to go hand in hand (producing the Marx-type labor unrest discussed in Chapter 1). Moreover, although autoworkers are better paid than the national average for workers, they are still an integral part of working-class communities, and thus are likely to play a leading role in national labor movements similar to that played by autoworkers in the twentieth-century labor unrest waves described earlier. And they are also likely to play an important role in widening and deepening processes of democratization, as was the case in earlier waves ranging from Spain to Brazil and South Africa to South Korea.

Yet, to the extent that the main trend in the world automobile industry is toward lean-and-dual production, then the most likely sites of future autoworker labor unrest will be among the lower-tier workers in the subcontracting system. Yet, in these sites, strong grievances do *not* go hand in hand with strong workplace bargaining power. Moreover, while upper-tier workers are likely to have strong workplace bargaining power, they are also likely to have fewer grievances, and at the same time they are likely to be physically and psychically separated from lower-tier workers with greater grievances and less structural power. And with the "leaning" of the industry, primary-sector workers will account for a tiny fraction of the automobile (and overall) working class. Finally, the distribution of upper- and lower-tier (secure and insecure) workers is likely to correspond to and reinforce the core–periphery geographical divide as well as to overlap with differences in ethnicity, place of residence, and citizenship – with important implications for world labor politics.

Nevertheless, whether the lean-and-mean or lean-and-dual version predominates in the future, globally autoworkers are unlikely to play the central role in the world labor movement of the twenty-first century that they played in the twentieth century. The automobile industry was widely acknowledged to be the quintessential industry of the twentieth century – the "leading sector" of capitalist development. Yet few, if any, commentators would suggest that this will remain true in the twenty-first century. Thus, with a few important exceptions (noted earlier), it is unlikely that the struggles of autoworkers will have in the future the same kind of symbolic and material impact that they have had for most of the twentieth century.

In this chapter, we traced the trajectory of labor unrest in the world automobile industry in the twentieth century, focusing on the interaction between labor unrest and capitalist strategies to maintain profitability and control through successive spatial and technological fixes. Nevertheless, capitalist strategies to maximize profitability and control are not limited to the geographical relocation of industrial capital or the reorganization of existing lines of production. Capital also "goes" into new industries and product lines in search of higher profits and greater control. If, as we have argued, "where capital goes, conflict goes," then we might do well to look to the new leading industries of the twenty-first century for the first rumblings of a renewed labor movement. In other words, we should expect to see not only a geographical shifting of conflict *within* industries over time (as documented in this chapter for the automobile industry) but also longer-term *intersectoral* shifts in the location of labor–capital conflict. It is this dynamic between labor unrest and what we will call the product fix that we now turn to in Chapter 3.

3

Labor Movements and Product Cycles

In the previous chapter our analysis of world labor unrest focused on the leading capitalist industry of the twentieth century. We followed the rise, globalization, and transformation of the mass production automobile industry. We found a cyclical pattern of labor militancy and capital relocation – a kind of *déjà vu* pattern in which strong labor movements emerged in each new favored low-wage site to which the industry relocated. In other words, spatial fixes re-created similar working classes and class conflict wherever capital went.

In this chapter, we widen the temporal scope of the analysis. On the one hand, we move back in time in order to compare the dynamic of the automobile industry with that of the leading industry of the nineteenth century – the textile industry. On the other hand, we move forward in time in an effort to identify the leading industries of the twenty-first century and to compare their likely dynamics with those of the past.

Two arguments are central to this chapter. The first is that the main location of working-class formation and protest shifts *within* any single industry along with shifts in the geographical location of production. In other words, we argue that a similar *déjà vu* pattern to that which we found for the world automobile industry can be observed also in the world textile industry. Moreover, we argue that, just as labor unrest shifts from location to location within any given industry, so the main sites of working-class formation and protest shift *from industry to industry* together with the rise/decline of leading sectors of capitalist development. While the first argument above relates to the trajectory of *intra-industry* working class formation and labor unrest, the second argument relates to the *inter-industry* dynamic of working-class formation and labor unrest.

To capture this inter-industry dynamic, we coin the term "product fix." Capitalists respond to a squeeze on profits in a given industry, with geographical relocation (a spatial fix) or process innovations (a technological/organizational fix), but they also attempt to shift capital into new innovative and more profitable product lines and industries. This product fix involves relocating capital from industries and product lines subject to intense competition to new and/or less-crowded industries and product lines. Successive new labor movements have risen (and established labor movements declined) with these shifts.

The chapter introduces a *critical reformulation* of product cycle theory to help link the inter- and intra-industry dynamics and to provide the foundation for a comparative analysis among the intra-industry cycles. From this reformulated perspective, historical capitalism has been characterized by a series of overlapping product cycles (product fixes) in which the late stages of one product cycle overlap with the initiation of new product cycles – the new cycle initiated almost invariably in high-income countries. Working-class formation and protest are key processes underlying both the shifts from phase to phase *within* a product cycle and the shift from one product cycle to the next.

Spatial fixes (the geographical relocation of production, emphasized in the original product cycle model) and technological/organizational fixes (process innovations) combine with labor unrest in historically specific ways. But there are also patterned variations in the way they combine, and hence in their implications for the evolution of world labor unrest in the nineteenth, twentieth, and twenty-first centuries. We seek to highlight these similarities and differences as we proceed with the comparative analysis, with the goal of being able to say something meaningful about the conditions that the world's workers are likely to face in the twenty-first century.

We begin in Section I by reconceptualizing the story of the world automobile industry as a modified "product cycle." This becomes the foundation for the comparative analysis with the textile industry (Section II) and emerging leading sectors of the twenty-first century (Section IV). From a micro-perspective, there are countless product cycles beginning/ending at any given time. But, as already hinted at, we single out the textile and automobile industries because these industrial complexes constitute two "macro" cycles that have been fundamental to the capitalist dynamic over the last 200 years. The textile complex – centered in the United Kingdom – was the leading capitalist industry of the nineteenth century, what Marx took to be the representative example of modern industry. The "peripheralization"

always looking for the door

of the textile complex in the early decades of the twentieth century coincided with the rise of an innovative mass-production automobile complex, centered in the United States – the new leading sector, not just in economic terms but in setting the social and cultural standards of the time. Following this logic, the final section of the chapter seeks to identify the likely successor(s) of the automobile complex as leading industry of world capitalism and to explore the implications of this shift for the bargaining power of labor and for the future of world labor unrest.

I. *The Automobile Product Cycle*

The trajectory of the automobile industry described in Chapter 2 (Section II) can be usefully reconceptualized as a product cycle, *but one in which labor unrest is a key component of the process*. In the original product cycle model proposed by Raymond Vernon (1966), newly innovated products tend to get produced in high-income countries, but as products (A) pass through their "life cycle," production facilities are dispersed to increasingly lower-cost (particularly lower-wage) sites of production. In the early "innovative" stage of the product's life cycle, competitive pressures are low and thus costs are relatively unimportant. But as products reach the stage of "maturity" and finally "standardization," the number of actual or potential competitors grows, as does the pressure to cut costs.

[handwritten margin note: (A) innovation becomes old news]

The trajectory of relocation described in Chapter 2 (Section II) for the automobile industry – at least in its Fordist incarnation – broadly corresponds to a product cycle, with automobile mass production successively being dispersed to lower-wage sites. But while product cycle theories tend to focus on "economic" variables (e.g., competition, factor costs) as the causes and effects of the cycle, a "social variable" – working-class formation and protest – is central to the product-cycle story we have told.[1] A major wave of labor unrest is one of the "push" factors leading to each new stage of production dispersal, and each new stage of production dispersal sets off a new round of working-class formation. Thus, the automobile's innovation life-cycle stage reached its limits with the CIO struggles in the United States. The limits of the second mature stage were reached with the European waves of labor unrest of the late 1960s and 1970s, and the third stage of standardization began to reach its limits with the various

---

[1] For a critique of the technologically deterministic and unidirectional nature of most of the product cycle literature, see Taylor (1986).

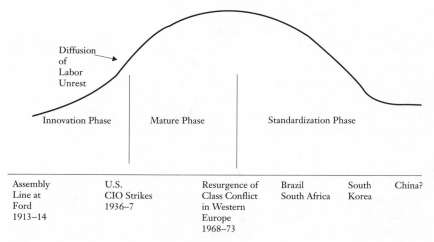

Assembly	U.S.	Resurgence of	Brazil	South	China?
Line at	CIO Strikes	Class Conflict	South Africa	Korea	
Ford	1936–7	in Western			
1913–14		Europe			
		1968–73			

Figure 3.1. The automobile product life cycle and labor unrest waves.

upsurges of labor militancy in NIC sites in the 1980s and 1990s. Figure 3.1 provides a graphic depiction of labor unrest waves and capital relocation in the automobile product life cycle.

Chapter 2 argued that geographical relocation of production in the automobile industry has not led to a race to the bottom in wages and working conditions because, wherever the automobile industry expanded, new working classes formed, and powerful labor movements tended to emerge. In other words, we emphasized an essentially cyclical process. Yet, the product life-cycle literature underscores how each phase of the product cycle takes place in an increasingly competitive environment as production disperses geographically and as the process of production becomes more routinized. Thus, the recurrent dynamic of labor militancy and capital relocation, described in Chapter 2, is not a simple repetition. Rather, each recurrence unfolds in a fundamentally different competitive environment. Monopolistic windfall profits – or what Joseph Schumpeter called "spectacular prizes" (1954: 73) – accrue to the innovator. But as we move through the stages of the product cycle, there is a decline in the industry's profitability. Moreover, in favoring low-wage sites for new rounds of expansion, production increasingly takes place in sites where the level of national wealth is relatively low.

These tendencies, in turn, have important implications for the *outcome* of the major waves of autoworker labor unrest that we have described – especially for the kind of labor–capital accords that labor movements can

I. The Automobile Product Cycle

achieve and the durability of the gains made. In Chapter 2, we emphasized that each major wave of autoworker labor unrest achieved significant
victories in terms of wages, working conditions, and expansion of the legitimate arena in which trade unions could operate. Nevertheless, from the
perspective introduced here, we can also see that the early starters were
in a position to finance a more generous and stable labor–capital accord
because they were the beneficiaries of the monopolistic windfall profits
that accrued to the cycle's innovators. Thus, the windfall profits that accrued to U.S. automakers helped them underwrite a stable labor–capital
accord and mass consumption social contract that lasted for more than four
decades after the CIO struggles of the 1930s. In contrast, the lower profit
levels associated with the intense competitive pressures toward the end of
the life cycle (and the relative national poverty of the favored new sites of
production) make such social contracts increasingly difficult to sustain economically. In other words, late-developers of mass production automobile
industries have experienced the social contradictions of capitalist development (including strong working classes) without the benefits that might
allow them to deal with those social contradictions successfully. Elsewhere,
we have labeled this phenomenon "the contradictions of semiperipheral
success" (Silver 1990; see also Arrighi 1990b).

Without stable labor–capital accords, militancy lingers, which in turn
creates a strong added motivation for further relocation of production.
Because of this, as well as the intensified competitive pressures that characterize the late stage of the product cycle, there has been a "speeding up"
of social history from one stage of the automobile life cycle to the next.
Whereas the dispersal and restructuring of production was a gradual process after the CIO struggles of the 1930s, in the increasingly competitive
environment of the 1970s and beyond, relocation/restructuring of production following upsurges of labor unrest was often rapid and devastating.
(See, for example, our discussion in Chapter 2 of the extremely rapid collapse of employment levels in the Sao Paolo area automobile industry in
the 1980s.)

From the foregoing, we might conclude that, even though a strong race-
to-the-bottom tendency did not exist in the first two stages of the product
cycle, by the end of the cycle it does indeed exist. Yet, our discussion so far
has only focused on the spatial fix. By the 1980s and 1990s, technological/
organizational fixes were at least as important in automaker strategies as the
spatial fix. Indeed, as we discussed in Chapter 2, automobile corporations'
intensive focus on pursuing process innovations fundamentally transformed

the spatial dynamics of the automobile product cycle. The process innovations introduced in the 1980s and 1990s helped restore the competitive position of high-wage production sites vis-à-vis low-wage areas. The introduction of robots and JIT production methods has pulled the rug out from under all but the lowest-wage sites of production (e.g., China, northern Mexico).[2]

This ability of high-income areas to recapture the competitive advantage in the later stages of the product cycle is consistent with some of the elaborations of the original product-cycle model. The original product-cycle model was rather unidirectional and deterministic, wherein competitive pressures effectively drove firms to relocate (or relinquish) production to lower-wage locations. As subsequent product-cycle formulations have emphasized, however, firms are not just passive agents but actively try to influence the pace and direction of the product cycle. In the words of Ian Giddy (1978: 92), "the product cycle pattern" is a "strategic business concept" rather than a descriptive model of actual events. It is "a tendency of international business that can be anticipated, followed or even reversed by alert international product managers" (see also Singleton 1997: 22; Dickerson 1991: 129–43; Taylor 1986).

In emphasizing the importance of agency in determining the trajectory of the product cycle, however, the product-cycle literature generally fails to make explicit the fact that not all *equally alert* entrepreneurs are *equally well positioned* to influence the product cycle in their favor. Innovations are most likely to take place in high-income countries. And this fact puts workers located in high-income countries in a fundamentally different structural position vis-à-vis their employers than workers in the same industries in low-income countries. As a result of extensive automation and organizational innovations at the firm level, and the higher levels of national wealth at the macro level, core regions can afford to offer high wages and "lifetime employment," albeit to a shrinking automobile labor force. More peripheral

---

[2] Firms have also attempted to divert the product cycle in their favor by seeking government aid and tariff protection. This strategy has been extremely important both in creating new sites of automobile industry production (import substitution industrialization) and protecting (even rejuvenating) declining sites. Indeed, the trajectory of the post-Fordist phase of the automobile industry discussed in Chapter 2 was strongly influenced by the quotas imposed on Japanese car imports into the United States, euphemistically called "voluntary" export restrictions. The role of protection has also been central to the trajectory of the working-class formation and labor unrest in the world textile industry. We will return to this theme in Chapters 4 and 5.

regions are left to compete on the basis of a more labor-intensive and labor-repressive strategy.[3]

Thus, we might distinguish two different periods. In both periods there was no significant race-to-the-bottom tendency. In the earlier period this was due primarily to the tendency of Fordist mass production to create new working classes and strong labor movements wherever it expanded; in the latter period it was due primarily to process innovations and political protection that succeeded in re-consolidating the North–South divide.

The combination of these strategies – the spatial fix and the technological/organizational fix – may be leading to the re-consolidation of a spatially bifurcated process. On the one hand, new innovations in organization and technology, to the extent they can be monopolized by the innovators, provide the basis for more consensual labor–capital–state social contracts, allowing legitimacy to be combined with profitability, albeit for a shrinking labor force. On the other hand, in poorer countries, where competitive advantage is based on a continuous drive to lower costs, profitability requirements lead to continuous crises of legitimacy. Finally, as we shall see in Section IV, this bifurcation is strongly reinforced by the dynamics of the product fix.

II. The Textile Complex Product Cycle in Comparative Perspective

A comparison of the dynamic of labor militancy and capital relocation in the automobile product cycle with the dynamic in the earlier textile product cycle reveals a similar pattern whereby, wherever textile capital went, labor–capital conflict emerged, and whenever conflict emerged, capitalists responded with spatial and technological fixes. Nevertheless, unlike the automobile industry, the world's textile workers, while extremely militant, faced almost universal defeat. There were only two exceptions to the chronicle of defeat. First, there were the significant victories of textile workers in the initial site of innovation – the United Kingdom – where

---

[3] Likewise, the ability of equally alert entrepreneurs to take advantage of protectionism (see previous footnote) depends on the differential ability of states to impose restrictions on the movement of people and goods across their borders – an ability that varies over space and time. To the extent that globalization is eroding the sovereignty of peripheral states more quickly than core states, entrepreneurs in core states are in a substantially better position to make effective use of a protectionist strategy. We will also return to this point in Chapters 4 and 5. (On the debate over whether state sovereignty is being eroded by globalization, see Chapter 1.)

Table 3.1 *High Points of Labor Unrest in the World Textile and Automobile Industries, 1870–1996*

	1870s	1880s	1890s	1900s	1910s	1920s	1930s	1940s	1950s	1960s	1970s	1980s	1990s[a]
Textiles													
United Kingdom	[X]						[X]						
Russia				X									
United States					X		X						
Spain					X		X		X				
Poland						X							
China						X	X						
Germany						X							
Australia						X							
India						X							
France							X						
Belgium							X						
Canada							X		X				
Mexico							X						
Egypt									X				
Pakistan									X				
Automobiles													
United States							X						
Canada							X						
United Kingdom									X				
France										X			
Italy										X			
Germany											X		
Spain											X		
Argentina											X		
South Africa												X	
Brazil												X	
South Korea												X	

[a] The 1990s decade includes 1990–96 only.

Note: The countries listed here are those that contribute at least 1% to the total mentions of textile (or automobile) labor unrest in the WLG database. "X" indicates the peak and/or periods in which at least 20% of textile (or automobile) labor unrest mentions for that country take place. See also Footnotes 4 and 5 in Chapter 3.

the monopolistic windfall profits that accrued to the innovators helped underwrite a relatively long-term, stable labor–capital accord. The second exception was that of textile workers involved in (and hence able to make use of) the rising tide of national liberation movements in the colonial world. This divergence between the outcomes of the struggles of textile and autoworkers, we shall argue, can be traced to differences in the organization of production of the two industries and related differences in workers' bargaining power.

Table 3.1 provides a bird's-eye view of the spatiotemporal distribution of high points of textile and autoworkers' unrest over the period covered by the WLG database, 1870–1996. Countries included in Table 3.1 experienced significant labor unrest in those industries.[4] Decades in which there were high-point waves of labor unrest are indicated with an "X".[5] Figure 3.2 provides a graphic depiction of labor unrest waves and capital relocation in the textile product life cycle. In what follows, we will highlight the similarities and differences between the dynamic of labor unrest in the two industries through a phase-by-phase comparison of their respective product cycles.

In both the textile and automobile product cycles, the first major successful wave of labor unrest takes place in the country in which the product cycle first arose (i.e., the United Kingdom for textiles and the United States for automobiles). Just as autoworkers were the vanguard of the U.S. labor movement in the mid twentieth century, setting the pace for standards of work and pay nationwide, so textile workers' unions were the strongest unions in the United Kingdom in the late nineteenth century.

But in both cases, strength came only after the crushing defeat of established craft-based movements. The major waves of labor unrest among Lancashire textile workers in the 1810s and 1820s[6] were spearheaded by craftworkers, and were mainly aimed at blocking the introduction of new technologies (e.g., powerlooms and self-acting mules) that eliminated their skill-based bargaining power (Sarkar 1993: 11; Chapman 1904; Lazonick

---

[4] Countries deemed to have significant labor unrest are those that account for at least 1% of the total WLG database mentions of labor unrest for the industry in question.

[5] High-point waves are defined as the peak year of labor unrest for the country and/or years in which the number of labor unrest mentions is greater than 20% of total mentions for the country. A different criterion was used for the United Kingdom since for the late nineteenth century the U.K. time series is based on only one source (the NYT Index), which is moreover the weaker of the two sources (see Appendix A). Since no year had 20% or more of the total U.K. textile mentions, the two highest years are marked.

[6] The WLG data begins in the 1870s and therefore is unable to capture the defeated labor unrest waves of the early and mid nineteenth century.

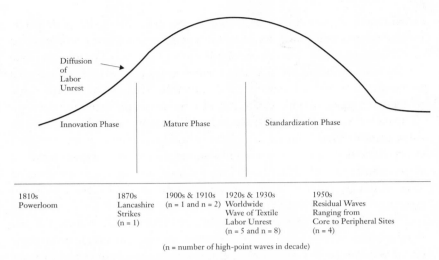

Figure 3.2. The textile product life cycle and labor unrest waves.

1990: 81; Thompson 1966). Yet, just as craftworkers' resistance in the metal trades failed to stop the spread of automobile mass-production techniques a century later, so these and later strikes (such as the 1842 general strike) failed to stop the spread of mechanization and the associated decline in wages in the textile industry.

One by-product of these defeats – in both cases – was the rise and expansion of a new category of workers who tended the machines. In the textile industry, spinners were turned into "minders." For the first half of the nineteenth century, the union power of this emerging group of textile workers was "virtually nonexistent" as technological unemployment constantly re-created an ample reserve army of labor (Lazonick 1990: 90). It was not until the 1870s that the minders were able to form an effective industrywide union and carry out a series of successful strikes between 1869 and 1875 (see Table 3.1) that led to major concessions from textile owners as a whole. The Amalgamated Association of Operative Cotton Spinners and Twiners, formed in 1870 as the mill-building boom was coming to an end, became one of the strongest workers' organizations in Britain over the next half century (Lazonick 1990: 103). Thus, while the process took longer in the case of textiles, in both the automobile and textiles industries, the first major labor victories were in the site of innovation, as the innovative phase drew to a close.

84

II. The Textile Complex Product Cycle

Moreover, in both cases, these struggles were able to obtain stable labor–capital accords that secured substantial material benefits for workers and provided the basis for decades of relative industrial peace. The labor–capital accord forged out of the U.S. labor movements of the 1930s and 1940s lasted into the 1970s. Likewise, the Lancashire struggles of the 1870s led to the emergence of widely recognized wage lists that lasted for decades. "Through the stipulation of wage lists, the minders were able to share in value gains derived from longer and faster mules as well as from increased effort. Backed by union power to enforce stipulated piece-rate agreements, the minders could work harder to increase their earnings without fear that rates would be reduced" (Lazonick 1990: 113; also see Cohen 1990 for contrast with the United States).

The ability of both textile and auto workers to make substantial and durable gains at the end of the innovation phase suggests that the monopolistic windfall profits reaped by the innovator in any given product cycle also creates favorable conditions (at least the material resources) for stable labor–capital compromises. Yet, as in the automobile industry, so in textiles, once the labor movement made a show of force, capitalists responded with a spatial-fix strategy that accelerated the diffusion of production to new sites, initiating the mature phase of the industry. Nonetheless, there were substantial differences between the two industries in the nature of the geographical diffusion of production. Diffusion was far more widespread in the mature phase of the textile industry than it was in an analogous (or even later) phase of the automobile industry product cycle. Whereas automobile mass production was largely limited to high-income countries in the 1950s and 1960s,[7] by the 1890s, there was significant mechanized textile production not just in the United States and continental Europe but also in India, China, and Japan.

The greater geographical spread of mechanized textile production was rooted in a number of differences between the textile and automobile industries. The barriers to entry into textiles were comparatively low. Start-up costs in terms of fixed capital were relatively small. Small firms could be competitive as economies of scale in textile production were relatively insignificant, and the necessary standardized machinery was easily available for import. Moreover, whereas in the 1920s and 1930s there was not yet

---

[7] The only exception was a handful of large middle-income countries that experienced some ISI-oriented growth, although this production was neither competitive on world markets nor amounted to a significant percentage of total world production.

a mass market for automobiles in Western Europe, in the late nineteenth century even poor countries had a mass consumer market for the textile industry's output, thus making import substitution strategies widely feasible. Last but not least, while mechanized textile production was new with the Industrial Revolution, textile production itself had been widespread since pre-modern times. Many of the countries that quickly adopted the new mechanized forms had a long proto-industrial history of textile production and, in many cases (most notably India and China), had been out-competing European textile producers. Indeed, Britain's textile industry took off only after it was protected from the flood of inexpensive and high-quality goods exported from India in the eighteenth century. Thus, areas with a long tradition of textile production had the means and motivation to respond to the onslaught of cheap British imports with local import-substituting production. This, combined with spatial-fix strategies pursued by British textile manufacturers, resulted in the wide and rapid spread of the industry.

In at least one instance – New England – the expansion of mechanized textile production and working-class formation had a *direct relational connection* to the dynamics of labor–capital conflict in the Lancashire textile industry. The migration of both entrepreneurs and skilled workers from the Lancashire area was critical to the growth and evolution of the New England textile industry, leading to an initial replication of patterns of labor–capital conflict (although not outcomes). Mule spinners in the northeastern textile workforce were overwhelmingly skilled workers who had emigrated from textile regions in the United Kingdom, bringing with them a strong union tradition. Some of these immigrants had been blacklisted or locked out at home for union activity; most were assisted by their unions to emigrate as part of a conscious union policy to reduce the size of the reserve army of labor in Lancashire (Cohen 1990: 140–4). While these immigrant workers never achieved the levels of control that their counterparts in Lancashire had, they nevertheless held up Lancashire as the standard for labor–capital relations in textiles. In an effort to reach that standard, they frequently struck over issues of craft control and wages. The bitterest disputes took place in Fall River – "the Manchester of America" – in the same decades that major disputes took place in Lancashire. But in contrast to the disputes in Lancashire, "every strike in Fall River result[ed] in a complete victory of capital over labor" (Cohen 1990: 116–17).

Nevertheless, there were some significant victories in New England, such as the 1912 strike in Lawrence, Massachusetts, which helped make the 1910s a high-point decade for textile labor unrest in the United States

II. The Textile Complex Product Cycle

(see Table 3.1). Such victories, together with the disruption to production brought about by frequent defeated strike outbreaks, led capital to reduce its dependence on this workforce. The mule spinners, in particular, produced an essential input (yarn) for a whole range of textile activities. As Isaac Cohen (1990: 127) pointed out, since the mules supply the necessary yarn, "a general mule spinners' stoppage, whether in Lancashire or Fall River, would sooner or later put out of employment the weavers, dressers, calico printers, and preparatory workers; in short, the entire mill work force."

Thus, U.S. textile firms, already in the late nineteenth century, began to pursue a combined strategy of spatial and technological fixes in an effort to resolve their labor-control problems. Employers aggressively replaced mule-spinning machinery with ring-spinning machinery during and after the 1870s strikes. Ring spinning was a machine-tending job filled by unorganized women and youth. Fall River manufacturers were aware that this transformation from mule spinning to ring spinning would eventually, as one manufacturer put it, leave "high and dry" (unemployed) the mule spinners "that cause all the trouble" (quoted in Cohen 1990: 131). Indeed, manufacturers openly threatened the union, suggesting that an "unwise use of [their] power" would inevitably hasten the replacement of mules by rings. Between 1879 and 1904, they proceeded to reduce the proportion of mule spindles in Fall River from 73 percent to 24 percent of the total number of spinning machines. Correspondingly, the total number of mule spinners employed in Fall River declined from 1,000 in 1879 to 350 in 1909 (Cohen 1990: 133).

At the same time an aggressive mill-building program (with ring-spinning technology) was begun in the U.S. South. The value of the textile industry's output in the South rose from about $13 million in 1880 to $85 million by the turn of the century, leaping to over $800 million in the 1920s and 1930s. By 1930 the value of Southern output was more than double the value of Northern output ($874 million versus $369 million) (Kane 1988; Sarkar 1993: 16). The Southern expansion was the combined result of the agency of Northern capitalists seeking a spatial fix to their labor/profitability troubles, and of Southern elites seeking a new economic basis for their social and political power in the post–Civil War South through investment in textile manufacturing (Wood 1991).

The U.S. South was but one of many rapidly expanding major textile centers in the late nineteenth century that were the combined result of import substitution strategies and capital relocation strategies. By the turn of the century, there would be numerous major textile-producing centers

87

around the world – many of which boasted far cheaper labor than could be found in Lanchashire or New England.

In the case of India, local merchants were the key agents in the initial growth of the mechanized cotton textile industry. In Bombay – where the industry was concentrated – the first mechanized cotton textile mill opened in 1856. By 1860, a Bombay newspaper boasted: "Bombay has long been the Liverpool of the East, and she has now become the Manchester also" (quoted in Morris 1965: 18). While this was quite a bit of hyperbole (there were only six mills open by that year), the cotton textile industry in Bombay proceeded to grow rapidly in the late nineteenth and early twentieth century. Already in 1862, British observer R. M. Martin expressed concern that "even the present generation may witness the Lancashire manufacturer beaten by his Hindu competitor" (quoted in Morris 1965: 25). In 1900, the number of mills built in Bombay reached 86, and the number and size of mills continued to expand rapidly until the early 1920s (Morris 1965: 27–8; see also Chandavarkar 1994).

In Japan, mechanized cotton textile production began to expand rapidly in the 1880s, once the Meiji government made it a priority. By the end of the 1880s, there were thirty-four cotton-spinning firms including ten that owned more than 18,000 spindles apiece (Tsurumi 1990: 35–6, 104). By 1890, Japan was an exporter of cotton textile products, and the industry continued to expand rapidly into the 1930s. One indication of this expansion is the average annual importation and consumption of raw cotton, which increased from 1 kiloton in 1860–79 to 294 kilotons in 1900–19 to 665 kilotons in 1920–1939. Moreover, Japan's share in world exports of textiles and clothing rose from 2 percent in 1899 to 22 percent by 1937 (Park and Anderson 1992: 23, 25).

In China, foreign direct investment contributed to the expansion of the textile industry in the late nineteenth century. It was no secret that this foreign direct investment was motivated by access to "cheap" and "submissive" labor. The Blackburn mission, sent from Great Britain to Shanghai in 1896, warned of a looming threat to British textile exports and suggested what amounted to a spatial fix for Lancashire's labor problems:

Comparing this Oriental labour and our own, there is on the one hand, cheap, plentiful, submissive, capable labour, plus the best machinery we can give it; on the other hand, dear, dictating and exacting labour, plus the same machinery. Can anyone call these equal conditions? Are they not in favour of the Shanghai capitalist, who can see that his money will be more profitably employed by utilising this labour than by selling English piece goods. (Quoted in Honig 1986: 16)

II. The Textile Complex Product Cycle

In 1895 and 1896, British firms opened large mills in Shanghai (shortly after the 1895 treaty opened the city to foreign direct investment). These were followed a year later by German and American firms. Japanese foreign direct investment expanded rapidly after 1911. During the First World War – with imports of cotton textiles cut off – several major Chinese families opened large mills and became major textile industrialists. By 1929, there were 61 spinning mills employing 110,882 workers and 405 weaving enterprises employing 29,244 workers (Honig 1986: 16–17, 24–5).

By the 1920s, this globalization of mechanized textile production had generated intense competitive pressures worldwide. And as was done by automobile producers when faced with analogous competitive pressures in the 1970s, textile industrialists sought to rationalize production and cut costs, which, in turn, unleashed a major world-scale wave of textile worker labor unrest in the 1920s and 1930s. As in the case of the automobile industry, intense labor–capital conflict arose in response to these rationalization efforts at the end of the mature phase. But the wider spread of the textile industry resulted in a wider spread of labor–capital conflict. Whereas major labor unrest at the end of the automobile's mature phase – the late 1960s and early 1970s – was largely a core (Western European) phenomenon, the mature phase of the textile complex ended with a virtually worldwide wave of labor unrest in the 1920s and 1930s. The location of massive textile workers' strikes ranged from Manchester to Bombay, Gastonia (North Carolina) and Shanghai (see Table 3.1).

This greater spread of textile workers' unrest in the mature phase of the textile complex should not be construed as a sign of greater bargaining power. On the contrary, the militancy of textile workers is not in doubt – indeed, Kerr and Siegel (1964) classified textile workers' propensity to strike as medium-high, second only to miners and maritime/longshoremen – but the success of their protests was less in evidence. In contrast to the stunning victories of the late 1960s and early 1970s labor upsurges in the automobile industry, textile militancy in the 1920s and 1930s led almost universally to defeat. Even in the United Kingdom, the bastion of textile worker strength, the 1920s and 1930s were decades of defeat.[8] To be sure, the social contracts that autoworker militancy won in the late 1960s were short-lived (overturned by the 1980s) relative to the four-decades-long social contract

---

[8] The general strike of 1926 was followed by five major textile strikes. Of the 30 million days lost in strikes from 1927 to 1933, over 18 million were accounted for by the five national textile strikes (Singleton 1990; Sarkar 1993: 14).

that emerged from the U.S. CIO struggles of the 1930s. Nevertheless, in comparison with the results of textile militancy at an analogous stage in the complex's product cycle, the gains were impressive.

Particularly telling in this respect was the fate of the major wave of labor unrest among textile workers in the U.S. South, including a general strike in 1934 – just two years before the flood of CIO victories in the auto industry. Although hard-fought, these strikes "were uniformly failures" including the 1934 general strike – the largest single strike in U.S. history – which culminated in a "crushing defeat" for labor (Truchil 1988: 94–103; Irons 2000). Striking textile workers in the northeastern United States fared slightly better in the same period due to their stronger associational bargaining power and the related more favorable political climate. However, these gains only strengthened the ongoing trend toward the relocation of U.S. textile capital to the South (Truchil 1988: 102–3).

Textile workers' successes in the industry's mature phase were almost exclusively limited to places where they could draw on the support of growing nationalist movements. In India, the post–World War I wave of strikes in the Bombay textile industry, including the general strikes in 1919 and 1920, occurred at a time of prosperity for the industry and growing nationalist agitation. Their outcome was certainly not a clear-cut defeat, and in some ways it could be interpreted as a victory. By the mid 1920s, prosperity had turned to intense competition, and mill owners sought to lower wages, cut employment, and speed up work. These efforts were met with violent strikes in 1924 and 1934. Again, the outcome was far from a clear-cut defeat. Increasingly, the nationalist leaders sought to incorporate workers' struggles within the nationalist movement. Moreover, the link between Britain's policy of keeping the Indian market open to Lancashire textile exports and their own wage/employment difficulties was sufficient to induce Indian workers to join various nationalist campaigns (Chandavarkar 1994). With the Indian Congress Party's rise to power in Bombay province in 1937, the process of rationalization was increasingly mediated by the government, which sought to coopt both workers and industrialists. Initially, Congress worked through an alliance with communist and socialist trade unions. In 1945, however, with independence in sight, a Congress-controlled union was formed, the RMMS (Rashtriya Mill Mazdoor Sangh). By 1951, the RMMS had become the dominant trade union in the Bombay textile industry, and was able to effectively channel workers' protest into official government-sanctioned channels (Morris 1965: 191–5; Sarkar 1993: 28).

II. The Textile Complex Product Cycle

In China, textile worker unrest was also intimately tied to the nationalist movement. These links at first strengthened the movement, but they also left it vulnerable to major shifts in the political wind. The cotton textile workers were swept up in the wave of unrest known as the May Thirteenth Movement of 1925. The movement began when a cotton mill worker was shot and killed by Japanese guards at a Japanese-owned mill. The incident triggered massive student demonstrations against foreign control in Shanghai, which were heavily repressed by foreign police forces. On May 31, 1925, in response to the killing of demonstrators, the Chinese General Chamber of Commerce declared a strike of workers, students, and merchants. The strikers' demands ranged from establishing Chinese control over the police in Shanghai and representation on the Municipal Council to improving labor conditions in Shanghai's factories. Strike activity, particularly in Shanghai's cotton mills, continued with increasing intensity under the direction of the Shanghai General Union. A general strike was mobilized in February 1927 and was successful in establishing a provisional municipal government in Chinese-controlled Zhabei. Chiang Kai-shek, leading his National Revolutionary Army, was able to enter Shanghai at the end of March without firing a single shot. Textile workers were able, at least for a time, to gain increases in wages and union recognition (Chesneaux 1968; Honig 1986). But the Chinese experience also shows the vulnerability of workers' movements dependent for their gains on associational bargaining power based on cross-class alliances with political movements. The textile workers' vulnerability to shifts in the political wind became clear when, on April 12, Chiang's soldiers, assisted by armed members of the (Mafia-like) Green Gang, launched a coup that devastated the labor movement and inaugurated the period known as the White Terror (Honig 1986: 27).

In sum, a comparison of labor unrest in the textile and auto industries through their respective mature phases reveals important analogies as well as differences. In both industries, spatial fixes to local crises of profitability and control were driven not just by intercapitalist competition but by labor unrest as well. Moreover, in both industries, spatial fixes only succeeded in a spatiotemporal "rescheduling" of profitability and control crises, while making them progressively more difficult to resolve through stable labor–capital accords.

We have nonetheless noted two important differences between the process of intra-industry diffusion of labor unrest in the two industries. First, the geographical spread of high-point waves of labor unrest in the mature

91

phase of the product cycle was much greater in the textile industry than in the automobile industry. Thus, as can be seen from a comparison of mature phases in Table 3.1, twelve countries experienced high points of labor unrest in the textile industry in the 1920s and 1930s compared to only five countries in the automobile industry in the 1960s and 1970s. Second, as described in the preceding narrative, the overall success of workers' struggles in winning concessions from capital was greater in the auto industry than in the textile industry. This difference in overall success is likely related to a third difference visible in Table 3.1 – the greater likelihood of repeated high points of labor unrest in any given country in the textile industry.[9] This, in turn, raises questions about the relationship between the strength of workers' bargaining power and the militancy of workers – a question to which we will return later.

The difference in the overall success rate of labor unrest can be traced in large part to differences in the way the two industries are organized and the resulting differential impact on workers' bargaining power. We have already discussed some of these organizational differences in relation to the greater geographical spread of textile production. We now turn to their implications for labor's bargaining power – workplace bargaining power, in particular. The workplace bargaining power of textile workers was significantly weaker than that of automobile workers. The disruptive power that continuous flow production puts in the hands of workers was largely absent in textiles. In contrast to the vertical integration and continuous flow production that characterized Fordist mass production, the textile industry was vertically disintegrated, and the labor process was divided into discrete phases. The work of one spinner/weaver did not require the completion of tasks by another spinner/weaver, and thus the collateral damage that could be caused by a work stoppage by only a few textile workers was minimal. One or more machines in a factory could be stopped without slowing down or disrupting the use of the remaining machines. Each machine could be operated (and each machine minder could work) independently of the other machines (and workers) – an organizational impossibility in the automobile industry and other continuous flow industries.[10] Moreover, because firms were small in size and production was vertically disintegrated, less fixed capital was

---

[9] Thus, whereas Italy is the only country to register more than one high-point wave of unrest in the automobile industry, five countries did so for the textile industry.

[10] See Cohen (1990) on U.S. textile strikes in which the owners were able to keep ring production going despite a full strike of the mule spinners.

II. The Textile Complex Product Cycle

idled by a strike in a single firm, and the damage done had no significant impact on the industry or region as a whole.[11]

This relatively weak workplace bargaining power of textile workers was generally not counterbalanced by a strong marketplace bargaining power based on scarce skills. Even for the Lancashire workers who operated the self-acting mules, craft status was more a construction based on union power than an actual monopoly over scarce skills. Moreover, the trend was toward a continual reduction of skill levels. If the self-acting mule required less skill than the common mule it replaced, ring spinning required even less experience and strength.

To be sure, the marketplace bargaining power of autoworkers based on scarce skills was probably no greater than that of textile workers. But the overall market-based bargaining power of textile workers was nonetheless weaker. First, there tended to be a much larger pool of surplus labor flooding textile industry labor markets as machine production displaced a large number of nonmachine producers – something that did not occur with automobiles, given that it was essentially a new industry. Second, the rise and spread of the textile industry occurred in a period characterized by widespread disruption of subsistence activities, leading to the continuous re-creation of freshly proletarianized labor in need of a wage in order to survive. Third, low barriers to entry led to the successive rise of new, lower-cost competitors, and a chronic tendency toward overproduction crises. The result was tremendous employment instability in any given textile community. Fourth, this cyclical drag on labor's marketplace bargaining power was reinforced by the periodic bouts of unemployment created by technological changes. Finally, the lower fixed capital requirements made relocation of production to new sites (as spatial fix or import substitution policy) easier and more profitable for textile firms, thus enlarging the

---

[11] In some ways, the workplace bargaining power situation of textile workers is analogous to that wielded by workers in supplier industries in the post-Fordist automobile industry. As we already noted in Chapter 2, subcontracting and just-in-time production has made auto assemblers vulnerable to the disruption of the flow of parts from their supplier networks. Likewise, because yarn is an essential input in a wide range of occupations, a *complete* and general strike in spinning could create substantial disruptions downstream. But given the fact that textile workers were operating in the context of an industry characterized by thousands of small firms, each owned by a different employer, organizing such a complete and general strike presupposed strong associational (trade union) power. Even in this analogy, autoworkers would need less compensating associational power than textile workers because the post-Fordist supply chain in automobiles may be most accurately characterized as a "one to few" relationship among firms in comparison to the "many to many" relationship that characterized textiles (cf. Gereffi 1994).

potential labor pool of the employer and further undermining the marketplace bargaining power of workers in textile communities.

Given the weak structural bargaining power of textile workers, it should not be surprising that associational power turned out to be an essential ingredient in those workers' victories described earlier. The victories of British textile workers in the late nineteenth century were based on solid trade union organizations that could organize and finance long region-wide general strikes as well as the emigration of surplus workers. As previously noted, however, British textile workers had advantages not shared by other textile workers. In particular, as the site of innovation (while it lasted), British firms were in a position to pay their workers a premium. In turn, this further strengthened both the organizational capacities of the British textile unions, as they relied on the financial backing *of their own membership*, allowing them to defend gains through a series of economic downturns.[12] Likewise, strong associational power in the form of cross-class alliances built around the national liberation struggles (while such alliances lasted) were critical to the workers' victories achieved in China and India. Nevertheless, these were the exceptional cases; more commonly, associational power was not sufficiently strong to compensate for the weak structural power of textile workers.

The end of the textile industry's mature phase corresponds to the world-wide upsurge of textile labor unrest in the 1920s and 1930s, just as the automobile industry's mature phase ended with the late 1960s and early 1970s auto strike waves. In both the textile and automobile industries, the heightened labor militancy and intercapitalist competition that marked the end of the mature phase led entrepreneurs to redouble their efforts to implement spatial and technological fixes, with contradictory results. On the one hand, the spatial fix of the standardization phase contributed to the further peripheralization of production. On the other hand, the technological fix of this phase contributed to a partial restoration of the competitive position of high-wage sites of production based on extensive automation.[13]

---

[12] For an emphasis on the extent (and specificity) of U.K. minders' shopfloor control as a basis of their strong trade union power, see Lazonick (1990: Chapter 3). Moreover, in Britain, much more than elsewhere, the industry was made up of small family firms. As a result, individual employers had fewer resources to deploy in a struggle with their workers, providing a further incentive to seeking industrial peace through the creation of a "labor aristocracy."

[13] As in the case of automobiles, the retention of significant production in high-wage areas in the standardization phase was in large part due to protectionism (see Footnote 2 for this

II. The Textile Complex Product Cycle

The combined outcome of these fixes was a rapid decline in the size of the labor forces employed in core locales, a further decrease in the marketplace bargaining power of the remaining (largely peripheral) workforce, and a corresponding waning of labor unrest. For the textile industry, as can be seen from Table 3.1, the WLG database registers some "residual" high-point waves of labor unrest in the 1950s, predominantly in very peripheral locales, followed by the disappearance of textile labor unrest waves sufficiently strong to reach our threshold criteria.[14] It is too soon to tell whether the automobile industry will follow an analogous trajectory. On the one hand, if labor unrest in the automobile standardization phase is following the same trajectory as that of the textile industry, we might interpret the high-point waves of the late 1970s and 1980s shown in Table 3.1 as the last gasps of a "residual" autoworker labor unrest. On the other hand, given the relatively strong workplace bargaining power of autoworkers, even in the standardization phase, powerful waves of labor unrest are still likely in the new sites of auto industry expansion (most notably in China). Moreover, given the size and global political–economic importance of China, we may witness not just the "last gasps" of "residual" autoworker labor unrest but rather autoworker labor unrest high points of world-historical significance.

So far our focus has been on a phase-by-phase *comparison* of the *intra-industry* dynamic of labor unrest in the textile and automobile product cycles. Yet the rise/decline of labor unrest in the textile and automobile product cycles are not just two instances of an independent phenomenon; rather these two trajectories are themselves interrelated through an *inter-industry* dynamic that we call the product fix. From this perspective, the textile and automobile product cycles overlapped and influenced each other.

chapter). In the United States, unions combined forces with textile manufacturers to lobby for protectionist legislation in the hope of slowing the decline in textile employment. "Buy American" campaigns – picked up by the autoworkers' union – had been initiated by the textile and garment workers' unions. Nevertheless, the protectionist legislation also had the unintended consequence of prompting textile/automobile producers subject to export quotas to relocate production to even lower-wage geographical areas that had not yet filled their quotas, thereby further intensifying competitive pressures. The recurrence of this dynamic is particularly striking in the case of Japan, which, in response to export quotas, first relocated textile production to lower-wage sites in Asia in the 1930s and then relocated automobile production to lower-wage sites in Asia in the 1980s.

[14] As we shall see when we widen the angle of vision to include world politics in Chapter 4, the postwar decline in textile labor unrest is also in part traceable to the fundamentally different world political circumstances that characterized the textile industry's mature and standardization phases.

As the textile industry reached the end of its mature phase (and labor unrest and competitive pressures escalated), capital moved into new and innovative product lines less subject to labor unrest and competitive pressures, including the automobile industry. And, as the textile industry entered the standardization phase and the automobile industry entered its own mature phase, high-point waves of textile labor unrest disappeared while high-point waves of auto labor unrest spread. This shift over time in the industrial epicenter of labor unrest can be seen in Table 3.1.

Thus, if we look at the two product cycles as a single interconnected phenomenon, we can see that the cyclical rise and demise of labor unrest *within* each leading industry of world capitalist development is embedded in a shift in labor unrest *between* industries as new product cycles emerge. Moreover, the shift from textiles to automobiles as the leading industry of world capitalism in the twentieth century also involved a fundamental transformation in the dynamics of labor unrest. As we have argued here, the structural bargaining power of workers in the new leading industry (automobiles) was far greater than that of workers in the old leading industry (textiles). The workplace bargaining power of autoworkers has been stronger as the industry has been more vulnerable to workers' disruptions at the point of production. And the marketplace bargaining power of autoworkers has been stronger as a result of the fact that the industry is less easy to relocate geographically than textile production.

The greater bargaining power of autoworkers was associated with far more successful outcomes to their struggles. However, it was not associated with greater levels of militancy per se. Indeed, from a simple count of the number of high-point waves of labor unrest in Table 3.1, we would conclude that the militancy of textile workers was greater than the militancy of automobile workers. Such an inverse relationship between militancy and bargaining power might be linked to the differential response of employers to structurally strong/weak labor movements. It is indeed reasonable to assume that, ceteris paribus, the greater capital's vulnerability to workers' direct action and the more limited the options of capital for pursuing a spatial-fix solution, the more employers would feel compelled to accommodate workers' demands and grievances. Such accommodation, in turn, would decrease workers' incentive for repeated militant action.[15]

---

[15] This inverse relationship between militancy and bargaining power was observed at various points in the preceding narrative. Deyo (1989: 79–81) also pointed it out in his discussion of the South Korean labor movement. Female textile workers have been among the most

In sum, the overall dynamic of world labor unrest has been embedded in the rise/decline of product cycles and the attendant shifts in the degree/nature of workers' bargaining power.[16] It follows that an understanding of the present and future dynamics of labor unrest requires an investigation of the most likely successor(s) of the automobile complex as the leading industry of world capitalism as well as the nature of workers' bargaining power therein. Before we turn to this investigation in Section IV, let us briefly digress to discuss a central part of the process of production that has been hidden from view by our focus on manufacturing, but that is nevertheless crucial for understanding the (past, present, and future) dynamics of world working-class formation and labor unrest.

III. *Cycles, Fixes, and Transportation Industry Labor Unrest*

Transportation industries "sell change of location" as their product (Harvey 1999: 376). The textile and automobile industries (indeed, all manufacturing) depend upon transportation systems at several "moments" in their production processes – acquisition of inputs (including getting workers to the workplace), moving intermediate products from one production site to the next, and bringing the final product to the market. Historically, rapid expansions in manufacturing output in any particular location have depended on the development of new transportation and communication networks for the distribution of goods and the acquisition of raw materials (Riddle 1986: 3, 7, 33, 37–8; Hartwell 1973: 373).[17]

Given this centrality of transport systems to historical capitalism, our theoretical framework would lead us to expect transportation labor unrest to account for a significant proportion of total labor unrest throughout the historical period covered by the WLG database. Moreover, just as we found shifts in the epicenter of labor unrest *within* manufacturing (i.e., from textiles to automobiles), so we should expect to find similar labor unrest shifts

militant workers in that country in the 1970s and 1980s; in fact, they are markedly more militant than automobile workers. Yet, the gains made by automobile (and other heavy industry) workers were far greater. (See Chapter 2 on the gains of the South Korean autoworkers.)

[16] This argument will be developed further when we introduce the dynamics of world politics into our analysis in Chapter 4.

[17] See Ciccantell and Bunker (1998) for a conceptualization of transport from a world-systems perspective.

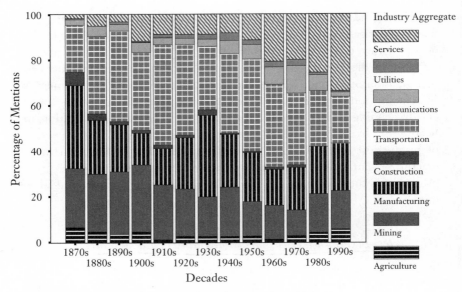

Figure 3.3. World labor unrest by industry, 1870–1996.

within transportation corresponding to shifts in the relative importance of different modes of transportation.[18]

The WLG data bear out both expectations. As can be seen from Figure 3.3, labor unrest in transportation has accounted for a large proportion of labor unrest – an average of 35% of the total industry-specific mentions from 1870 to 1996. As such, transportation labor unrest is the largest category, surpassing even manufacturing (which accounts for 21% of total industry-specific mentions over the entire time period) and mining (which accounts for 18%).[19] Indeed, the percentage of total labor unrest accounted for by transportation workers surpasses all other categories in every decade except three: the 1870s and 1930s when manufacturing takes

---

[18] The same argument about centrality (*and* shifts) could be made with respect to energy industries, and hence about the expected centrality of workers in coal, oil, and other energy sectors for world working-class formation and labor unrest. We will not attempt such an analysis here, but see Podobnik (2000) for a study of the relationship between labor/social unrest and historical transformations in world energy regimes, especially coal and oil.

[19] Within mining, coal mining is by far the most important category. For an analysis of the pattern of world labor unrest in coal mining using WLG data, see Podobnik (2000).

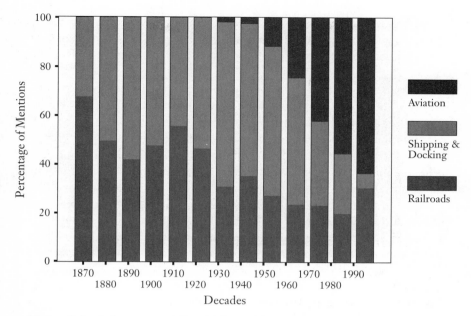

Figure 3.4. Labor unrest shifts within transportation, 1870–1996.

the lead and the 1990s when the aggregate service category jumps into the lead.[20]

Moreover, as can be seen from Figure 3.4, which charts the distribution of labor unrest for three major transportation subsectors, there has been a shift in the overall weight of labor unrest within transportation over the course of the twentieth century. The shift is most dramatic for shipping/docks in relation to aviation. Labor unrest among ship and dockworkers accounts for 52% of the total transportation labor unrest mentions over the entire 1870 to 1996 period, whereas the corresponding figure for railroad and aviation workers is 35% and 13%, respectively. Yet by the 1970s, the relative weight of labor unrest mentions in aviation was 42%, surpassing the 35% registered for docking/shipping in the 1970s. Moreover, the rise of aviation labor unrest relative to docking/shipping continued into the 1980s (55% aviation, 24% docking/shipping) and 1990s (63% aviation, 7% docking/shipping). A similar, though less dramatic

---

[20] The steady increase in the overall weight of the aggregate service category from the 1960s (to be discussed in more detail later) produces the steady relative decline in transportation labor unrest over the same period visible in Figure 3.3.

relative decline in railroad labor unrest is also visible with the percentage of mentions declining from an average of 43% in the first half of the twentieth century to an average of 25% in the second half of the century.

Transport workers have possessed and continue to possess relatively strong workplace bargaining power. This is especially clear after we conceptualize their workplace as the entire distribution network in which they are enmeshed. Thus, the source of their workplace bargaining power often is to be found less in the direct impact of their actions on their immediate (often public) employers and more on the upstream/downstream impact of the failure to deliver goods, services, and people to their destination. The "relative fortunes of capitalists in different locations" are greatly impacted by the development of new transportation networks (Harvey 1999: 378), as well as by the disruption of existing transportation networks, including disruptions caused by workers' struggles.

Moreover, in transportation industries, it is not easy to devise (much less practically carry out) spatial fixes as counterweights to labor's strong workplace bargaining power. Particularly troublesome nodes might be eliminated entirely from the distribution network – that is, unruly or otherwise unprofitable nodes can be cut off from networks of trade and production. But the upstream and downstream ramifications for all other industries of such a spatial fix in transportation makes it a heavy-handed solution at best (especially if the region as a whole to be cut off is not plagued by generalized problems of profitability and control). Moreover, "roads, railways, canals, airports, etc., cannot be moved without the value embodied in them being lost," creating the paradoxical situation whereby the mobility of capital requires relatively immobile investments in the transportation industries (Harvey 1999: 380). Thus, the disincentives to geographical relocation facing the transportation industries are on average significantly higher than the deterrents facing even the most capital-intensive manufacturing industries. Indeed, the fact that the reports of transportation workers' unrest in the WLG database are consistently spread widely across the globe throughout the 1870–1996 period suggests that spatial fixes have not been the main response to transport worker unrest.[21]

---

[21] The wide geographical spread of transportation labor unrest can be seen from the following comparison. Whereas eleven countries met the 1 percent threshold that we have been using to identify significant sites of labor unrest for automobiles, and fifteen countries met that threshold for textiles, twenty-seven different countries met the threshold for the

III. Cycles, Fixes, and Transportation Labor Unrest

Technological fixes have, on the other hand, been far more significant in the arsenal of employer responses to transportation worker labor unrest. The most widely studied case is that of containerization and dock automation in the shipping industry. These process innovations dramatically downsized the historically militant dock labor force in the second half of the twentieth century and in large part account for the dramatic decline in labor unrest mentions discussed earlier. Where substantial transformations in the transport labor process have been less forthcoming, product fixes have been the more prominent response. Thus, for example, railroads and railroad workers have come under increasing competitive pressure from new alternatives: trucking and aviation for cargo and the automobile and aviation for passengers.

Finally, the role played by state regulation has been far more central and direct in the dynamics of transportation labor unrest than in other industries. The importance of smoothly functioning transportation systems to capital accumulation – combined with the strong workplace bargaining power of transportation workers and the limited scope for spatial fixes – helps explain why states have felt it necessary to intervene extensively and precociously in transport industry labor unrest. For example, railroad workers, in country after country, were among the first to gain legal rights (e.g., legalization of trade unions). Simultaneously with the adoption of these new rights, however, laws that restricted their activities (e.g., the outlawing of strikes) were also passed.

For manufacturing industries, we made the argument that as the product cycle advances, competitive pressures increase; thus, late industrializers have fewer resources with which to accommodate labor unrest. For transportation industries, in contrast, different parts of a (railroad, airline) network are not in direct competition with each other (or the nature of that competition is exceedingly complex), and thus our product-cycle arguments seem far less relevant for explaining spatially differentiated outcomes to labor unrest in transportation. Thus, we might also expect outcomes to labor unrest in transportation to be less spatially differentiated along core–periphery lines than outcomes to labor unrest in manufacturing. Moreover, this combination of less direct competition and less spatial differentiation among workers may mean that the material basis of labor internationalism

three transport subsectors (seventeen in railroads, twenty in docking/shipping, seventeen in aviation).

is stronger among transport workers than among workers in manufacturing industries.[22]

In line with this expectation are the emergent international pilot alliances – an unexpected side effect of the late 1990s and early 2000s trend among major airlines to set up global alliances sharing routes, airplanes, and marketing. Pilots in each of the major airline alliances have set up their own corresponding pilot alliances (e.g., the Star Alliance Pilots for the United Airlines–led Star Alliance). These pilot alliances are quite active. The Oneworld Cockpit Crew Coalition encompassing pilots from the American Airlines/British Airlines–led Oneworld Alliance, for example, held a meeting in Miami in 2001 in which pilots from American Airlines' union shared information and discussed union strategy in solidarity with pilots from Lan Chile and Aer Lingus. For airline executives, this international solidarity among airline pilots is a "world-wide trend" that is "very worrying" (Michaels 2001: 23, 28).

So far we have emphasized similarities among the transportation industries. But what are the implications of the shifts (or product fixes) *within* transportation for the contemporary dynamics of labor unrest? The increasingly dense networks of trade and production created by the latest round of globalization mean that transportation workers are at least as central to processes of capital accumulation as they were in the past. Moreover, there is no reason to think that the workplace bargaining power of aviation workers is any less strong than that of dock/shipping or railroads workers – indeed, it may well be greater, especially with respect to its potential impact on global networks. Yet, aviation workers have been less militant on average than railroad or dock/shipping workers.[23] As we shall argue in Chapter 4, this is in part traceable to the different world-political contexts in which labor movements were operating in the 1920s, 1950s, and 1970s – the peak

---

[22] The only caveat relates to the central role of the state (as employer and/or conflict mediator) in transportation industries. Assuming that governments of wealthier countries have more material resources (larger tax base) with which to mediate conflict than governments of poorer countries, divergent outcomes to labor unrest are to be expected. Nevertheless, this is a different dynamic than that of direct competition among differently located factories (and workers) and hence poses fewer barriers to cross-border cooperation and solidarity.

[23] Because it is difficult to conceptualize meaningfully a product cycle in the transportation industries, it is also difficult to single out comparable periods (e.g., mature phases). If we compare the peak labor unrest decade for the three transport subsectors, we find the lowest levels of labor unrest for aviation. Thus, while dock/shipping labor unrest peaks at 1,887 mentions in the 1950s and railroad labor unrest peaks at 1,165 mentions in the 1920s, aviation's peak decade *to date* – the 1970s – registered only 637 mentions.

decades for WLG reports of labor unrest in the railroad, dock/shipping, and aviation industries, respectively. But as suggested previously with respect to the textile–auto shift, it might also be related to an *increase* in workplace bargaining power – an increase that compels employers and states to offer more concessions and therefore reduces workers' incentive for ongoing labor unrest. If so, then the relative shift to aviation represents a continuation of the century-long trend toward increased workplace bargaining power.

Nevertheless, as we shall see in the next section, the overall impact on workplace bargaining of post-Fordist product fixes has been far more mixed than would appear to be the case from a focus on transportation industries. In other words, although this section argues that transportation workers continue to have strong workplace bargaining power, and Chapter 2 argued that autoworkers' workplace bargaining power also remains strong, many of the sites of rapidly growing employment are producing workers with relatively weak workplace bargaining power. In terms of the overall outcomes for workers in the early twenty-first century, one critical question will be how those with strong workplace bargaining power will deploy it – will it be in struggles that benefit workers broadly (including those with weak bargaining power) or in more narrow struggles?[24] This is a theme to which we shall return in the conclusions of both this chapter and the book.

IV. A New Product Fix?

This chapter has argued that the locus of major waves of labor unrest shifts together with geographical shifts in production *within* the leading capitalist industry of a given epoch as well as *among* industries with the successive rise/fall of overlapping product cycles. A critical next task, from this perspective, is to identify the likely successor(s) of the automobile complex as leading industry of world capitalism and to explore the nature of workers' bargaining power therein. Yet it is difficult to identify a single product that plays a role equivalent to that played historically by the textile complex in the nineteenth century or the automobile complex in the twentieth century.

---

[24] As Chapter 2 showed, the initial major waves of autoworker labor unrest in country after country were intertwined with broader struggles of working and poor people in general and often with struggles for democracy as well. This tendency was no doubt rooted in a combination of structural conditions (e.g., autoworkers lived in broad working-class communities) and political choices. A key question is whether analogously favorable structural conditions exist today to incline workers with strong bargaining power to use that power in a way that links up with demands beyond their own specific interests.

As observers of post-Fordism have emphasized, one striking characteristic of contemporary capitalism is its eclecticism and flexibility, visible in the dizzying array of choices in consumer goods and the rapid emergence of new commodities and new ways of consuming old commodities. In the remainder of this chapter, we will identify several "industries" that deserve close monitoring as potentially critical sites of ongoing world-scale working-class formation and labor unrest.

The Semiconductor Industry

This dizzying array of products is in large part made possible by a single product – the semiconductor. Indeed, Peter Dicken (1998: 353–4) suggested that microelectronics has replaced the automobile as today's "industry of industries." Like "textiles, steel and automobiles before it," the microelectronics industry "has come to be regarded as the touchstone of industrial success." Even more so than in the case of the automobile industry, the microelectronics industry's most striking impact is indirect, through the incorporation of semiconductors into a wide range of products and processes. The automobile industry brought with it a host of ancillary changes in daily life ranging from residential and industrial suburbanization to the transformation of the geopolitics of energy acquisition and the cultural symbols of the era. The semiconductor industry – through the "computerization of everything," including automobile and textile production – has had at least as profound an impact on the experience of everyday life and work.

Nevertheless, employment in the semiconductor industry itself has not had a direct impact on working-class formation equivalent to the historical impact of textiles or automobiles. Despite the phenomenal growth in output since the 1970s, the number of manufacturing jobs created in the semiconductor industry has been relatively small because wafer fabrication is automated. Design and wafer fabrication, the innovative and technologically sophisticated part of semiconductor production, is located in high-income countries. It requires high-level scientific, technical, and engineering personnel as well as expensive plant and equipment providing a "pure" environment for production, but little direct labor input in the manufacturing process.[25] The labor-intensive part of the production process is

---

[25] At the highly automated semiconductor production facility to be opened by IBM in Fishkill, New York, in 2003, the 300-millimeter silicon wafers will go through more than five

board assembly, which has been relocated to low-wage countries, especially in Asia, since the early 1960s (Dicken 1998: 373).

Thus, on the one hand, few manufacturing jobs have been created in high-income countries by the expansion of the semiconductor industry. On the other hand, the industry's expansion has further contributed to the growth of an industrial proletariat in lower-wage countries. More specifically, it led to the rapid growth of a young, female industrial proletariat – a phenomenon that attracted substantial scholarly attention in the 1970s and 1980s under the rubric of "the global assembly line" (see, e.g., Fernandez-Kelly 1983; Lim 1990; Ong 1987). Nevertheless, in recent years, board assembly itself has become increasingly automated, and job growth in low-wage countries in this sector has also slowed (Dicken 1998: 383–6).[26]

Likewise, the expansion of (and proliferation of products in) consumer electronics has been associated with a similar employment pattern – that is, a shrinking of the industrial proletariat in the core together with a further enlargement of the industrial proletariat in select low-wage locales. Even though research and development (R&D), marketing, and coordination remain in the hands of multinational corporations and are carried out mainly in high-wage countries, virtually all manufacturing and assembly takes place in low-wage countries. In this sphere, China looms large. In the case of television sets, China "came from nowhere" to become the world's largest maker of televisions in 1987 (Dicken 1998: 357).[27]

This pattern whereby the size of the industrial working class is shrinking in high-wage countries but simultaneously increasing in lower-wage countries replicates the pattern we identified previously for the textile and automobile industries. As a result of these combined processes, the mass-production industrial proletariat has continued to grow rapidly in size and centrality in many lower-wage countries. More specifically, since the mid 1980s, Asia, and especially China, has been the key site of industrial expansion and new industrial working-class formation. Our analysis of the past would lead us to expect the emergence of vigorous workers' movements in China in the near future. And given the size and centrality of China – in the

---

hundred processing steps, typically lasting twenty days, without the wafers ever being touched by human hands (Lohr 2002).

[26] Software jobs, in contrast to hardware, have become a significant source of employment in India – a point to which we return later.

[27] See Cowie (1999) on the successive relocation of RCA's consumer electronics production facilities to lower-wage, less-unionized sites of production within North America over the course of the twentieth century.

East Asian region and globally – the impact of this movement, if it emerges, will likely be world resounding, analogous to the impact of China's peasant-based revolution in the mid twentieth century.

Indeed, there have been reports of mounting labor unrest in China; for example, an official report estimated some 30,000 demonstrations in the year 2000 alone. Yet most of these were protests against job loss and unpaid wages and pensions, as the rapid industrialization fueled by foreign direct investment has gone hand in hand with the dismantling of state-owned industrial enterprises. Thus, the growing labor unrest in China to date has largely taken the form of what we have called Polanyi-type movements against the disruption of established ways of life and livelihood. On the one hand, the impetus for these types of protest is not over. With China's entry into the WTO, another 40 million laid-off workers from state-owned enterprises are expected to join the 45 million to 50 million who have been laid off so far (Solinger 2001; see also Solinger 1999). On the other hand, our analysis so far gives us every reason to expect that what we have called Marx-type labor unrest will also emerge. Workers in different industries will have varying amounts of bargaining power, but some (like autoworkers) will possess strong workplace bargaining power. Exactly when this Marx-type labor unrest will emerge and how these workers will interact with protests by the unemployed are open questions. Nevertheless, the importance of the Chinese industrial working class to the future of world labor unrest would appear to be incontrovertible.

Producer Services

The geographical decentralization of manufacturing activities discussed earlier has taken place together with the growth and centralization of global "command and control" functions, as well as a growing financialization of capital.[28] "Increased capital mobility," wrote Saskia Sassen (2001: 24) "generates a demand for types of production needed to ensure the management, control, and servicing of this new organization of manufacturing and finance." These new types of production range from telecommunications to specialized services such as legal, financial, advertising, consulting, and

---

[28] In Chapter 4, we will reconceptualize this growing financialization of capital as a financial fix. This financial fix can be seen as a continuation of the product cycle by other means. As competition becomes intense, rather than invest in new manufactured products, capital is pulled out of trade and production entirely and reinvested in financial deals and speculation (Arrighi 1994; Arrighi and Silver 1999).

accounting. Although these producer services support business organizations that are managing vast global networks of factories, offices, and financial markets, they are themselves subject to economies of agglomeration, according to Sassen. Thus, the geographical dispersal of manufacturing production and the hypermobility of financial capital has as its other side the centralization in select core cities of multinational corporate headquarters and the producer services they require. These are the "places where the work of running global systems gets done" (Sassen 2000: 1). And, as we shall argue, these also are critical sites to be monitored for ongoing processes of working-class formation and emerging labor unrest.

Since the 1970s, employment in producer services has grown faster than any other economic sector in most core countries (Sassen 2000: 62–4; see also Castells and Aoyama 1994; Marshall and Wood 1995: 9–11). In the United States, for example, while total employment grew from 76.8 million in 1970 to 102.2 million in 1996, producer services grew from 6.3 million to 17.6 million. In contrast, manufacturing grew only from 19.9 million to 20.4 million (see Sassen 2000: Exhibit 4.1). Some observers have taken these figures to indicate that post-industrial societies are generating mainly well-paying professional, technical, and managerial jobs. Such a diagnosis was made almost three decades ago by Daniel Bell (1973) in *The Coming of Post-Industrial Society*, which posited that "advanced capitalist economies" were producing both highly educated workforces and more pacific labor–capital relations. This view has been stated even more baldly in some of the 1990s odes to the "New Economy." Nevertheless, the evidence increasingly contradicts this view. This is because producer services require – as an integral part of their production – support from a host of traditionally pink- and blue-collar positions ranging from secretaries, telephone operators, building maintenance crews, and janitors to waiters, dishwashers, and childcare workers. Thus, where producer services have grown rapidly, there has been a polarization of the labor force between high-wage professionals and low-wage workers (Wall Street Journal 2000; Greenhouse 2000).[29]

---

[29] Reporting on a just-released study on employment trends in New York City, Steven Greenhouse (2000) wrote: "New York City's rebounding economy has produced a record number of jobs, but a new study shows that the number of low-wage jobs, those paying less than $25,000 a year, is growing much faster than the number of middle- or high-wage jobs. The study . . . found that while the city had added thousands of high-paying Wall Street and Silicon Alley jobs in recent years, the fastest job growth had been among low-wage service employees, like restaurant workers, security guards, day care workers, and home

The theoretical framework developed in this book suggests that we should look to the sites of significant new job growth as the critical arenas for emergent working-class formation and protest. We cannot disaggregate producer services from other services in the WLG database. Nevertheless, Figure 3.3, which charts the distribution of WLG labor unrest mentions by industry, reveals a pattern that is in line with this expectation. Taking services as a whole, we can see a rapid increase in their relative importance as a site of world labor unrest in the last four decades of the twentieth century. Thus, whereas services accounted for between 9% and 12% of the total number of industry-specific mentions of labor unrest in the first half of the twentieth century, this figure jumps to 21% in the 1960s, 26% in the 1980s, and 34% in the 1990s.[30]

At first sight, many of the low-paid support workers in the producer services sector would appear to have little bargaining power. Yet, Sassen suggested a source of power that is often overlooked – perhaps even purposely deemphasized. If the logic according to which producer services operate is one of economies of agglomeration, then the industries involved in the command and control functions of the global economy (and their support) are relatively place-bound themselves. Moreover, certain types of investments that make global cities function are extremely capital-intensive[31] and cannot be easily abandoned without a huge loss in terms of sunken fixed capital. These include telecommunication networks and the wiring of modern office buildings with advanced communications capabilities. In other words, the producer services complex cannot easily respond to labor unrest with the spatial fix of geographical mobility.

It is interesting to note how the dominant economic narrative argues that place no longer matters, that firms can locate anywhere thanks to telematics, that major

---

attendants for the elderly." The study "also found that for the city's low-wage workers, the median wage dropped by 2 percent from 1989 to 1999, after taking inflation into account." Growth of employment in Europe has also been based on expansion of part-time, relatively low-paid positions (see Sassen 2000).

[30] In this connection it is interesting to note that in the United States the Service Employees International Union (SEIU) and its former President John Sweeney have been in the forefront of efforts to bring about the new activist turn in the AFL-CIO.

[31] There has been a general trend toward increasing capital-intensity of services. According to Riddle (1986: 8): "In the United States, a significant proportion of services are capital-intensive, not labor-intensive." Of the 145 industry divisions ranked by R. E. Kutscher and J. A. Mark (1983) on the basis of capital stock per employee, "service industry divisions made up nearly one-half of the 30 divisions in the first two deciles of the ranking" (cited by Riddle 1986: 29).

industries now are information-based and hence not place-bound. This line of argument... allows the corporate economy to extract major concessions from city governments [and workers] under the notion that firms can simply leave and relocate elsewhere, which is not quite the case for a whole complex of firms. (Sassen 2000: 144)

Of course, this place-bound nature of producer services can be overstated. There is a point at which rising costs in the sites in which producer services are concentrated would eventually provide capital with the incentive for a spatial fix, even a very costly one. Moreover, as national and local governments have come to realize that attracting investment from producer service industries (the new shining star) requires providing advanced telecommunications infrastructures, they have also begun to organize and subsidize the building of such infrastructure as part of a competitive bid to host new producer services centers.

Likewise some segments of producer service production processes do not need to take place at the central office. We can distinguish two different labor process types within the producer services complex: for the first type, spatial fixes are not in fact a real option, but for the second type they are very much an option. Thus, the buildings in which corporations are headquartered cannot be sent to low-wage countries each night to be cleaned. Janitorial work must be done on site. In contrast, however, much of the routine work of data entry and word processing on which producer services depend can (and are) being sent to low-wage countries on a regular basis. We will discuss these two different types in turn.

Let's take the case of janitors who clean the skyscrapers in the downtown commercial district in Los Angeles. These workers would appear to have little bargaining power. Their jobs do not require scarce skills. The positions are generally part-time and/or temporary jobs with no benefits, career ladders, or job security, and with high turnover. The workers are disproportionately immigrant or minority women who often hold second jobs and/or have childcare responsibilities that leave them little time for union activity. Moreover, the "employers" are often phantom or subcontracting organizations, set up with the goal of cutting costs by evading existing union (or customary) contracts with workers. Yet in the late 1990s these workers, and other workers in the lowest rung of producer services complexes of other U.S. cities, succeeded in winning significant victories. These include the spread of a campaign for a Living Wage in Baltimore, and from Baltimore to over thirty other U.S. cities, and the victorious Justice for Janitors campaign in several cities, most notably in Los Angeles.

These campaigns have secured improved wages and working conditions for low-wage service workers such as cleaning crews in major office buildings. In addition, they have sparked a burst of labor movement social activism at a time of historically low levels of labor unrest in the United States.

What was the basis of these victories? On the one hand, they probably derived some structural power from the place-bound nature of their employers. As already mentioned, while employers could seek out low-paid immigrant labor to clean the buildings, they could not send the buildings elsewhere to be cleaned. Yet, given the analysis carried forward so far in this chapter, it would seem that this is insufficient to explain even the limited successes achieved in the context of the overall weak structural bargaining power of these workers. Rather, it would appear that victories have been based on a significant strategic rethinking of how to leverage "associational power." In particular, these campaigns involved a major reassessment of the established workplace-focused organizing model and a shift to a new model of organizing that was more community-based. With workers spread among multiple work sites and employment relations characterized by a high degree of contingency and turnover, organizing individual workplaces would be a Sisyphean task. Thus, the Living Wage campaign in Baltimore sought to build a citywide movement to improve the wages and working conditions of the working poor. According to one of the campaign's organizers, the goal was to build a new type of labor organization – one that is "transportable for people from workplace to workplace" (cited by Harvey 2000: 126). Thus, as for the U.K. textile workers who faced multiple employers, regionwide associational bargaining power was essential.

The Justice for Janitors campaign also avoided established workplace organizing procedures, in part because they realized that the real power to change conditions lay not with the ostensible "employers" – the cleaning subcontracting companies – but with the property owners who used the subcontracted firms as a union avoidance strategy. Thus, instead of pursuing National Labor Relations Board (NLRB) elections for union recognition in what were essentially phantom enterprises that could be closed with a union victory and reopened as nonunion shops, the campaign emphasized "in your face" street protests directed at the building owners and business tenants (Waldinger et al. 1998: 110). Likewise, the Living Wage campaign seeks to make governments, large corporations, and universities responsible, not only for the treatment of the workers in their direct employ but also for the behavior of the subcontractors they hire. The spread of subcontracting has created a "byzantine system that disguises responsibility and accountability"

(Needleman 1998: 79). Successful campaigns have been able to counter this by identifying and targeting the "responsible" agent with the power to change conditions.[32]

All these campaigns have relied heavily on "allies in those social layers not directly interested in the question" (Harvey 2000: 125, paraphrasing Marx). In the case of Baltimore's Living Wage campaign, a church-based interfaith alliance took the initial lead and provided much of the resources (Harvey 2000). In the case of the Justice for Janitors, the crucial role was played by intervention from the headquarters of a revitalized and (now) centralized trade union organization – the Service Employees International Union – that bypassed the more conservative local union leadership. While the Justice for Janitors campaign involved extensive grass roots mobilization and would not have been successful without this, it also involved extensive resources that could only be provided by the pooling and redistribution capacities of a large organization. Waldinger et al. (1998: 112–13) pointed to some of the costs involved in a campaign that was research-intensive (with at least one staff researcher studying the structure of the industry and its weaknesses), lawyer-intensive (with high-risk confrontational tactics as well as "guerilla legal tactics"), and organizer-intensive. The Justice for Janitors campaign cost half a million dollars a year in Los Angeles alone.[33]

Finally, because these transformations in the organization of production have also gone hand in hand with a transformation in the gender and ethnic composition of the working class, the campaigns have had to confront simultaneously issues of race, gender, citizenship, and class. Successful campaigns have transformed the face of the labor movement activist to better reflect the face of the workers. And they have addressed the specific needs and demands of this new workforce – including such things as adequate childcare and English language lessons.[34] Given that the new labor force simultaneously raised issues of gender, race, national, and class oppression,

---

[32] This byzantine structure has also been characteristic of the garment industry. Finding ways to hold retailers and fashion houses accountable for the behavior of their subcontractors has likewise been a key strategy in labor organizing in this sector (see Bonacich and Appelbaum 2000; Ness 1998). Needleman (1998) makes the same point with regard to home health care workers (a case of privatized social service workers).

[33] Waldinger et al. (1998) also pointed to the role of class-consciousness that workers brought with them from their (mainly Central American) countries of origin. As such, there is a parallel with the story we have told of New England textile workers who brought with them from Lancashire a tradition of militancy (although not the structural conditions for success).

[34] On the importance of labor–community centers, see Needleman (1998) and Ness (1998).

it also more naturally drew support from a variety of social movement organizations including civil rights and women's organizations (Bronfenbrenner
et al. 1998).

Thus, it would appear that the relative immobility of capital is insufficient
to explain the victories achieved. Nevertheless, if workers are able to *hold
on to their gains* in the coming decade, an important part of the explanation
will no doubt be found in the barriers to a spatial-fix response by capital.

What then of the more mobile segments of producer service labor
processes, such as routine data entry? One of the most important de-
velopments in this regard is the investments being made by U.S. and
European companies designed to tap India's supply of educated, English-
speaking workers. Data processing offices, telephone call centers, and other
"information-based" job sites are being established including ones involved
in higher-end producer service activities such as software and engineering.
Ireland, Jamaica, and the Philippines also have been providing low-cost
"back-office" staff for foreign companies, yet the number of Indian workers employed in this manner is expected to swamp all previous cases. An
estimated 40,000 Indians are now working in the so-called remote service industry, and the industry is expected to experience enormous growth,
employing as many as 700,000 people by 2008 (Filkins 2000).

"Overseas companies send [the work] via satellite, and Indian workers
key it into files, categorize it, analyze it, and ship it back home...for a
small fraction of the cost back home." British Airways, for example, "beams
a scanned copy of every one of the 35 million tickets it sells each year to
India, where workers reconcile the tickets with billing information sent
from travel agents." And General Electric plans in the next two years to
quadruple the size of its current 1,000-strong workforce that is employed
in New Delhi to "process loans, perform accounting tasks and call people
in the United States who are late on their loan payments"(Filkins 2000).

Here, then, is another important industrial and geographical site of new
working-class formation and potential labor unrest in the early twenty-first
century. Yet, what kind of bargaining power might these workers rely upon?
This work makes use of the Internet and other advanced communication
systems for receiving the raw materials, transmitting the final product, and
in many cases handling intermediate steps in the production process as well.
The vulnerability of cyberspace to disruptions is far greater than the vulnerability of the assembly line or JIT production systems, as we know from
experience with hackers and viruses. Nevertheless, how this vulnerability
might translate into effective workplace bargaining power is something that

remains to be demonstrated by workers' creativity in innovating new forms of struggles for the new environment (cf. Piven and Cloward 2001).

In such a highly mobile industry, the response to any labor unrest might be immediate geographical relocation. Indeed, if one is to believe management, the production process itself is hypermobile. "I could take this operation anywhere in the world. It is completely portable," claims a supervisor of 120 employees who process claims for a Cincinnati-based insurance firm in Bangalore, India (quoted by Filkins 2000: 5). Nevertheless, as a permanent spatial fix to labor unrest, such statements might contain a bit of hyperbole. The industry has already relocated to one of the lowest-income countries in the world. Where does it go from there? Moreover, once new forms of workplace bargaining power are uncovered and deployed in these information-based industries, is it not possible that employers will find, like the automobile corporations before them, that working-class struggles reemerge in each new favored site of expansion?

To be sure, these jobs are far more mobile than the janitorial work discussed previously. And this does have important implications for associational power. As discussed previously, the victories by janitors were built in large measure on community-based associational power – a power that is particularly effective when the employers cannot move out of the community. Community level associational power would be far less effective for workers whose jobs are easily moved to other communities or countries. Any short-run gains built on community-level power would be overturned when the work left the community. In this situation, for associational bargaining power to be effective, it would have to be not at the community level, but at the level at which capital is mobile – that is, globally. This, in turn, brings us back to the need for – *but also the difficulties and limits of* – labor internationalism, an issue raised in Chapter 1 and to which we will return in Chapter 5.

A prerequisite for the mass expansion of this information-based workforce has been the expansion of mass education. One might even argue that the "education industry" has become the central capital-goods-producing industry of the late twentieth and early twenty-first centuries. It is to a discussion of this industry and its workers that we now turn.

The Education Industry

In attempting to capture the overall nature of post-Fordist transformations, diverse analysts have emphasized the new centrality of "information" or the emergence of a knowledge-based economy. Manuel Castells (1997) conceptualized "the informational economy." David Harvey (1989: 186) saw capitalism as depending more and more on "mobilizing the powers of intellectual labour as a vehicle for further accumulation." For Peter Drucker (1993: 8), the "basic economic resource" is no longer capital, land, or labor, rather " *it is and will be knowledge.*" Yet as Michael Hardt and Antonio Negri emphasized, knowledge itself has to be produced. Moreover, the production of knowledge "involves new kinds of production and labor" (2000: 461–2). Seen from these combined perspectives, mass education appears as one of the most important "capital goods industries" of the twenty-first century – in part producing "knowledge" and, more importantly, producing the workers who have the necessary skills for the new knowledge-intensive form of capital accumulation.[35] Like textile workers in the nineteenth century and automobile workers in the twentieth century, education workers (teachers) are central to processes of capital accumulation in the twenty-first century.

Teachers are proletarians. Indeed, it has been some time now since a significant number of teachers owned their own means of production; in order to survive they sell their labor power (generally to the state). Nevertheless, social scientists often do not classify teachers as workers, perhaps because their jobs are seen as skilled and/or they are deemed to have some autonomy and control over the curriculum and the classroom and/or they are public employees. Moreover, while states have been subject to recurrent fiscal crises that have seriously affected the working conditions of teachers, educational systems by and large have not been run with strictly "for-profit" criteria. From the perspective of this book, the central question would be whether these characteristics (assuming they are accurate) fully insulate teachers from the negative effects of the commodification of their labor power. Otherwise, we would expect "unrest" in response to these negative effects, and we would classify it as "labor unrest."[36]

---

[35] Teachers produce "a labour force, a commodity improved in value" (Lawn and Ozga 1988: 84).

[36] For conceptualizations of teachers as workers, see the essays collected in Ozga (1988b). Jenny Ozga (1988a: x) hypothesized that teachers' experience as workers varies dramatically over time depending on whether or not there is a fiscal crisis of the state and/or general crisis of capitalism. In times of economic crisis, "the central state tends towards strong, directive management which imposes controls on teacher recruitment, training, salaries and status, and curriculum and examination content." In periods when resources are abundant, management "relies heavily on the promotion of teacher professionalism as a form of control." Beyond this cyclical dynamic, there is a secular trend: the more central the role of teachers in creating value (i.e., a trained labor force), the more the teaching labor process

IV. A New Product Fix?

The rapid increase in the size of the world's teaching force dates from mid century, increasing from 8 million in 1950 to 47 million in 1990, according to UNESCO data (Legters 1993).[37] Not only has the education industry been the site of rapid employment growth, it has also been the site of growing labor unrest worldwide in the second half of the twentieth century. According to the WLG data, the education industry is one of the few industries that has experienced a rising trend of labor unrest in the final decades of the twentieth century. Moreover, the geographical spread of teacher labor unrest has been far greater than was the case historically for the textile and automobile industries. As Table 3.2 shows, twenty-three countries made our threshold cutoff for inclusion in the teacher labor unrest chart as compared with fifteen countries for the textile industry and only eleven for the automobile industry (compare Tables 3.1 and 3.2). Using the same threshold criteria, the geographical spread of teacher labor unrest (23) is even greater than that of railroads (17), aviation (17), or docking/shipping (20).

Major changes in the nature of educational systems may be in progress – a point to which we shall return. Nevertheless, let's look at how teachers' bargaining power, at least until recently, has compared with labor's bargaining power in other industries discussed so far. On the one hand, in comparison with auto workers, the workplace bargaining power of teachers would seem to be weak. Unlike auto workers, teachers are *not* enmeshed in a complex *technical division of labor* at the point of production. Generally, teachers work alone in self-contained classrooms. If one teacher stops work (e.g., strikes, is out sick), other teachers in the same school can go on with

will be "analyzed and restructured to increase its efficiency (productivity)" (Lawn and Ozga 1988: 87–8). Ozga's empirical reference point is the United Kingdom. Reformulating and deploying these hypotheses at the world-historical level is an intriguing proposition, but one beyond the scope of this book.

[37] Since education has been a very labor-intensive industry (i.e., more students generally require the hiring of more teachers), school enrollment growth rates is another good indicator of teacher employment growth. School enrollments at all levels, but especially primary, started to mushroom in Latin America in the 1960s, in Africa and the Middle East during the 1970s, and in Asia during the 1980s. In high-income countries, primary school enrollment was nearly universal by mid century, and the main growth in the second half of the century was at the secondary level. Secondary school enrollments had reached nearly universal levels in high-income countries by 1990 and around 50 percent in poorer countries (UNESCO data cited by Legters 1993: 6–7). The weight of the education industry is also suggested by the example of the United States where, in 1990, employment in public education accounted for almost half of total government employment (Marshall and Wood 1995: 11).

Table 3.2 *High Points of Labor Unrest in the World Education Industry, 1870–1996*

	1870s	1880s	1890s	1900s	1910s	1920s	1930s	1940s	1950s	1960s	1970s	1980s	1990s[a]
Ireland								X		X			
Japan								X	X				
Belgium									X			X	X
Italy									X	X	X		
Bolivia									X	X		X	
Chile									X			X	
Mexico									X			X	
India									X				
United States										X	X		
Sweden										X	X		
United Kingdom										X			
Greece										X			X
Argentina										X			
Kenya										X			
Canada											X	X	
France											X		
Spain											X	X	
Australia												X	X
New Zealand												X	X
Israel/Palestine												X	
South Africa												X	X
Russia/USSR													X
Nigeria													X

[a]The 1990s decade includes 1990–96 only.

Note: The 23 countries included here met threshold criteria of having at least 1% of total mentions of education labor unrest in WLG database. "X" indicates peak decade and/or decades in which at least 20% of teacher labor unrest mentions for that country occurred.

IV. A New Product Fix?

their work without any significant disruption. Moreover, there is little interdependency among the separate school sites in a school system. Thus, unlike in the automobile industry, where a stoppage in a key supplier plant can bring an entire corporation to a halt, a strike in one school may have little or no impact on the operation of other schools in the system. While even in the case of textiles, a general strike in spinning could eventually bring weaving and other downstream activities to a halt, a general strike of secondary school teachers, by itself, does not stop work in the primary schools, or vice versa.

On the other hand, teachers are strategically located in a *social division of labor*. Whereas the raw material inputs that go into textile or automobile production can be stored for the duration of a strike, the same cannot be done with the raw material inputs in the education industry (students). Teachers' strikes have ripple effects throughout the social division of labor – disrupting family routines and making it difficult for working parents to do their own jobs. Moreover, where there have been exceptionally long and/or frequent strikes in education (or widespread teacher hostility toward their employers), fears have been raised about the longer-term impact of teacher labor unrest on the final product – that is, students' educational accomplishments as well as their proper socialization as citizens.

At the same time, teachers generally have more marketplace bargaining power than either automobile or textile workers. To date, the education industry has remained relatively impervious to technological fixes. This means that an expansion of the educational system leads to expanding employment of teachers. Whereas the introduction of new labor-saving technologies in textiles and automobile production continually created bouts of technological unemployment that weighed on the bargaining power of the active labor force, teaching so far has been largely unaffected by this dynamic. Indeed, Larry Cuban's (1984) examination of nearly a century of instructional activities shows little change in the practice and technology of teaching.[38]

The difficulty involved in raising productivity through technological innovation means that cost-cutting pressures take the form of the intensification of work in terms of longer hours or more students per teacher (Danylewycz and Prentice 1988; Lawn 1987). Nevertheless, these speed-up efforts have themselves touched off major waves of labor unrest – such as those in response to transformations driven by the fiscal crisis of core states in the 1970s. The major waves of teacher labor unrest in low- and

---

[38] Cuban's study focuses on the United States, but his findings are no doubt widely applicable.

middle-income countries in response to speed-ups and cutbacks associated with IMF structural adjustment packages in the 1980s and privatization drives in the 1990s is another important example.

In addition to the difficulties involved in implementing technological fixes, the education industry is also particularly impervious to spatial fixes. Whereas manufacturers (and many service sector employers) can credibly threaten their labor forces with competition from global labor reserves (either through relocation of productive capital or importation of immigrant labor), the threat to teachers is not very credible. On the one hand, the production site generally must be located near the key raw material – the students – thus making geographical relocation largely unfeasible. On the other hand, language and cultural barriers protect teachers, to some extent, from competition from cheaper immigrant teacher labor. Certainly, we cannot discern any meaningful product cycle through geographical relocation in the education industry. With the partial exception of elite university education (where there is substantial "migration" of students), there is no substitutability between (competition among) the various national (or even local) education complexes. Finally, even though teachers are dispersed among multiple work sites (as was the case for textile workers), they generally share a single employer (the state – minimally at the citywide level and more frequently at the national level), giving a certain coherence to the organizational task of coordinating teacher labor unrest. Thus, the imperviousness of the education industry to spatial and technological fixes (in particular, geographical relocation and automation) may be at the root of a great deal of teacher bargaining power.[39]

Current educational reform drives can, in part, be seen as an effort to find alternative ways of putting competitive pressure on teachers. School voucher programs threaten public school teachers with the dismantling of public education by facilitating the movement of students to alternative

[39] As we suggested in Chapter 1, when bringing labor's bargaining power under control is particularly difficult, boundary drawing takes on particular salience as a strategy for reducing costs (for resolving the system-level problem). Indeed, boundary drawing has been particularly evident among teachers, both through the ideology of professionalism and through boundary drawing based on gender. Male teachers have been paid more than female teachers and secondary school teachers have been paid more than primary school teachers. Yet, boundary drawing is a double-edged sword for labor control. For example, the 1960s strikes in New York City initially took the form of male secondary school teachers with postgraduate degrees protesting loss of status vis-à-vis (predominantly female) primary school teachers (Cole 1969).

schools. Merit-based resource allocation to schools puts schools/teachers in competition with one another for resources necessary to make their work experience bearable. Privatization, on the one hand, and community control, on the other hand, are reforms that eliminate the single, large, visible object of the state as employer. All these reforms are ways of mobilizing market pressures against teachers. Nevertheless, in comparison with other industries, the education industry's ability to mobilize global reserves of labor in competition with teachers is likely to remain very limited. After all, even voucher programs open up competition only as far as the intracity or intranational level.[40]

Although teaching has been historically impervious to technological transformations, it is difficult to anticipate to what extent the Internet and other advanced communications technologies might be used to bring effective competitive pressures to bear on teachers, analogous to those that automation brought to bear on manufacturing workers (see, e.g., Traub 2000). Yet, as noted in discussing the automobile industry, we do know that the same processes that undermine marketplace bargaining power often enhance workplace bargaining power. Thus, any such technological changes in the teaching labor process can be expected to enmesh teachers in a complex technical division of labor vulnerable to disruption in a way that the autonomous classroom model never was.

Personal Services

A last area of rapid employment growth is in personal services. We might also call this area reproductive services since they are constituted by the commodification of activities previously carried out in the home (from food preparation and childcare to entertainment). Personal services provide what seems to be the clearest example of a type of job growth that reverses the twentieth century trend toward stronger workplace bargaining power. With weak workplace and marketplace bargaining power, workers in this sector have been obliged to accept informal work practices with a high proportion of the labor force working on a part-time and/or temporary basis.

The weak workplace bargaining power of personal service workers is in part rooted in the geographical dispersion of the sector. Personal services are oriented toward the individual consumer and therefore have a

---

[40] See Ball's (1993) discussion of school vouchers as class strategy.

pattern of dispersion that is largely proportional to the distribution of the population and/or the distribution of wealth.[41] Thus, in personal services, work sites tend to be small scale and dispersed, making coordination of labor action across multiple sites difficult. Moreover, this weak workplace bargaining power is not counterbalanced by a strategic location within the social division of labor, as is the case for teachers.

In contrast to the automobile industry, in the fast food industry, for example, a strike in just one or a few outlets within a large chain will not interfere with the operation of other outlets in the same chain. Moreover, while a strike in an entire chain may damage a corporation, fast food workers (unlike teachers) are not strategically enmeshed in the social division of labor. If an entire fast food chain goes on strike, people will not starve. Unlike the case of public education, there are multiple competing alternative sources of prepared food. And given the multitude of prepared food outlets, the level of coordination among workers necessary to bring about a general stoppage in prepared foods production (and hence a stoppage that would begin to impact on the social division of labor) is very hard to attain. Finally, even without the pressures of technologically induced unemployment, marketplace bargaining power in personal services is also generally weak because of the existence of a large supply of workers with the necessary skills.

We have argued that where workers' strategic bargaining power is weak, victories depend on strong associational power (either autonomous trade union organization as in the case of British textile workers or cross-class political alliances as in the case of Indian and Chinese textile workers). The historical pattern of labor unrest for personal service workers that emerges from the WLG data is consistent with this argument. Taking the case of hotel and restaurant workers, we find that waves of labor unrest in this industry during the twentieth century almost invariably take place together with widespread labor unrest in the city or region in which these workers are situated. Thus, we might say that they rely on the "reflected" power that comes from community-level organization and/or the strategic bargaining power of more favorably situated workers. Likewise, 1990s union organizing victories in the United States in personal services (e.g., in nursing

---

[41] State-sponsored social services (such as education) are generally backed by a state commitment to provide these services to everyone; therefore, their actual dispersal comes close to the theoretical standard of matching population dispersal. In the case of personal services, on the other hand, their geographical spread in large part follows the dispersal of wealth rather than that of population per se.

IV. A New Product Fix?

homes and among home health care workers) also were based on the kinds of associational power displayed in the Justice for Janitors case discussed earlier (Needleman 1998).

Thus, the late-twentieth-century growth of personal services suggests a significant trend toward the overall weakening of labor's workplace bargaining power. This is especially so if we take into account the fact that many formerly state-sponsored social services in the late twentieth century have been "privatized" and/or subcontracted, bringing many social service jobs closer in form to the personal service model (e.g., without a single, visible employer as a target). Yet, a countertrend is worth noting. There has been a growing tendency to "decouple" the production of personal services from their delivery to take advantage of economies of scale (Riddle 1986: 143). And where there are economies of scale, we have argued, there is also generally greater workplace bargaining power.

Indeed, many personal services are no longer organized spatially in a simple, dispersed fashion. Some of the most-lucrative and fastest-growing arenas for personal services now have multiple layers of mediation between the final delivery of the service to the consumer and the production of the service. One example is the entertainment industry. In the early twentieth century, most of the entertainment industry involved direct contact with the final consumer (e.g., live performances), and the *historical* pattern of labor unrest in the industry visible from the WLG database was similar to that identified for hotel and restaurant workers. Labor unrest, that is, took place together with more generalized labor unrest in a particular city. In today's movie industry, however, only the very final stage – showing films in theaters – involves direct contact with the final consumer (and in television there isn't even that point of contact). The production process involved in bringing the film to the screen now involves a complex technical division of labor, subject to economies of agglomeration rather than dispersion.

Thus, it is not surprising that recent strikes and strike threats in Hollywood depart from the personal service model previously described. The surge of technological change in the industry (e.g., cable, video, DVD, Internet distribution, and the globalization of markets for films and television series) has brought new types of grievances to the fore with regard to pay and status. Moreover, with the growing complexity of the technical division of labor and the new economies of agglomeration, including the concentration of the industry in Hollywood, strikes by one job category (e.g., writers) have tremendous "ripple effects." Thus, for example, a recent estimate of the impact of any entertainment industry strike starts by

121

pointing to the ripple effects of $680 million in lost wages a month in Los Angeles for the 272,000 people working in the entertainment industry.[42]

In sum, even in the personal service sector, the trend in labor's bargaining power is not as clear-cut as it would at first appear. To be sure, labor unrest in the entertainment industry has tended to be seen as a squabble within the more privileged segments of the population over the distribution of the spoils. Moreover, such labor unrest brings us back to the question of how workers located in industries with strong workplace bargaining power will interact with workers whose bargaining power is weak, either in other industries in their own community or in the same industry in other countries.

V. Conclusion

This chapter has argued that the main location of working-class formation and protest has shifted *within* industries along with the geographical relocation of production as well as *between* industries along with the rise of new leading industries and the decline of old ones. As such, we would expect the main sites of twenty-first-century labor unrest to be found in the new leading industries of the day. Yet, in the last section, we argued that it is not possible to identify a manufacturing industry that plays a leading role in world-scale processes of capital accumulation analogous to that played by the textile industry in the nineteenth century and the automobile industry in the twentieth century.

The only manufacturing industry that, in some respects, would qualify for the title of new leading industry – the semiconductor industry – has

---

[42] On the labor unrest in Hollywood, see Bernard Weinraub (2000: A1, A25). In addition to the issues raised earlier, Weinraub emphasized that conglomerates now own the entertainment industry. The article quoted Ken Ziffren, a top entertainment industry lawyer: "Time Warner is AOL and cable, Sony is a consumer electronics company, Fox is a television network and a station group and a satellite operator and a media empire. Universal is really a music company. Disney is theme parks and cable channels as well as the ABC network. It goes on and on. The business of feature films and television is now a very small part of the corporate set-up of some of these companies. There are divergent issues and interests now, much more than management versus labor." Weinraub went on to point out that "[t]he sheer size of many of the conglomerates can weigh heavily now in labor negotiations. For example, if the television division at Fox or Disney is facing a poor year, it could adopt a hard-line approach to negotiations because the parent company would have little to lose. These conglomerates themselves would financially support the television unit through the collective bargaining process. But if, say, Warner's television division was successful – and Time Warner's magazine and cable units were lagging – it would probably be a corporate priority to resolve a strike quickly in order for various series to continue and prosper" (2000: A25).

departed substantially from the trajectory of successive geographical re-location to lower-wage sites that characterized both the textile and automobile industry. Manufacturing jobs in the semiconductor industry were located virtually from the start (i.e., in the innovative phase) in low-income countries, while R&D, managerial, and other high-value-added jobs were (and still are) concentrated in high-income countries. Moreover, the semiconductor industry (including board assembly) is increasingly automated, making it a weak source of employment growth worldwide.

In the early twenty-first century, then, the labor forces for new leading manufacturing industries such as semiconductors as well as old established industries such as textiles and automobiles are concentrated in low- and middle-income countries. The epicenter of world labor unrest in manufacturing in the twenty-first century is thus also likely to be concentrated in these same countries.

At the same time, employment and labor unrest in services has been growing worldwide and will likely continue to grow in the future. Because of the heterogeneity of services, the impact of the rise of service employment on workers' overall average bargaining power is not easy to summarize. On the one hand, we have argued that some of the most rapidly expanding service industries (e.g., aviation) endow their workers with considerable workplace bargaining power, while others (e.g., the education industry and producer services) are far more impervious to spatial fixes (geographical relocation) than most manufacturing industries. On the other hand, we have argued that the vertical disintegration of production and the corresponding proliferation of sites of production and (actual or phantom) employers faced by workers have weakened labor's structural bargaining power. This structural weakness has placed a renewed premium on the importance of associational power. Indeed, the organizing environment faced by workers in the early twenty-first century in certain respects has more in common with that faced by nineteenth-century textile workers than twentieth-century automobile workers.

We shall return to a discussion of the likely future dynamics of labor unrest in Chapter 5. But first we must widen the angle of vision of our analysis. The trajectory of twentieth-century world labor unrest has been embedded not only in product cycles but also in cycles of world politics. It is to the interrelationship between the dynamics of world labor unrest and world politics that we turn in Chapter 4, enriching our understanding of twentieth-century labor unrest as well as strengthening the base from which to assess likely future trends.

4

Labor Movements and World Politics

The previous two chapters focused on labor and global economic dynamics – especially the interrelationship between transformations in the organization/location of production, workers' bargaining power, and world-historical patterns of labor unrest. In this chapter, we shift the angle of vision, bringing to center stage the interrelationship between global politics and labor movements. For as we argued in Chapter 1, global economic processes are themselves deeply embedded in global political dynamics ranging from state formation and citizenship bounding to interstate conflict and world war.

In Chapter 1, we also suggested that the twentieth century – viewed through a Polanyian lens – traces a pendulum-like trajectory between the commodification of labor and the breakdown of established social compacts, on the one hand, and the decommodification of labor and the establishment of new social compacts, on the other hand. The first swing of the pendulum – the late-nineteenth- and early-twentieth-centuries movement toward the "commodification of labor" and the initial countermovement response from growing labor movements – is the focus of Section II of this chapter. Section V, in turn, focuses on the pendulum's swing back – the establishment of new national and international social compacts binding labor, capital, and states, which partially protected labor from the vagaries of an unregulated global market in the post–Second World War decades.

This swing of the pendulum was a response to four decades of world war, depression, explosive labor militancy, and worldwide revolutionary upheaval. This intervening period, characterized by a widening and deepening vicious circle of war and labor unrest, is the focus of Sections III and IV.

The post–Second World War swing of the pendulum toward the decommodification of labor was short-lived. The social compacts could not be sustained in the long run without becoming a growing fetter on profitability – a fetter that was broken with the late-twentieth-century wave of globalization – the subject of the sixth and final section of this chapter. The contradictions of these postwar social compacts have been analyzed elsewhere as the limits of "liberal corporatism" (Panitch 1977, 1981; Apple 1980) and of "hegemonic factory regimes" (Burawoy 1983: 602–3; Burawoy 1985) – analyses that we build on in Section V.

Before we narrate the first swing of the pendulum, the next section lays out the empirical picture of world-scale labor unrest for the twentieth century as derived from the World Labor Group database. On the one hand, this picture points to the centrality of the world wars in shaping the overall trajectory of world labor unrest in the twentieth century. On the other hand, it also suggests that the twentieth century can be divided into two phases, corresponding to our Polanyian pendulum swings, but also, and relatedly, to phases of world hegemony.

I. World Wars and Labor Unrest

The most immediately striking feature of the aggregate picture of world-scale labor unrest for the twentieth century derived from the WLG database is the interrelationship between world labor unrest and the two world wars. Figure 4.1 presents a time series of the number of mentions of labor unrest worldwide from 1870 to the present in the WLG database. Figures 4.2 and 4.3 chart the same series, but for metropolitan and colonial/semi-colonial countries as distinct aggregates. All three figures display the series with a three-year moving average. (See Appendix C for a list of countries included in the three figures.)

All three figures show the profound impact that the two world wars have had on the temporal pattern of labor unrest. The two highest peaks in overall world labor unrest are the years immediately following the two world wars. The years 1919 and 1920 are the peak years of the series with a total of 2,720 and 2,293 mentions, respectively. The next highest peak is 1946 and 1947 with a total of 1,857 and 2,122 mentions, respectively.

The early war years themselves are among the low points of the time series.[1] The low points fall into three categories: the years from 1898 to

---

[1] These findings with regard to both the world war and post-world-war periods correspond with those of Douglas Hibbs (1978: 157). In a long-run analysis of strike activity in eleven Western European and North American countries, he found industrial conflict to

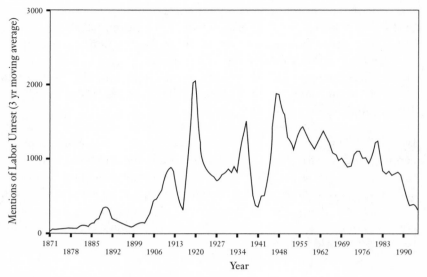

Figure 4.1. World labor unrest, 1870–1996.

1904, the war years (1915 has only 196 mentions and 1940 and 1942 only 248 and 279, respectively),[2] and finally (with 301 and 202 mentions for 1995 and 1996) the mid 1990s.[3]

Finally, the years just prior to the outbreak of the wars are years of rapidly rising labor unrest leading to local peaks in the series. Thus in the decade leading up to the outbreak of the First World War, the total number of mentions of labor unrest increases from 325 in 1905 to 604 in 1909 and 875 in 1913. Likewise, the total number of mentions of labor unrest is rising

"decline markedly" during both the First and Second World Wars. He also found that "most countries experienced strike explosions towards the end or just after the end of the World Wars."

[2] Labor unrest waves by no means disappeared for the entire span of the world wars. For example, the WLG data shows labor unrest waves in the middle of the First World War (particularly in Germany and Russia in 1917–18 as well as elsewhere in Europe). In the middle of the Second World War, there were labor unrest waves in the United States (1941, 1943), in Canada (1943), and the United Kingdom (1943), as well as in some African and Asian colonies such as Zambia (1940–1) and Singapore (1940). Nevertheless, the overall effect of the world wars (especially with the onset of war) was to decrease the levels of overt labor militancy on a world scale. See Sections III and IV for further discussion of the degree and durability of the world wars' dampening effect.

[3] We shall return in Section VI to a discussion of the similarities between the late-twentieth-century (1990s) trough and late-nineteenth-century (1890s) trough.

I. World Wars and Labor Unrest

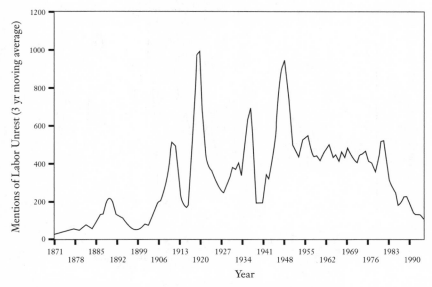

Figure 4.2. Labor unrest, metropolitan countries, 1870–1996.

in the decade leading up to the Second World War (from 859 in 1930 to 1101 in 1934 and 1186 in 1938) – although the rise is less steep, and, as we shall see in Section III, its interpretation is less straightforward.

This interrelationship between the world wars and the temporal patterning of labor unrest is most striking for the metropolitan aggregate (see Figure 4.2). Yet, even for the colonial/semi-colonial aggregate, the link is clearly visible: labor unrest is rising on the eves of both world wars, and there are short-lived but major declines in overt unrest with the onset of war and major waves in the aftermath of the world wars (see Figure 4.3). The most conspicuous difference between the metropolitan and colonial/semi-colonial patterns is the relative size of the two postwar labor unrest waves. For the metropolitan aggregate, the wave of labor unrest following the First World War is higher (but not longer) than the wave of labor unrest following the Second World War. For the colonial/semi-colonial aggregate, however, the opposite is true, with the post–Second World War wave of labor unrest being far higher and longer than the post–First World War wave.[4]

---

[4] See Appendix A for a discussion on the post–Second World War paper shortage at *The Times* (London) as a potential source of underestimation of the size of the post–Second

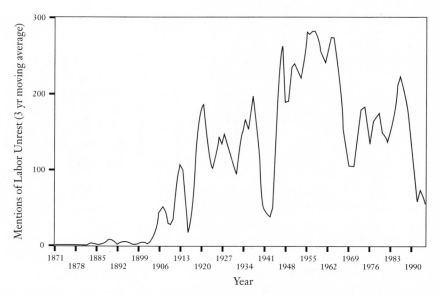

Figure 4.3. Labor unrest, colonial and semi-colonial world, 1870–1996.

Perhaps these links between world wars and labor unrest should come as no surprise. Indeed, there is a long tradition within the social sciences linking wars to labor militancy or to social conflict more generally.[5] Michael Stohl (1980: 297) suggested that the "presumed nexus of civil conflict and international conflict" is "one of the most venerable hypotheses in the social science literature" – although he also points to the extensive debate around the exact form of this nexus as well as the nexus' spatial–temporal relevance.

Stohl (1980: 297–8) identifies three (seemingly contradictory) subvariants of the "nexus" hypothesis that have been widespread in the scholarly literature:

(1) involvement in war increases social cohesion at the national level and thus brings about internal peace;

(2) involvement in war increases social conflict at the national level and increases the chances of revolution; and

World War wave of labor unrest. Nevertheless, the comparative (metropolitan–colonial) difference pointed to earlier would not be affected by the paper shortage.
[5] See for example, Lenin ([1916] 1971), Semmel (1960), Laqueur (1968), Hibbs (1978), Tilly (1978), Skocpol (1979), Mann (1988, 1993), cf. Goldstone (1991). See Levy (1989, 1998) and Stohl (1980) for extensive reviews of this literature.

(3) social conflict at the national level encourages governments to involve themselves in wars.

Curiously, the patterns discussed here may be interpreted as providing support for all three of these hypotheses (with *labor unrest* and *world wars* as the two sides of the equation).[6] Although often cast as mutually exclusive alternatives, we will argue here that they are complementary hypotheses, but of different temporal relevance. That is, hypothesis 3 (the oft-called scapegoat or diversionary hypothesis) best describes the period leading up to the world wars; hypothesis 2, the aftermath of the world wars; and hypothesis 1, the duration of the hostilities.

Thus, as the next section argues, late-nineteenth-century globalization undermined existing social compacts and created/strengthened new working classes, setting the stage for the growth of both Marx-type and Polanyi-type labor unrest waves.[7] Moreover, as argued in Sections III and IV, this growing labor unrest was both fed by and fed into interimperialist rivalries, producing a widening and deepening "vicious circle" of war and labor unrest during the first half of the twentieth century.

The vicious circle of war and labor unrest in the first half of the twentieth century contrasts with the trajectory of world labor unrest in the second half of the century. World labor unrest in the first half of the century is rising and explosive in character; in the second half of the century world labor unrest is both declining and far less explosive. The contrasting pattern is visible in Figures 4.1 and 4.2 (but significantly, not Figure 4.3) as well as in the summary descriptive statistics provided in Table 4.1. Both periods have about the same mean level of labor unrest per year: 935 and 984 average annual mentions of labor unrest, respectively. However, the rising trend of

---

[6] The three hypotheses cited by Stohl are formulated vaguely, with generic war on one side of the equation and social conflict and/or revolution on the other side. Indeed, Stohl points to this vagueness as a serious problem in the literature. For the war side of the equation, there has been substantial debate in the nexus literature (and in war studies more generally) as to whether all wars can be understood with reference to the same theoretical framework. For a sample of the debate, see the Midlarsky (1990) edited collection entitled "Big Wars, Little Wars – A Single Theory?" Likewise, Levy (1998) has complained that substantial confusion has been created in the domestic–international conflict literature by the variety of ways in which the relevant variables are conceptualized and measured. Domestic conflict has been measured using anything from surveys to presidential popularity to revolutions. The international conflict variable has been measured using anything ranging from open warfare to posturing and threats. To be clear, the two sides of the equation examined here are *labor unrest* and *world wars*.

[7] See Chapter 1 on the distinction between Polanyi-type and Marx-type labor unrest.

Table 4.1 *World Labor Unrest in the Twentieth Century*
(Descriptive Statistics)

	1906–49	1950–96
Trend[a]/significance	.257 (.09)	−7.8 (.00)
Mean mentions	935	984
Explosiveness: standard deviation of mentions series	573	352

[a] Standardized linear coefficient.

labor unrest in the first half of the twentieth century contrasts sharply with the declining trend of world labor unrest in the second half of the century. Moreover, whereas labor unrest is highly explosive in character in the first half of the century (as measured by the standard deviation from the mean), it is far less explosive in the second half of the century.

The transition from a pattern of escalating and explosive labor militancy to a pattern of relatively smooth and declining labor militancy is tied to the establishment of a new world hegemonic regime at the close of the Second World War (see Section V). The transition is especially apparent for the metropolitan aggregate of countries (compare Figures 4.2 and 4.3). Labor movements – especially core labor movements – were accommodated through various interlinked firm-level, national and international social compacts (and structural transformations supporting those compacts). Labor unrest remained at relatively high levels in the metropolitan aggregate of countries for several decades after the war, but the partial de-commodification of labor brought about by these compacts brought an end to intense, politically revolutionary labor militancy in the core.[8]

The fifty years after the Second World War, however, do not fall into a single homogeneous pattern. For as Section VI argues, the social compacts on which stabilized labor–capital relations were based, were full of contradictions from the start. When these social compacts collapsed in the 1980s, overt labor unrest in the core at first rose and then also collapsed. The collapse appeared to be just a core country phenomenon in the 1980s (see Figure 4.2). Yet, by the early 1990s, a similar (lagged) pattern appeared in the post-colonial world – that is, a (larger) rise in overt labor unrest in the late 1980s followed by a (smaller) collapse in the early 1990s (see Figure 4.3).

[8] For a discussion of periods of escalating (versus declining) social conflict, conceptualized within the context of cycles of world hegemony, from seventeenth-century Dutch hegemony to twentieth-century U.S. hegemony, see Silver and Slater (1999).

130

II. Late-Nineteenth-Century Globalization and Labor

A final point to which we shall return is that of the relationship between the product-cycle dynamic discussed in Chapter 3 and the world war/hegemonic dynamic introduced here. The product cycle and world war dynamics have had opposite impacts on the overall temporal–spatial profile of world labor unrest. The world war dynamic has a clustering effect, leading to periods of explosive *world-scale* outbreaks of labor militancy such as the two post–world-war periods. In contrast, the successive spatial fixes associated with the product-cycle dynamic tend to have a "smoothing" effect, as the geographical relocation of production leads to spatial shifts across time in the epicenter of labor unrest. Upsurges in one place are counterbalanced by (not unrelated) declines in other places. In the first half of the twentieth century, the world war dynamic overwhelmed product-cycle dynamics. In the period of U.S. hegemony, in contrast, the reconstruction of the world market and the transformed world political environment allowed the product-cycle dynamic to flourish.[9]

II. Late-Nineteenth-Century Globalization and the Rise of the Modern Labor Movement

The major mid-nineteenth-century expansion of the world economy – the so-called Golden Age of Capital – culminated in the Great Depression of 1873–96, a period of intense intercapitalist competition on a world scale. This competitive pressure, in turn, sparked a series of major transformations in world-scale processes of capital accumulation. It is in the context of these deep, rapid, and varied transformations that the modern labor movement in Western Europe and North America was born.

These transformations involved four types of fixes, three of which have been introduced in earlier chapters (the spatial, technological/organizational, and product) and one that we will introduce here for the first time (the financial fix). The transformations brought about by these fixes, we will argue, undermined established customs and livelihoods (producing Polanyi-type movements of self-protection among craftworkers and peasants). Simultaneously, however, they created and strengthened new working

---

[9] In Chapter 3, where we found a cluster of labor unrest waves (such as for the textile industry in the 1920s and 1930s), we traced this clustering to the organization of production and product cycle. That is, the widespread and simultaneous geographical diffusion of mechanized textile production, it was argued, produced simultaneous and widespread waves of labor unrest. This chapter suggests an additional explanation rooted in the world political context of the 1920s and 1930s.

classes with strategic bargaining power in the expanding and profitable segments of the global economy, laying the foundations for waves of Marx-type labor unrest.

In the third quarter of the nineteenth century, as competition intensified on a world scale, commodity prices in both agriculture and industry collapsed, and profits shrank (Landes 1969: 231). Among the responses by firms was a combination of spatial and technological/organizational fixes. In the textile industry, as we saw in Chapter 3, mechanized textile production spread rapidly to lower-wage areas in the late nineteenth century while ring spinning displaced mule-spinning technology, thereby creating a surge of unemployment among textile workers in established sites of production. This period was also characterized by the first major moves toward both the horizontal and vertical integration of production. These organizational innovations reduced the competitive pressures faced by capitalists – the vertically integrated firm in particular would become an imposing "barrier to entry" (Chandler 1977: 285, 299) – while increasing the size and resources of the capitalist organizations confronted by workers and workers' movements.

The search for product fixes – the movement of capital into new industries and product lines subject to less competition – also intensified. Capital goods at first seemed to provide one such outlet. Yet, as more and more investment poured into the capital goods sector, competitive pressures also mounted there, prompting concerted efforts to decrease costs and increase control, in particular through technological fixes. By the end of the late-nineteenth-century Great Depression, the capital goods sector had become the focal point of labor process transformations – in David Montgomery's words, it became the "cradle" in which "scientific management" was born (1987: 56).

Another crucial product fix was to be found in the armaments industry. With the escalation of interimperialist rivalries in the 1880s and 1890s, the "global, industrialized armaments business" (McNeill 1982: 241) became a major new sphere for profitable private investment. And, as we shall see in the next section, the armaments industry also became one of the most important sites of rapid new working-class formation and militancy.

Finally, the arms race also opened up the space for the pursuit of yet another kind of fix, which we may call the financial fix.[10] The financial

---

[10] This concept is derived from a related concept of financial expansions as recurrent phases of capitalist development on a world scale (Arrighi 1994; Arrighi and Silver 1999). Seen

fix shares analogies with the product fix – for just as capitalists attempt to shift into new lines of trade and production less subject to competitive pressures through a product fix, so they shift capital entirely out of trade/production and into money lending, financial intermediation, and speculation. The profitability of the late-nineteenth-century financial fix was closely tied to the escalation of the arms race. The arms race created intense competition among states for access to borrowed funds to pay for military buildups, thus increasing the profitability of finance (Arrighi 1994: 171–3). This financialization of capital weakened the marketplace bargaining power of labor in those "overcrowded" industrial activities from which capital was withdrawing. To what extent this weakening was compensated for by a growing demand for labor in armaments industries is unclear.

What is clear is that, by the 1890s, the combination of the financial fix and other fixes began to reduce the competitive pressure on capital while increasing the competitive pressure on labor. Prices started to rise faster than wages, structural unemployment became persistent and there was a trend toward a growing polarization of wealth between rich and poor (Gordon, Edwards, and Reich 1982: 95–9; Boyer 1979; Phelps Brown and Browne 1968; Silver and Slater 1999). For the European bourgeoisie – and the British in particular – the period from 1896 to the outbreak of the First World War went down in history as the *belle époque* (Hobsbawm 1987: 168–9).

The initial reaction of workers in metropolitan countries to capitalist restructuring was a major upsurge of labor unrest in the 1880s (see Figure 4.2). Labor unrest then declined in the late 1890s – coincident with the take-off of the financial expansion.[11] Nevertheless, within a decade, labor unrest was once again rising rapidly, and it continued to do so until the outbreak of the First World War. This rising labor militancy took a variety of forms. By the end of the 1890s, trade unions and working-class parties were proliferating throughout Europe and the Americas. The Second International was established, a significant number of socialists were getting elected to

as a recurrent phenomenon, the financial expansion/fix of the late nineteenth century has important similarities with that of the late twentieth century, a point to which we shall return at the end of this chapter and in Chapter 5.

[11] Whether this decline was just a coincidence or whether the late-nineteenth-century financial fix actually weakened labor movements is a question to which we will return when we discuss the late-twentieth-century financial fix and its impact on labor movements in the final section of this chapter.

parliaments, and union membership was mushrooming (Abendroth 1972: Chapter 3; Hobsbawm 1987: 130).

In sharp contrast to 1848 (or 1871), any success in repressing this upsurge proved to be temporary. The size and scope of the industrial working classes had grown enormously in the course of the second half of the nineteenth century. In Germany, while only 600,000 workers (or about 4 percent of the total labor force) were employed in mining and manufacturing in 1850, by 1873 the number had tripled, and by 1900 it had reached 5.7 million workers, or 22 percent of the total labor force (Kocka 1986: 296–7). In the United States between 1840 and 1870, employment in manufacturing increased fivefold. In Boston, the numbers employed in major industries doubled between 1845 and 1855 and doubled again between 1855 and 1865. In the three decades after the Civil War, the advances in industrial output and employment, the emergence of giant factories, and the disappearance of artisanal establishments were even more rapid (Gordon et al. 1982: 82–3; Shefter 1986: 199–200; Bridges 1986: 173).

The various technological/organizational fixes attacked craft standards and chipped away at the "consent" of the "labor aristocracy," inducing skilled workers to reach out to the growing ranks of unskilled workers. In Britain, the discontent of the artisanal elite and the growing size and power of unskilled workers combined to produce the "new unionism" of the late 1880s. In only four years following 1888, union membership doubled from 5 percent to 11 percent, with industrial unions in mining and transport leading the way. An employer offensive in the late 1890s was followed by another forward burst of unionism in the decade prior to the world war, with membership jumping to over 4 million and union density reaching 25 percent.[12] Trade unionism became more aggressive and political and *less sectional*, "absorbing unskilled, semiskilled, and skilled workers alike" (Mann 1993: 601–9).

The trend toward greater unity of action and purpose across skill levels was visible wherever the old craft elite felt threatened while the new industrial workforce mushroomed in size. In France, this period saw a "second great burst of socialist ferment and organization," but it was also the first time that "factory workers and artisans were integrated into a common class-conscious movement" (Sewell 1986: 67–70). In the United States, union membership increased fourfold between 1880 and 1890, while strike

[12] A similar timing of labor unrest ups/downs for those years is visible for the metropolitan aggregate in Figure 4.2

activity swelled in the 1890s and the first decade of the twentieth century. The spark for strikes in this period was often attacks on the customary rights of craftworkers. But strikes tended to spread quickly and envelop the full labor force in large factories. Cooperation between skilled and unskilled workers (and men and women) could also be seen in the widespread community support in manufacturing towns that striking workers received. Late-nineteenth-century strikes were frequently accompanied by marches from factory to factory, and through working-class neighborhoods, calling for support. Nonstriking members of these working-class communities commonly participated in these marches and open-air meetings (Shefter 1986: 217–18; Brecher 1972; Gordon et al. 1982: 121–7; Montgomery 1979).

The mushrooming size of the unskilled workforce and its concentration in downtown factory districts and working-class neighborhoods facilitated both the rapid spread of protest across categories of workers and plants, and a growing common class consciousness. Protests launched in one plant or neighborhood quickly spread, leading contemporary observers to use the epidemiological metaphor of "contagious diseases" to describe the diffusion of protest. "This density and intensity of 'communicable' protest," wrote Gordon et al. (1982: 126), "both took root in the increasingly homogenous working conditions of masses of wage workers and helped to contribute to these workers' spreading consciousness of common problems and conditions."

While the most spectacular trade union growth took place in Britain, and the most violent class warfare erupted in the United States, the most stunning example of working-class party growth was in Germany. The German Social Democratic Party (SDP) quickly became the largest political party after the abrogation of the antisocialist laws in 1890. The electoral strength of the SDP doubled from 10 percent of the vote in 1887 to 23 percent in 1893. They attracted "nearly one and a half million votes in 1890, over two millions in 1898, three millions out of an electorate of nine millions in 1903, and four and a quarter millions in 1912." The German case was the most striking example of a general process. While mass working-class parties barely existed in 1880, by 1906 they were "the norm" in industrializing countries wherever they were legal. In Scandinavia and Germany, they were already the largest party (although still not a majority) (Barraclough 1967: 135; Piven 1992: 2).

The rise of working-class parties and the general agitation for universal manhood suffrage presented a profound challenge to the British-centered world capitalist system. In Polanyi's words: "Inside and outside

England... there was not a militant liberal who did not express his conviction that popular democracy was a danger to capitalism" ([1944] 1957: 226). A common response to the challenge was repression (the German Social Democratic Party was outlawed in 1879), but pure repression was no longer a sufficient response. In 1890, the ban on the German SDP was removed, and major extensions of the franchise were won throughout most of Europe around the turn of the century. To be sure, as suffrage rights were broadened, various tactics (e.g., limiting the constitutional powers of directly elected bodies and gerrymandering) were introduced as safeguards (Hobsbawm 1987: 85–99, 116–18). Nevertheless, the emergence of politically organized working classes was a profound transformation and required more than a modification of tactics; a fundamental change in ruling class strategies was required (Therborn 1977: 23–8).

This fundamental change might be dubbed "the socialization of the state." By the end of the late-nineteenth-century Great Depression, writes Polanyi ([1944] 1957: 216–17), "all western countries... irrespective of national mentality or history" moved toward the implementation of policies designed to protect citizens against the disruptions caused by a self-regulating market. Social insurance schemes (old-age pensions, health and unemployment insurance) were introduced as part of an effort to take the steam out of socialist agitation. Germany was precocious with the first moves in the 1880s, but others soon followed suit (Abbott and DeViney 1992).[13]

These measures were part of a more general development of a cross-class alliance in favor of a strong and activist state. The intense competition that characterized the Great Depression prompted clamors for protection from all segments of the class spectrum. The agrarian classes in continental Europe were especially hard hit by the massive inflow of imported grains as the steamship and railroads (and free-trade policies) allowed cheap American and Russian supplies to flood the continental market (Mayer 1981). Moreover, the national bourgeoisies of continental Europe,

---

[13] When the slump of 1873–9 hit Germany, the spread of unemployment, labor unrest, and socialist agitation, combined with a crippling fiscal crisis of the Reich, induced Chancellor Bismarck to intervene to protect German society, lest the ravages of unfettered market competition destroy the imperial edifice he had just built. At the same time, the growing convergence of agrarian and industrial interests in pressing for governmental protection from foreign competition provided Bismarck with unique opportunities to use the political power invested in the Reich executive "to secure a new balance of power between the *Reich* and the states... and to complete the national unification by cementing it with unbreakable economic ties" (Rosenberg 1943 67–8; Arrighi and Silver 1999: 124–5).

which had tended to see international free trade as being in their own as well as Britain's interest during the mid nineteenth century, changed their tune by the 1878 Congress of Berlin. They joined agrarian elites in demanding that government action be oriented toward obtaining exclusive spheres of influence, protected markets, and privileged sources of supply.

In the United States, repeated overproduction crises in agriculture led to vigorous demands from farmers for government action aimed at expanding their markets and providing them with cheap railroad transportation (LaFeber 1963: 9–10; Williams 1969: 20–2). The depression of 1893 (the first crisis in the United States to hit manufacturing harder than agriculture) cemented the alliance between agriculturalists and industrialists in favor of aggressive overseas expansion. The fact that this depression was accompanied by widespread social unrest contributed to the sense of urgency. As William A. Williams (1969: 41) noted: "The economic impact of the depression [of 1893], and its effect in producing a real fear of extensive social unrest and even revolution," led U.S. business and government leaders to finally accept "overseas expansion as the strategic solution to the nation's economic and social problems." One immediate outcome was the U.S. government decision to fight Spain on two fronts in 1898 – a war in large measure designed to expand U.S. access to the markets of Asia.

These colonial wars and growing interimperialist rivalries, in turn, provided another incentive for the "socialization of the state." Rulers were increasingly dependent on the active co-operation of their citizens for imperial expansion and war. Prior to the nineteenth century, states relied mainly on paid professional mercenaries and "gentlemen" to fight wars, and these could drag on for years without provoking mass social unrest. The mobilization of citizen armies during the Napoleonic Wars was a first premonition of things to come – a premonition that led Europe's rulers to end experiments and restore old-style armies after the war. As William McNeill has pointed out, the experience of warfare in the age of revolution convinced Europe's rulers that "the fierce energy of the French conscripts in 1793–95, and the nationalist fervor of some German citizen soldiers in 1813–14, could challenge constituted authority as readily as it could confirm and strengthen it." By restoring the old-style armies, Europe's rulers "refrained from tapping the depths of national energies that the revolutionary years unveiled." But they also kept "the specter of revolutionary disorder at bay" (McNeill 1982: 221).

Nevertheless, by the end of the nineteenth century, states were once again developing nationalism and patriotism as the new civil religion and as a basis for mobilizing soldiers as citizens (Tilly 1990; Mann 1988). Moreover, with the growing industrialization of war in the late nineteenth and early twentieth centuries (McNeill 1982: Chapters 7–8), workers became critical cogs in the war machine, not only at the front, but also behind the front lines in factories. Thus, the successful prosecution of wars increasingly required the support of worker-citizens. The extension of democratic and workers' rights was aimed at shoring up the loyalty of the working classes and at keeping the specter of revolution at bay, but, given the destructiveness of modern warfare, it was, as we shall see, at best an unstable solution.

Thus by the eve of the First World War, world politics and labor politics were already deeply (and dysfunctionally) intertwined. If we were to judge from the direction of mass labor protest in the decades leading up to the First World War, it would appear that national hegemonic projects fusing national and social protection were not successfully containing social tensions. As Figure 4.2 shows, labor unrest in the metropolitan countries escalated in the decade leading up to the outbreak of the First World War. During the *belle époque*, strategically located working classes continued to grow rapidly in size. Moreover, these working classes took advantage of their strategic location in an increasingly planned and conscious fashion to launch mass strikes in the sectors that were the lifeblood of the world capitalist system, especially coal mining, maritime transportation, and railways.

III. The Vicious Circle of International and Domestic Conflict

The moves and countermoves leading up to the outbreak of the First World War have been widely taken to provide support for the validity of the scapegoat hypothesis (hypothesis 3, in Section I). That is, the outbreak of the war is widely seen as, in large measure, being prompted by "diversionary" moves on the part of some of Europe's leaders. A. J. P. Taylor (1954: 529) wrote of a direct link, arguing that Europe's leading statesmen in 1914 believed "that war would stave off their social and political problems." Likewise, Kaiser (1983) argued that "a far-reaching consensus now agrees that German foreign policy after 1897 must be understood as a response to the internal threat of socialism and democracy."

In addition to these direct links, more roundabout linkages between labor unrest and the outbreak of the First World War can be seen in the colonialist adventures of the late 1890s and 1900s. These conflicts – motivated at least in part by an effort to divert increasing class antagonisms – directly contributed to the tensions leading to the outbreak of the First World War. (Semmel 1960; Fischer 1975; Mayer 1967, 1977; Berghahn 1973; see also Levy 1998; Rosecrance 1963; Lebow 1981: chapter 4; Ritter 1970, vol. 2: 227–39.) Moreover, to the extent that the state's growing social-protectionist role could only be successfully implemented through the expansion of markets and access to resources, the likelihood of interimperialist clashes increased, especially given the fact that a growing number of rivals were pursuing similar strategies.

By the turn of the century, rulers had learned that little victorious wars could provide a "diversion" and bolster governments. The Spanish-American War (for the United States) and the South African War (for the United Kingdom) were two such examples. However, the revolutionary upheavals that shook the Russian Empire in the wake of its 1905 defeat by Japan also showed the potential boomerang effect of lost (or otherwise unpopular) wars. On the eve of the Russo-Japanese War of 1904, the Russian interior minister had openly stated that "this country needs . . . a short victorious war to stem the tide of revolution" (Levy 1989: 264). If European rulers hoped in 1914 for a popular little war, they badly misjudged the changed conditions that the industrialization and nationalization of warfare had brought about.

If the behavior of rulers in the buildup to the First World War is widely seen as supporting hypothesis 3, then the collapse of the Second International and the general decline of labor militancy with the outbreak of the war are widely seen as providing strong support for hypothesis 1 (linking war to social cohesion). Given the militancy of European working classes in the decades leading up to the war, it surprised most contemporary observers when European citizens (including most of the working class) went to war in 1914 with apparent enthusiasm. It now appeared that the ruling elites of metropolitan countries had successfully fashioned national hegemonic projects that brought cross-class allegiance to the state. Indeed, once the masses were in a position to make demands on their respective states for social and economic protection, workers backed their states, nationalism waxed, and international socialism collapsed (Carr 1945: 20–1; also Abendroth 1972; Haupt 1972).

To the surprise of the war planners, draft evasion was virtually nonexistent. Labor militancy and socialist agitation declined precipitously in the belligerent countries during the first years of the war (cf. Figure 4.2). To be sure, this decline in part had coercive roots[14] but it was also rooted in active government efforts to secure the consent and cooperation of trade unionists. Tripartite agreements between trade unions, employers, and governments secured no strike pledges from union leaders in exchange for government and employer recognition of trade unions and the establishment of collective bargaining and grievance procedures. For the union movement in many countries (e.g., the United States), the First World War marked the first time that employers relaxed their implacable hostility to trade unions (Hibbs 1978: 157; see also Feldman 1966; Brody 1980; Dubofsky 1983; Davis 1986; Giddens 1987).

Not only were trade union rights expanded during the war, but major expansions of the right to vote also took place during the war and its aftermath. Thus, John Markoff has emphasized that the "vital national interest" in labor peace during wartime made wartime propitious for the successful expansion of suffrage rights for both propertyless men and women (the latter were drawn into wartime factories in large numbers). In Belgium, for example, there had been mass strikes in 1886, 1888, 1891, 1893, 1902, and 1913 for which universal suffrage was a central demand, yet Belgium entered the First World War with a voting system in which older men owning property had three votes. By the war's end, however, Belgium had equal male suffrage (1996: 73–4, 85).[15]

Nevertheless, a central characteristic of the early twentieth century was the extremely unstable nature of all these national hegemonic compacts. The brutality of the war soon disabused many of the idea that a successful formula for protecting citizens had been found. Once the wheel turned from nationalist to revolutionary fervor, the arms used to defend the constituted order were used to challenge it. Demobilized and deserting soldiers

---

[14] Tilly (1989: 441–2) saw a general tendency for the repressive capacity of governments to increase during wartime. This increased coercive capacity of the state is further enhanced, he argued, as a result of the decreased organizational capacity of workers' movements in wartime. Organized workers are called into military service or shifted to war-related industries, while new proletarians without organizational traditions are brought into the factories en masse.

[15] Looking at it from the opposite side, military strategists developed campaigns designed to undermine "popular support" among the enemies' population. During the First World War, new military strategies (such as naval blockades) aimed at cutting off food supplies and raising the threat of mass starvation among noncombatants. Designed to create domestic instability on the enemies' home front, such strategies recognized the importance of retaining popular loyalty (and the danger of losing mass support) for success in war (Offer 1985).

returned to their towns and villages from the battleground, carrying both the message of revolution and the guns with which to fight for it (Wolf 1969). A major wave of rebellions and revolutions exploded in the midst of the war and continued in its aftermath.

If the collapse of the Second International is among the most vivid images in support of hypothesis 1, then widespread revolutionary crises in the final years of the First World War and its aftermath are among the most vivid images in support of hypothesis 2 linking war and revolution. Indeed, in the case of the First World War, the dampening effect of war on labor unrest did not last until the end of the war. By 1916, mushrooming strikes, desertions, and revolts gave lie to the conclusion that stable national hegemonies had been formed. By the time of the 1917 Russian Revolution, antiwar feeling among the populations of Europe was probably a majority sentiment. And in 1918, it seemed like socialist revolution would spread throughout Europe.

The strikes in the 1905–14 period revealed the vulnerability of capital to labor agitation in transportation and mining industries. During the war itself, the vast and rapidly expanding armaments industries (see Section II) proved most vulnerable to labor militancy. The industrialization of war meant massive private and public investments in weapons manufacture. Workers in the metalworking industries became critical cogs in the war machine, supplying the soldiers at the front. But the industrialization of war also meant a confrontation with craftworkers as efforts to mechanize arms production were pushed forward. It was in the metalworking industries that the Tripartite Agreements first floundered, for it was here that "the traditional force of labour organization" (the skilled craftworkers) "met the modern factory." The vast armaments industries – in Britain, Germany, France, Russia, and the United States – became the centers of industrial and antiwar militancy by both skilled and unskilled workers. The metalworkers in the factories turned to revolution during and after the war, as did "the new high-tech navies" or "floating factories" at Kronstadt and Kiel (Hobsbawm 1994; 1987: 123–4; Cronin 1983: 33–5).

In the wake of the Great War, a deep fear of revolution gripped the ruling elites of Europe. All the defeated powers – Germany, Hungary, Turkey, Bulgaria, and Russia – suffered revolutions and state breakdowns. Moreover, even those countries that had won the war faced massive social unrest. In 1919, the British prime minister Lloyd George observed: "[T]he whole of Europe is filled with the spirit of revolution. There is a deep sense not only of discontent, but of anger and revolt among the workmen against prewar conditions. The whole existing order in its political, social and economic aspects is questioned by the masses of the population from one end of Europe to the other" (quoted in Cronin 1983: 23). Lenin's 1916 prediction that imperialism would intensify all the contradictions of capitalism and thus would mark "the eve of the social revolution of the proletariat" seemed confirmed ([1916] 1971: 175).

Yet, with the failure of revolution in Germany and the fascist takeover in Italy, the waves of labor unrest and revolution began to subside. In what Polanyi ([1944] 1957) has labeled the "conservative twenties" a consensus developed among Europe's political and economic elite in favor of policies designed to turn the clock back to the nineteenth century. The proponents of this restorationist program argued that a return to the gold standard and international free trade was necessary to reestablish the virtuous circle of international and domestic peace that had characterized the mid-nineteenth century. But as predicted by a prescient contemporary (Keynes [1971] 1920), such an effort was doomed to create a new round of social dislocation and unleash once again the vicious circle of international and domestic conflict.

A global self-regulating market was even more of a utopian project in the 1920s than it had been in the nineteenth century. The mechanisms that, for a short period in the nineteenth century, had absorbed the social tensions produced by laissez-faire policies were no longer there. First, the new center of wealth and power (the largely self-sufficient and protectionist United States) was a poor substitute for the British entrepôt, which had been prepared to absorb a large share of the world's nonindustrial exports in the nineteenth century. Second, the largest industrial countries – first and foremost the United States – closed their frontiers to large-scale immigration after the war, thus eliminating "one of the most effective and necessary safety valves of the nineteenth-century international order" (Carr 1945: 22–3; see also O'Rourke and Williamson 1999: Chapter 10).

This change in immigration policy was partly a response to labor-movement demands for protection from intense labor-market competition. As such it was related to yet another difference between the mid-nineteenth-century environment in which the British-sponsored world-economic liberalization took place and the environment in which the 1920s restoration was attempted. That is, despite the widespread defeats suffered by labor and socialist movements, the power of the working classes to resist laissez-faire policies was far greater in the 1920s than it had been in the 1840s and 1850s. Democratic governments now had to demonstrate concern about wage levels and living standards of their own workers (and citizens more generally) – something that was of little concern to nineteenth-century economic liberals.

In this highly unpropitious environment, the international gold commission in Geneva began forcing on countries what today have become known as "structural adjustment" policies to promote healthy (convertible) currencies. These policies created immense social dislocations. Governments were forced to choose between sound currency and improved social services, between the confidence of international financial markets and the confidence of the masses, between following the dictates of Geneva and following the results of the democratic ballot box. For those governments tempted to make the wrong choice, the mechanism to punish noncompliance was most effective. "Flight of capital . . . [played] a vital role in the overthrow of the liberal governments in France in 1925, and again in 1938, as well as in the development of a fascist movement in Germany in 1930." In Austria in 1923, in Belgium and France in 1926, and in Germany and England in 1931, labor parties were eliminated from government, social services and wages were reduced, and unions were busted in vain attempts to "save the currency" (Polanyi [1944] 1957: 24, 229–33).

Restoring the gold standard became "the symbol of world solidarity" in the 1920s. But within a year or two after the Wall Street crash, it became clear that the restorationists' efforts had failed abysmally. Although unsuccessful, the effort to restore the gold standard had important social and political effects: "free markets had *not* been restored though free governments *had* been sacrificed." Democratic forces "which might otherwise have averted the fascist catastrophe" were weakened by the "stubbornness of economic liberals" who had, in the service of deflationary policies, supported the authoritarian policies of (often democratically elected) governments throughout the 1920s (Polanyi [1944] 1957: 26, 233–4). But in the 1920s, no amount of repression could reestablish the nineteenth-century world order, and the façade of international elite unity collapsed together with the restorationist effort.

In the wake of the Crash of 1929, with the political credibility of high finance and liberal governments destroyed, experiments with fusing national and social hegemonic projects were taken much further than they had been in the period leading up to the First World War. The New Deal, the Soviet Five-Year Plan, fascism, and Nazism were different ways of jumping off the disintegrating world market into the life raft of the national economy. These competing national projects shared two common characteristics. First, they discarded laissez-faire principles; second, they promoted rapid industrial expansion as part of an effort to overcome the social and political crises caused by the failure of the market system, and mass unemployment in particular (Polanyi [1944] 1957: Chapter 2).

But rapid industrial expansion relieved unemployment only by exacerbating other sources of domestic and international tensions. First and foremost, it increased pressures to seek out new markets and new sources of raw materials. These pressures, in turn, brought about a renewed escalation of interimperialist rivalries as the major powers sought out exclusive and protected overseas domains. Britain, with its huge head start in overseas territorial expansion, already controlled a vast empire in Asia and Africa. The United States was itself a continental empire and was expanding with ease in Latin America by replacing Britain as the center of an informal empire. Russia likewise was continental in size, but it had no informal empire of its own and far less secure frontiers than the United States. The Axis powers, in contrast, felt constrained by their relative backwardness as empire builders and their relatively small geographical home bases; thus, they began to challenge actively and aggressively the existing distribution of political–economic space (Neumann 1942).

As interimperialist rivalries re-ignited, the pressure to industrialize intensified given the now intimate links between industrial and military capabilities. The vicious circle of escalating domestic and international conflict of the Edwardian era resurfaced in core countries in the 1930s and 1940s with a vengeance. Figure 4.2 shows a virtual repeat of the pattern of escalating labor unrest on the eve of the war, declining overt militancy with the outbreak of the war, and a major explosion in the aftermath of the war itself. Nevertheless, the causal link between labor unrest and the outbreak of war – the role of "diversionary" hypothesis 3 – is more mediated in the case of the Second World War in comparison with the First World War. The main sites of metropolitan labor unrest in the years immediately prior to the outbreak of the Second World War (e.g., the United States, France) were not the countries that initiated the Second World War. Instead, in the case of the Second World War, the link appears to be to the major waves of labor unrest and revolutionary crises in countries such as Germany, Italy, and Japan *in the 1920s*. Labor was roundly defeated, but antilabor, counterrevolutionary alliances brought aggressively expansionist regimes to power in the process.

The geographical scope of the second round of the vicious circle was far greater than the first. The military–industrial complexes brought into confrontation during the war were of incomparably greater destructive power.

IV. Labor Unrest, World War, National Liberation

Not unrelated was the fact that the labor unrest and revolutionary upheavals that followed the Second World War engulfed a much greater proportion of the globe. It is to this mid-twentieth-century globalization of labor unrest and revolutionary processes that we now turn.

IV. Labor Unrest, World War, and National Liberation in the Colonial World

So far our discussion has focused on the metropolitan or core countries. Yet, the dislocations and transformations associated with growing interimperialist rivalries and spreading colonialism also produced rising labor militancy and social conflict of both the Marx-type and the Polanyi-type throughout the colonial and semi-colonial world. The period from the late-nineteenth-century Great Depression to the First World War was characterized by massive new waves of proletarianization throughout the world. With the spread of railroads and steamships, the intensification of competition that marked the late-nineteenth-century Great Depression shook local class relations from South America to Asia and Africa. From the sugar plantations of Morelos in Mexico to the vineyards of western Algeria and the rubber plantations of southern Vietnam, the new opportunities to sell cash crops in the world market initiated a race by foreign and local capitalist entrepreneurs to grab land, labor, and other resources. The result was a crisis of livelihood for the peasantry and a crisis of legitimacy for existing social contracts upon which political stability had been based (Wolf 1969; Walton 1984).

A major spark for labor unrest in the late-nineteenth-century colonial and semi-colonial world was resistance to being proletarianized – a subtype of what we have called Polanyi-type resistance.[16] At the same time, however, new, strategically located working classes were being created – hence creating the foundation for future waves of Marx-type labor unrest.

In the decade leading up to the First World War, WLG mentions of labor unrest in the colonial and semi-colonial world concentrate in mining and transportation industries. The growth in labor unrest (see Figure 4.3)

---

[16] We have defined resistance to proletarianization as a form of labor unrest, but the newspapers tend to report on these actions as "native revolts," which we did not record in the WLG database. (See Appendix A.) As a result, the overall degree of labor unrest in the late-nineteenth-century colonial world is no doubt underestimated in the WLG database and, as such, in Figure 4.3. Resistance to proletarianization was also an important component of overall labor unrest in Europe during this period, particularly in response to disruptions in the agrarian sector (Mayer 1981).

145

takes place in the context of a first wave of nationalist revolts led by Westernized elites, increasingly disillusioned with both the *ancien régimes* and Western supremacy.[17] While labor unrest declined during the war, the war itself nevertheless had a radicalizing effect on labor movements in the colonial world. The long arm of the European state reached into its colonies and pulled out workers to fight as soldiers in colonial armies on faraway battlefields. Resentments against such mobilizations fueled worker radicalism and anti-colonialism (Chandavarkar 1994).

In the aftermath of the First World War, WLG labor unrest mentions in the colonial and semi-colonial world reach a new historical peak (see Figure 4.3) with mining and transportation still accounting for the bulk of labor unrest mentions. There is a slight dip from the immediate postwar peak, but then unrest mentions start to rise again in the 1920s and 1930s up to the eve of the Second World War. Throughout, export industries (especially mining) and allied transport industries remain important (Bergquist 1986; Brown 1988; Silver 1995b: 179). Nevertheless, by the 1920s and 1930s, the number of labor unrest mentions among factory workers is also rising, reflecting the spread of manufacturing (especially textiles) to the colonial and semi-colonial world in the previous three decades (see Chapter 3).[18]

The disruptive power of this mass mobilization was enhanced by the fact that, by the eve of the Second World War, the colonies and semi-colonies were tightly interwoven into the supply structures of the imperial powers (as suppliers of both men and material). The Second World War (and the buildup to it) led to rapid urbanization and growth in the size of export enclaves and provided workers in these enclaves with strong bargaining power. Just as the metropolitan workers in the armaments industries occupied a

---

[17] Japan's military victory over Russia in 1905, even more than the 1905 Russian Revolution itself, had an electrifying effect on colonial elites throughout Asia. According to Sun Zhongshan, "the Russian defeat by Japan [was regarded] as the defeat of the West by the East. We regarded the Japanese victory as our own victory." And Jawaharlal Nehru recalled how as a schoolboy in India: "Japanese victories stirred up my enthusiasm. . . . Nationalistic ideas filled my mind. I mused of Indian freedom. . . . I dreamed of brave deeds of how, sword in hand, I would fight for India and help in freeing her" (quoted by Stavrianos 1981: 389).

[18] Looking back at our discussion of the textile industry in Chapter 3, we can now see that the global political environment was surely important in magnifying the worldwide textile labor unrest wave of the 1920s and 1930s. Likewise, the contrasting world political environment of the 1920s/1930s and the 1960s/1970s provides an additional explanation for the mature-phase differences between labor unrest patterns in the automobile and textile industries, apart from the differences in the two industries' structural characteristics already noted in Chapter 3.

strategic position within the military–industrial complexes of the belligerents, so the colonial export enclaves occupied strategic positions within the resource-needs structures of the imperial powers (Bergquist 1986; Brown 1988).

To be sure, war did not everywhere lead to a strengthening of the working class. In Shanghai, which had been the center of the textile industry and of working class formation, the war essentially wiped out the working class as factories closed and workers returned to the countryside so as to be able to survive (Honig 1986).[19] But in the areas that were being incorporated into resource provisioning, rather than being plundered, the war strengthened the strategic bargaining power of workers. One indication of the effectiveness of strikes in these sectors is Britain's decision to introduce trade unions and conciliation and arbitration mechanisms throughout its empire during the Second World War. During the First World War, tripartite agreements among trade unions, employers, and states only emerged in metropolitan countries and were rapidly eliminated after the war. The tripartite agreements concluded during the Second World War were more permanent, involved far greater concessions to labor in metropolitan countries, and were much broader in geographical spread. (On Britain's colonial trade union policy, see Cooper 1996; Brown 1988; Burawoy 1982.)[20]

Growing labor militancy intertwined with growing nationalist agitation. The elites who led the nationalist movements in the years leading up to the First World War made little or no attempt to mobilize the mass of the population into the nationalist struggle. However, in the interwar years, partly in response to the 1917 Russian Revolution and the spread of socialist ideology, the (successful) nationalist leaders – both communist and noncommunist – began "broadening . . . the basis of resistance to foreign colonial power by the organization of a mass following among peasants and workers and the forging of links between the leaders and the people" (Barraclough 1967: 178).

In India, the shift from "nationalist agitation on a relatively narrow middle-class basis" to mass mobilization took place in 1920 when Gandhi launched the first national civil disobedience campaign. Gandhi's

[19] Such dislocation, on the other hand, fostered "peasant" mobilization for revolution.

[20] To be sure, the extension of the idea of workers' rights to the colonial world by the imperial power raised problems of system-level profitability that prompted new boundary-drawing schemes – an issue already introduced in Chapter 1 and to which we will return below.

"outstanding contribution in the phase immediately following the First World War was to bring Congress to the masses and thus to make it a mass movement" (Barraclough 1967: 180; see also Chatterjee 1986).

In China, an analogous shift was made around 1924 when Sun Zhongshan reorganized the Guomindang (GMD) after a wave of labor militancy in China induced him to rethink the role of the popular classes in the nationalist movement. Prior to 1924, social issues played little part in his program. But by 1924 he had made contacts with the Russian Bolsheviks, placed the economic question at the head of his program, allied with the Communist Party, and reorganized the GMD into a mass party with a revolutionary army as its spearhead (Barraclough 1967: 182).

Likewise, by the 1940s, the leading nationalist movements in Africa (e.g., the Gold Coast and Nigeria) had moved from being "middle-class parties with limited popular contacts, to mass parties which mobilized support by combining national with social objectives for the attainment of which the whole people could be stirred to action" (Barraclough 1967: 189). Thus, nationalist movements in Asia and Africa increasingly merged with social revolutions. It became clear that a successful independence movement required mass agitation. As Kwame Nkrumah put it, "a middle class elite, without the battering ram of the illiterate masses could never hope to smash the forces of colonialism." But the loyalty of the masses could not be secured without promising that radical social change ("the building of a new society") would be high on the agenda of the nationalist movements (Barraclough 1967: 190; Nkrumah 1965: 177).

As in the aftermath of the First World War, so in the aftermath of the Second World War, major waves of labor unrest spread through the colonial and semi-colonial world. But the post–Second World War wave is far higher and lasts far longer (see Figure 4.3).

With the communist victory in China in 1949, the problem of repressing or accommodating the social revolutionary challenge from the non-Western world moved to center stage in the global strategies of the new hegemonic power. Until 1949, attention had been focused on Europe where, as a U.S. undersecretary of commerce reported to President Truman in 1947, "most . . . countries were standing on the very brink [of revolution] and may be pushed over at any time; others are gravely threatened" (quoted in Loth 1988: 137). By 1949, the social revolutionary threat was unmistakable. Instead of "a single, weak and isolated USSR, something like a dozen states had emerged, or were emerging, from the second great wave of global revolution. . . . Nor was the impetus of global revolution exhausted, for the decolonization of the old imperialist overseas possessions was still in full progress" (Hobsbawm 1994: 82).

V. U.S. Hegemony and Mass Consumption and Developmentalist Social Contracts

With the establishment of U.S. world hegemony in the aftermath of the Second World War, the vicious circle of war and labor unrest was brought to a close. In the first half of the twentieth century, labor movements worldwide had grown in strength and militancy, while efforts to accommodate and/or repress them failed. Waves of labor unrest intertwined with widespread revolutionary upheavals across the globe. Yet, as noted in Section I, a clear shift in the dynamics of world-scale labor unrest occurred, from rising/explosive in the first half of the century to stable/declining in the post–Second World War period (see Figure 4.1 and Table 4.1).

The shift was in part related to the unprecedented concentration of military and economic power in the hands of the United States at the close of the Second World War, thus putting to an end the great power rivalries that fed the vicious circle of war and labor unrest. Nevertheless, this concentration of economic and military power in itself is insufficient to explain the shift. Of equal importance were deep institutional reforms at the firm, national, and especially global levels that partially de-commodified labor. The reforms outlined here were a response to the growing strength of labor worldwide and to the major successes of revolutionary movements (especially the Soviet and Chinese) in achieving state power in the first half of the century.[21]

---

[21] The importance of the ongoing global revolutionary challenge in determining the relatively reformist bent of U.S. world hegemony in the immediate post–Second World War period becomes clearer if we contrast the situation faced by Britain in the early years of British world hegemony with that faced by the United States in the early years of U.S. world hegemony. At the outset of British world hegemony, France (the main great-power embodiment of the revolutionary challenge of the late eighteenth and early nineteenth centuries) had suffered a decisive military defeat, as did the British labor movement domestically. Britain did not face a serious popular revolutionary challenge, and thus the initial thrust of British domestic and international policy in the immediate aftermath of the Napoleonic Wars was repression at home and the restoration of *ancien régimes* on the Continent. Reform policies only emerged later. In contrast, at the outset of U.S. hegemony, the Soviet Union (the main great-power embodiment of the revolutionary challenge of the first half of the twentieth century) emerged from the Second World War battered, but much stronger politically and militarily. Moreover, both labor and nationalist movements emerged from the twentieth-century world wars strengthened and radicalized. The

Institutional transformations at the global level were especially important for they provided the context in which national social compacts could attain some stability. In the first half of the century, as we argued earlier, the various efforts at national social compacts had the unintended effect of fostering the movement toward global economic instability and warfare. In sponsoring global institutional transformations that allowed for a *partial* de-commodification of labor power at the firm and national level, the United States became hegemonic in a Gramscian sense. It led the world capitalist system as a whole in a direction that could be credibly presented as meeting *some* of the challenges and demands thrown up by the intense social and labor unrest of the previous half century (see Arrighi and Silver 1999, especially Chapter 3).

While the various reforms amounted to an effort to accommodate the growing strength and bargaining power of labor in the world capitalist system, such accommodation took place on extremely unstable foundations. As we shall argue, it proceeded along the knife's edge between a major crisis of profitability, due to the costs of the reforms, and a major crisis of legitimacy, due to the failure to deliver on the promised reforms fully. This contradiction eventually exploded in the crisis of the 1970s.[22]

The way this contradiction played out over time was strongly influenced by strategies of differentiation in space. The balance between reform and repression tilted more strongly toward repression in the colonial/post-colonial world than in the metropolitan countries.[23] As a result, crises of legitimacy were in evidence both earlier and to a greater degree in the colonial/post-colonial world than in the metropolitan countries. Time series derived from the WLG database are consistent with such a bifurcation (see Figures 4.2 and 4.3). In the metropolitan aggregate of countries, although mean levels of labor unrest remain at historically high levels for several decades after the Second World War, there was nonetheless a slow and steady decline in labor unrest mentions. Moreover, labor unrest waves were increasingly dissociated from revolutionary crises. In contrast, labor unrest waves in the colonial/semi-colonial world remained at historic highs

*counter*revolutionary challenge of the Axis powers was defeated in the war, while the power and prestige of the revolutionary challenge was enhanced (see Silver and Slater 1999: 202–3).

[22] See Chapter 1, which lays out the tension between crises of profitability and crises of legitimacy as a fundamental contradiction within historical capitalism.

[23] This tilting of the balance toward repression in the colonial/post-colonial world can in part be understood with reference to the product-cycle argument developed in Chapter 3.

throughout the 1950s and 1960s, declining once the waves of decolonization had run their course, only to rise again shortly thereafter.

In the remainder of this section, we will look more closely at the transformations affecting postwar patterns of labor unrest, focusing first on the
extent and nature of the reforms pursued and then on the role of repression. Finally, we will look at the role played by processes of world economic
restructuring – in particular, the ways in which spatial, technological/
organizational, and product fixes weakened "behind workers' backs" the
bargaining power of labor. This restructuring/weakening, in turn, helped
set the stage for a particularly unfavorable outcome to the crisis of the 1970s
for labor, especially for metropolitan labor movements.

Reform

The continuing global revolutionary challenge in the postwar period, combined with the experience of the Great Depression and fascism, convinced
the ruling groups of the leading capitalist states that a serious reform of the
world capitalist system needed to be a leading element in the strategy for
postwar reconstruction. According to Franz Schurmann (1974: 4–5):

The collapse of capitalism and the rise of fascism convinced people that the systems of peace and progress that had been growing ever since the beginning of the
nineteenth century were finally doomed. There was hunger for experimentation
with new social and world orders even at the highest levels of interests, while the
pessimism was even greater at the bottom.

There was a widespread perception that laissez-faire economics and
laissez-faire politics had contributed to the social and political chaos of
the interwar and war years. This, in turn, contributed to a shift in the
philosophies guiding the construction of international institutions. Thus,
according to Inis Claude, while the image that inspired the founders of the
League of Nations was the nineteenth-century night-watchman state, the
supporting image for the United Nations was the twentieth-century welfare state. To do the job of keeping the peace, international organizations
had to be empowered to deal with "the wide-spreading economic, social,
and ideological root structure of the problem of war" (Claude 1956: 87–9).

Likewise, international monetary and trade institutions were reformed
in a direction that recognized the right and duty of nation-states to protect their workers, businesses, and currencies from annihilation by unregulated world-market forces. In the 1950s and 1960s, there was thus no

attempt to move toward nineteenth-century-style free trade. Instead, the GATT (General Agreement on Tariffs and Trade) rounds set up a system of multilateral negotiations designed to promote a controlled process of trade liberalization over time (Ruggie 1982; Maier 1987: 121–52; Ikenberry 1989; Mjöset 1990; Burley 1993; cf. Cronin 1996). Moreover, the Bretton Woods system accepted that governments would use monetary policy as an instrument for reducing unemployment and inflationary pressures. At Bretton Woods, the regulation of high finance was shifted from private to public hands (Ingham 1994: 40). As Henry Morgenthau himself later boasted, he and Roosevelt "moved the money capital from London and Wall Street to Washington, and [the big bankers] hated us for it" (quoted in Frieden 1987: 60).

Global economic institutions were designed to mesh with the pursuit of Keynesian policies at the national level. In the words of Albert Hirschman, U.S. economic advisers fanned "out to the far corners of the U.S.-controlled portion of the globe" preaching the Keynesian gospel – their message backed up by military government in defeated countries and Marshall Plan aid for the Allies (1989: 347–56; also Maier 1978, 1981). Keynesianism was seen as supplying an attractive third way between the Soviet model of centralized planning (which had gained in power and prestige during the 1930s and 1940s) and traditional laissez-faire policies (which had lost all credibility in the course of the Great Depression and the related social–political catastrophes of the era).

There was, however, a core–periphery differentiation in economic prescriptions. While Keynesianism was promoted as the recipe for the "developed" countries, a new brand of development economics with strong Keynesian overtones was promoted for poorer countries. We focus first on the Keynesian package for the core and then move to a discussion of the core–periphery differentiation of economic prescriptions and its implications.

The broad Keynesian package presupposed a truce in the labor–capital conflict based on a tripartite exchange among governments, unions, and business enterprises. Governments and big business accepted the permanence of unionism, while unions accepted the right of management to make ongoing changes in the organization of production to increase productivity (a point to which we shall return later in the subsection on restructuring). Governments promised to use the macroeconomic tools at their disposal to promote full employment, while businesses would pass on a share of the increased profits from productivity increases in the form of rising real wages.

V. Mass Consumption and Development Social Contracts

This, in turn, assured a mass market for the growing output of industry and opened up a vast field for the pursuit of product fixes. Likewise, rising real wages helped bring about the depoliticization and taming of labor–capital conflict through the promise of "high mass consumption" – that is, through the promise of universal access to the "American Dream" (Aglietta 1979; Gordon et al. 1982; Arrighi and Silver 1984; Harvey 1989).

These trade-offs constituted efforts to accommodate labor strength and quell labor militancy within the context of a reformed capitalism. Yet, full-employment policies and the compulsory recognition of trade unions reduced both the weight of the reserve army of labor on the employed as well as the arbitrary power of management at the workplace, effectively strengthening further labor's bargaining power. Therefore, for these agreements to remain compatible with capital accumulation (i.e., to produce profitable outcomes for firms and to avoid hyperinflation), they had to be accompanied by the creation of new institutional structures at the national level and the firm level.

At the national level, Leo Panitch (1980: 174) emphasized the importance of "liberal corporatist" structures that gave trade unions a role in macroeconomic policymaking in exchange for union leaders agreeing to keep wage demands in line with "capitalist growth criteria." Trade union leaders (often in partnership with social-democratic parties) were expected to impose wage restraint on their members, actively controlling rank-and-file militancy in exchange for a seat at the policymaking table (see also Panitch 1981). At the shopfloor level, Michael Burawoy (1983: 589) emphasized a related transition from "despotic" to "hegemonic" factory regimes, in which the productivity of workers depended far more on the active mobilization of workers' consent than on heavy-handed coercion. The promotion ladders of internal labor markets provided an incentive for workers' cooperation and loyalty, while detailed work rules and grievance procedures created a legal framework at the level of the firm for the resolution of conflict.

Yet, both Burawoy and Panitch also emphasized the limits of these institutional solutions. For Burawoy (1983: 602) hegemonic factory regimes placed "such constraints on accumulation" that competition from firms and/or countries with greater shopfloor flexibility threatened the viability (profitability) of hegemonic factory regimes. In contrast, Panitch emphasized the internal tensions produced *within* the labor movement itself by participation in corporatist structures. The role assigned to trade-union leaders of disciplining the rank-and-file constantly threatened to drive a wedge between the trade union leaders and their membership. To the extent that such a wedge was driven, trade union leaders could no longer effectively control rank-and-file militancy. And to the extent that trade union leaders responded to the grievances thrown up from their base, they were obliged to withdraw from corporatist structures. Thus, either path obtained the same result – that is, the inability to control rank-and-file militancy (Panitch 1981: 35–6). Given these contradictions, both Burawoy and Panitch concluded that there is a built-in tendency for these consent-based structures either to collapse or to take on increasingly authoritarian (less consensual) tones, and thus for their legitimating functions to weaken or crumble (Panitch 1977: 87; Burawoy 1983: 590; see also Apple 1980; Burawoy 1985).

Nevertheless, as argued in Chapter 1, how such contradictions between profitability and legitimacy play out over time is deeply intertwined with strategies of spatial differentiation and boundary drawing. Thus, while internal labor markets protected those workers within their walls from the full effects of commodification, most major firms with internal labor markets kept a percentage of their workforce outside the wall of protection, treating them as part-time or temporary, with fewer rights and benefits. Critical to the supply side of this process was the massive entry of married women into the paid labor force in core countries after the Second World War. Their incorporation into these more "flexible" jobs was facilitated by a widespread ideology that viewed women as secondary and/or temporary breadwinners – a view that became increasingly untenable as their incorporation into the wage labor force became clearly permanent (Arrighi and Silver 1984: 203–4).

Equally important as a corporate strategy for lowering the percentage of workers within the "wall of protection" was the transnational expansion of capital to lower-wage areas – a strategy built on the historical legacy of North–South inequalities in wealth and power as well as on their ongoing reality. This transnational expansion of capital would take place in the context of a package of world-level reforms directed at the colonial/post-colonial world. To be sure, the Keynesian package prescription discussed previously was only meant for the "developed" countries. High mass consumption and full employment – touchstones of the welfare state – were deemed to be beyond the reach of "underdeveloped" economies. Consensus politics at the national and/or shopfloor level were also deemed luxuries that might have to be sacrificed in the effort to industrialize and modernize (Huntington 1968; but also Rostow 1960). Nevertheless, it was clear to U.S. policymakers that postwar global reform efforts could not be limited to the metropolitan world. Labor movements had proven themselves to be

154

V. Mass Consumption and Development Social Contracts

significant forces that could provide a mass force for social revolution in many Third World countries (see Section IV). Moreover, the Cold War competition was more and more being fought out in the Third World. In the words of Arturo Escobar, by the late 1940s "the real struggle between East and West had already moved to the Third World" and it "was commonly accepted in the early 1950s that if poor countries were not rescued from their poverty, they would succumb to communism" (1995: 33–4).[24]

Yet, a rapid rescue from poverty was not in the cards. The rhetoric of the reformed international regime established under U.S. hegemony spoke of the *universalization* of mass consumption (the American Dream). Yet, while workers in First World countries were promised that they would share in the fruits of capitalist growth immediately, workers in Third World countries were told that there would first have to be a vigorous drive for industrialization and "development." The hegemonic promise – made explicit in Walt Rostow's (1960) "stages of economic growth"[25] – was that all the peoples of the world could achieve the American Dream. Each country would pass through a set of similar stages on the road to the same (desirable) destination – the "Age of High Mass Consumption." This discourse of development[26] thus implicitly dealt with the system-level problem that the universalization of mass consumption posed (see Chapter 1) by attempting to postpone the problem. That is, to the extent that rising real wages and shopfloor rights for Third World workers could be postponed into the future, crises of profitability could also be postponed in time. And, as long as, and to the extent that, workers found credible the promise of future redemption, crises of legitimacy might also be postponed.

Nevertheless, such promises were insufficient to control labor militancy, especially once the impulse to sacrifice tapped by national liberation and

---

[24] The effects of the Cold War pulled U.S. policy in two different directions at once. On the one hand, the competition with the USSR and China encouraged the United States to back social reform as part of an effort to demonstrate capitalism's superiority to communism in producing social welfare. On the other hand, the U.S. government's skeptical attitude toward the feasibility of democracy and its widespread support for dictatorships in the Third World was also strongly influenced by what were deemed to be the exigencies of the Cold War competition – especially when and where the struggle over "hearts and minds" was failing. This is a point to which we will return in the next subsection focusing on repression.

[25] The press of the Cold War competition on U.S. official and semi-official thinking and policy on the Third World was made explicit in the subtitle of Rostow's book – *The Stages of Economic Growth: A Non-Communist Manifesto*.

[26] On postwar development discourse, see Escobar (1995), Esteva (1992), and McMichael (1996).

revolutionary movements subsided. Just as the appeal to worker sacrifice in the name of "the national interest" was insufficient to provide a stable basis to liberal corporatism in the core, so the appeal to cross-class cooperation in the name of national development was weak by itself in the Third World. As in core countries, however, national- and firm-level reforms were implemented in Third World countries that protected at least some of the working class from the full brunt of commodification. These reforms provided a material basis for cooperation. They took a wide variety of shapes, but certain common tendencies prevailed.

Thus, while there was no Marshall Plan for the Third World, in those countries allied to the United States, import substitution industrialization was allowed, even encouraged, so long as there was an open door to direct investment by U.S. multinational corporations. Likewise, in areas allied to either the United States or the USSR, it was assumed that government should play a vigorous role in promoting growth and employment (Hirschman 1979: 1–24). Finally, some of the protections afforded by internal labor markets in core countries were replicated in Second and Third World countries (Stark 1986; Walder 1986; Cooper 1996; Solinger 1999). Just as in the core, the costs of such internal labor markets were contained by the drawing of boundaries that divided the labor force between those who were within the wall of protection and those who were outside of it. In contrast to the core, however, because of the relative poverty of Second and Third World countries, the percentage of workers who fell outside was far greater. Thus, for example, as discussed in Chapter 1, in late-colonial and post-colonial Africa, efforts were made to define small, compact stable working classes set off from the rural masses and urban underclass (Cooper 1996; Mamdani 1996). Likewise, as Bryan Roberts (1995: 4) pointed out, in Latin America's "cities of peasants," only a tiny fraction of the urban poor were employed in the formal sector enterprises fostered by import substitution industrialization or were the beneficiaries of state-sponsored social services or infrastructure. A variation on the same theme was found in Maoist China where the household registration system (*hukou*) limited access to urban areas, thereby protecting a small urban working class from competition over jobs and housing with a sea of peasants who remained tied to the rural areas (Solinger 1999).[27]

---

[27] The loosening of these restrictions on rural–urban migration is one of the key reforms of the post-Mao era that provided a new "flexibility" for capitalist development in China. It went hand in hand with the massive layoffs of workers from state-owned enterprises and

V. Mass Consumption and Development Social Contracts

Repression

Given that the reform basket offered to Third World workers was far emptier than that offered to First World workers, it should not be surprising that repression of labor was a far more significant mechanism of control in the Third World than in the First World. To be sure, even in the metropolitan countries, co-optation of the "responsible" elements of the labor movement was supplemented by fierce repression of the "irresponsible" elements. In the United States, the radical and communist left was purged from the ranks of organized labor, starting with the 1947 Taft-Hartley Act loyalty oaths and culminating with McCarthyism. And in Western Europe, reformism and repression also went hand in hand as responsible U.S. labor leaders were invited to assist the U.S. government in the postwar reconstruction of Europe by setting up noncommunist unions in competition with the existing trade union movement (McCormick 1989: 82–4; Radosh 1969; Rupert 1995).

Nevertheless, in the balance between reform and repression, the latter weighed far more heavily in the Third World. Decolonization – the extension of juridical sovereignty to all nations – was the immediate global reform won by the colonial world from the period of war and revolution. For the nationalist elites who had never embraced social revolution (or for those segments for whom the alliance was one of only tactical convenience), their central aim of political independence and sovereignty had been achieved. Even those among the nationalist elites who believed that the social and national revolutions could not be separated for the most part accepted the idea that development (read industrialization) was a prerequisite for meeting the needs of the people. With no Marshall Plan for the Third World as a whole,[28] poor countries were "instructed to look to private capital, both foreign and domestic." But to attract private capital, it was necessary to create the right investment climate, including guaranteeing a

---

the breaking of long-existing social compacts with the established urban working class. This breaking of the "iron rice bowl," in turn, sparked waves of Polanyi-type labor unrest from workers in state-owned enterprises in the late 1990s and early 2000s (Eckholm 2001; Pan 2002; Solinger 2001). We shall return to this issue in Section VI.

[28] With the exception of a handful of countries that were built up as showcases of successful capitalist development (Arrighi 1990b; Grosfoguel 1996), few public funds were sent by the United States to support the development project, in sharp contrast to the role of U.S. governmental funds in European reconstruction. Curiously, the supplies that the United States bought in Asia for wars fought in Asia (Korea and Vietnam) played a key role in boosting the economies (and hence industrialization/proletarianization) of subordinate allies in that region.

disciplined and hard-working labor force (Walton 1984; see also Escobar 1995: 33; Bataille 1988).[29]

Thus, decolonization undermined one of the central bases of labor movement strength in the colonial world. As each colony achieved independence, the cross-class alliance of the nationalist movements tended to dissolve. Once nationalist movement leaders controlled state power, workers' and peasants' struggles invariably lost much of their former support from other classes within society (see, for example, Walton 1984 on Kenya; Post 1988 on Vietnam; and Beinin and Lockman 1987: 14–18 on Egypt as well as more generally). Moreover, as part of the global anti-Communist struggle, U.S. policy further strengthened the trend toward antilabor repression by actively supporting dictatorial regimes – from military governments in Brazil to the Shah in Iran and the puppet regimes in South Vietnam.

Yet, repression alone is a very unstable form of rule, and given that reforms are expensive, the postwar resolutions to labor unrest in the Third World were also crisis-prone. This is especially the case once we take into account the impact of the world-scale restructuring of processes of accumulation in rapidly industrializing regions of the Third (and Second) World.

Restructuring

A third component of the postwar reaction to strong labor movements was the extensive world-scale restructuring of processes of capital accumulation. By the late 1970s, these restructuring processes were to grow rapidly in speed and scope, coming to be seen as a defining characteristic of world capitalism after the 1970s. Yet, already in the 1950s and 1960s, these restructuring processes – with the exception of the financial fix – were taking place and having significant impacts on the bargaining power of labor.

In shifting control of monetary policy from private to public hands, Bretton Woods dramatically reduced the scope for the profitable pursuit of financial fixes, forcing capital back into investment in trade and production and away from speculation. At the same time, however, steps were taken to widen significantly the scope for the profitable pursuit of

[29] The Soviet challenge, on this front, represented no challenge at all. The Soviet version of "development" also prioritized industrialization as a prerequisite for achieving communism and thus also emphasized the importance of a disciplined and hardworking labor force. The fruits of this discipline and hard work would be reaped with the transition from socialism to communism.

spatial, technological/organizational, and product fixes. We already mentioned that the postwar social contracts in the core were premised on trade union support for the introduction of new technologies designed to increase productivity. And we already mentioned the role of mass consumption in opening new vistas for profitable product fixes. Likewise, we already mentioned that U.S. support for import substitution industrialization in the Third World was conditioned on an open door for foreign direct investment, a condition that simultaneously created a favorable environment for spatial fixes (vis-à-vis core workers) and technological/organizational fixes (vis-à-vis workers in sites to which multinational corporate capital flowed).

In Western Europe, the U.S. government promoted the formation of the European Community – a sufficiently large market to make U.S. corporate investment profitable and to support the kinds of technological/organizational transformations characteristic of Fordist mass production. Moreover, the U.S. government created various fiscal and other incentives designed to increase the flow of U.S. capital to Western Europe (and abroad more generally). Nevertheless, with liquidity shortages and political uncertainty, private capital was slow to respond to the incentives. It was only with the heating up of the Cold War that the transnational expansion of U.S. capital into Western Europe took off. With the communist victory in China in 1949 followed by the 1950 outbreak of the Korean War, a previously reluctant U.S. Congress released massive public funds to finance a global U.S. military buildup, thus overcoming the liquidity shortage that had plagued Europe and helping to create conditions favorable to private foreign direct investment (Block 1977: 114; Arrighi and Silver 1999: 87; Borden 1984: 23; McCormick 1989: 77–8; Maier 1978, 1981).

The wave of U.S. corporate investments in Western Europe in the 1950s and 1960s, in combination with the European response to the "American challenge," fostered the rapid spread of Fordist mass-production techniques in Western Europe. As argued in Chapter 2 with specific reference to the automobile industry, the immediate result of this relocation was a weakening of the strongest segments of the labor movement in both Western Europe and the United States. As mass-production techniques spread in Western Europe, craftworkers – who had been the backbone of the militant European labor movement of the first half of the twentieth century – were progressively marginalized from production, and their bargaining power was undermined. At the same time, as the geographical relocation of U.S. corporate capital proceeded, the semiskilled mass-production workers – who had formed the backbone of the U.S. labor movement in the 1930s and 1940s – were progressively weakened. (See also Arrighi and Silver 1984; Edwards 1979; Goldfield 1987; Moody 1988.)

By the 1950s and 1960s, the industrial sociology literature began to talk about "the withering away of the strike," which was seen as the inevitable and beneficial outcome of "modernization" (Ross and Hartman 1960). Our analysis would suggest that this decline resulted from the combination of reforms, repression, and restructuring discussed in this section. Yet just as the "withering" thesis became hegemonic in industrial sociology, a major wave of labor unrest spread through Western European mass-production industries. One side of the restructuring process had led to a weakening of European craftworkers, but the other side involved the creation/ strengthening of a class of semiskilled factory workers, who became the main protagonists of the labor unrest wave (see Chapter 2).[30] The late 1960s and early 1970s wave of labor unrest, in turn, was an important spark in the take-off of the transnational expansion of Western European corporate capital to lower-wage areas, as well as the intensification and widening of the scope of U.S. foreign direct investment.

To summarize, this section has put forward the argument that the various efforts to accommodate and control strong labor movements in the postwar decades all had limits and contradictions. Reforms – to the extent that they were fully realized and embraced more than a tiny fraction of the world's labor force – were expensive. Moreover, by protecting workers from the full brunt of market forces, reforms strengthened labor's bargaining power,

---

[30] While the labor unrest decline visible in Figure 4.2 for the 1950s and 1960s is less dramatic than one would expect from the withering thesis, the upsurge in the late 1960s and early 1970s is less prominent than would be expected from the "resurgence of class conflict" literature on Western Europe. Yet, if we disaggregate the data by country, there are indeed waves where and when we would expect them (e.g., France in 1968, Italy in 1969–70). The fact that it does not show up in the aggregate time series for metropolitan countries is probably due to several factors. First, the explosions were not simultaneous in all European countries; thus, they tend to average each other out in the aggregate time series. Second, the wave, while intense, was relatively short-lived. Third, much of the social unrest of the period was tied to student protests, feminist movements, and protests against the war in Vietnam. These other movements were sometimes fueled by an element of labor unrest. In particular, with the mass incorporation of women into the paid labor force as "cheap labor" in the postwar decades, some of the impetus for feminist protests came from demands such as "equal pay for equal work." Likewise, in the United States, there was a significant labor unrest component to some of the Black civil rights protests (Arrighi and Silver 1984: 204; Piore 1979: 160–1). Nonetheless, most of this protest activity was not classifiable as labor unrest. Even when it was, it would not get reported by the newspapers as labor unrest; hence, it would not make it into the WLG database.

creating tensions that corporatist structures were designed to (but could not fully) resolve. Repression – still an important tool in the repertoire of labor control – was also an unstable solution. Finally, the world-scale restructuring of processes of capital accumulation that took place in the postwar decades also had contradictory effects. Spatial fixes largely relocated strong workplace bargaining power and militancy from one site to another, while technological/organizational and product fixes did not clearly weaken (and in some cases strengthened) the bargaining power of labor. We have also argued that the same contradictions were visible in the First, Second, and Third Worlds – with important variations on the basic theme and with important links among them. That is, the contradictions did not unfold within isolated national cases, but rather as the outcome of a dynamic interaction among the cases. Economic linkages through trade and investment were important, but, as we have seen, the political–ideological competition of the Cold War also drove the processes of accommodation and conflict.

An unresolved impasse thus existed in the way in which the strength of labor movements was accommodated within a reformed world capitalist system. It was bound to lead to another world-scale crisis. That crisis erupted in the 1970s. At first it took the form of a crisis of world capitalism and of U.S. world power, but by the end of the 1980s, it had become instead a world-scale crisis of labor movements.

VI. *From Crisis of U.S. Hegemony to Crisis of World Labor*

The U.S.-sponsored restructuring of the world capitalist system provided the foundations for two decades of sustained and profitable growth in the 1950s and 1960s – a "Golden Age of capitalism." This unprecedented growth and profitability, in turn, furnished the material resources with which to fund the social compacts of the postwar decades. Yet, like the Golden Age of capitalism in the mid nineteenth century (see Section II), the rapid growth of world trade and production in the 1950s and 1960s eventually sparked an overaccumulation crisis characterized by intense intercapitalist competition and a general squeeze on profits. It was in the context of this crisis that the postwar social compacts accommodating labor exploded.

Initial efforts by corporate capital to resolve the crisis of profitability in the 1960s by intensifying the pace of work were counterproductive, as these speed-ups tended to provoke a combination of open revolt and non-cooperation. The "Lordstown Blues" (named after the labor unrest at the General Motors plant in Lordstown, Ohio) came to symbolize this

161

non-cooperation. Likewise, the massive strike waves and labor radicalism centered in Fordist mass-production industries that swept Western Europe in the late 1960s and early 1970s (referred to earlier) were in important measure sparked by factory speed-ups designed to meet the intensifying intercapitalist competition. The labor unrest wave resulted in an unprecedented explosion in wages and in the widespread sense that capitalists, states, and unions had lost control over workers and the workplace (Crouch and Pizzorno 1978; also Chapter 2 in this volume).

In the 1970s, counterattacks by capital and states against labor movements took an *indirect* form, suggesting that labor movements were too strong (or at least perceived as too strong) to attack directly. In Western Europe, the wave of rank-and-file militancy at first led to a crisis of liberal corporatist structures as union leaders "ran after their members, not merely in a cynical attempt to retain organizational control, but often as a genuine response to their base" (Panitch 1981: 35). When coercive measures (e.g., outlawing strikes) failed to control labor militancy, new corporatist deals reflecting the greater bargaining power of labor were struck. Partly in response to demands from unions, the new corporatist structures integrated unions in decision making down to the shopfloor level, creating or strengthening what Burawoy calls "hegemonic factory regimes."[31] Unions were expected to discipline the rank-and-file in exchange for participation in shopfloor decision making. Nevertheless, tensions and instabilities still characterized these factory regimes, as they constituted real constraints on the flexibility of capital. Thus, as a solution to the crisis, they were at best temporary (Dubois 1978: 30; Panitch 1981: 35–8).

In the United States, an open repudiation of the mass-consumption social contract by major corporations and/or the government also seemed to be out of the question in the 1970s. In the private sector, collective bargaining institutions remained intact. Internal labor markets and other firm-level strategies that partially de-commodified labor were eroded through subcontracting but were not directly attacked. Finally, a direct attack on real wages was still out of the question in the 1970s. Instead, nominal wage rates continued to rise rapidly, while inflation ate into real wages (Goldfield 1987; Moody 1988).

---

[31] Whereas union involvement in corporatist structures regarding macroeconomic policy was common in Western Europe prior to the late 1960s, the involvement of unions in shopfloor decision making was largely an outcome of the wave of labor unrest in the late-1960s.

162

VI. From U.S. Hegemony Crisis to World Labor Crisis

The mass-consumption social contract presupposed not only that real wages would expand steadily but also that unemployment would be contained – by expansion of government hiring if needed. But meeting these hegemonic promises brought national, state, and local governments face to face with deep fiscal crises, and fostered rising levels of taxation that further squeezed profits. In the United States, the difficulties were further increased by the escalating costs (financial and human) of the war in Vietnam. As opposition to the war grew and as a mobilized civil rights movement turned its attention to issues of poverty and employment, the U.S. government responded with another giant step forward toward the "socialization of the state." The War on Poverty (a major expansion of social welfare programs) in combination with the war in Vietnam precipitated a deep fiscal crisis of the U.S. state. They also helped create strong global demand conditions that strengthened the marketplace bargaining power of labor in many parts of the world.

Thus, in the 1970s, when faced with the choice between meeting the demands from below for the fulfillment of the hegemonic promises or the demands from capitalists for a restoration of favorable conditions for capital accumulation, metropolitan states attempted not to choose. In response, capital went "on strike." An increasingly mobile capital "voted with its feet," not only by intensifying and deepening the geographical relocation of productive capital to lower-wage areas but also by accumulating capital in liquid form in proliferating offshore tax havens. And to the extent that industrial production still took place in the core, technological fixes and a growing reliance on immigrant labor became increasingly important capitalist strategies.

A combination of spatial, technological/organizational, and financial fixes thus seriously weakened workers "behind their backs" in the 1970s, allowing for an open assault by states and capital on core labor movements in the 1980s. By the early 1980s, the shopfloor gains of core labor movements had been largely overturned. Liberal corporatist structures either failed to deliver gains and lost most of their credibility with workers (e.g., as unemployment skyrocketed throughout Western Europe) or collapsed entirely with a shift in government strategy toward outright repression (e.g., with Thatcher's election in Britain). Workers fought to defend the established social contracts – struggles visible in the surge of labor unrest reports for the metropolitan aggregate in the early 1980s (see Figure 4.2). The British miners' strike, the U.S. air traffic controllers' strike, and the showdown at Fiat in Italy are among the events contributing to the early 1980s surge of labor unrest reports. These strikes were largely defensive struggles (i.e., resistance to the undermining of established ways of life and existing social contracts), or what we would call Polanyi-type waves of labor unrest. They all met with defeat.

The deep crisis into which core labor movements fell in the 1980s was not immediately replicated elsewhere. On the contrary, in the late 1970s and 1980s, major waves of labor militancy hit "showcases" of rapid industrialization in the Second and Third Worlds. These labor unrest waves were what we would call Marx-type rather than Polanyi-type waves. Strong new working-class movements had been created as a combined result of the spatial fixes pursued by multinational corporate capital and the import substitution industrialization efforts of modernizing states. In some cases, like Brazil's automobile workers, labor militancy was rooted in the newly expanding mass production consumer durable industries (see Chapter 2). In other cases, like the rise of *Solidarnosc* in Poland's shipyards, militancy was centered in gigantic establishments producing capital goods (Silver 1992: chapter 2; Singer 1982). In still other cases, like Iran's oil workers, labor militancy was centered in critical natural resource export industries (Abrahamian 1982).

Initially, the financial fix further strengthened the bargaining power of workers in the Second and Third World states. In the 1970s (in sharp contrast to what would happen in the 1980s), loan capital flowed freely to Second and Third World countries. With capital "on strike" in the First World, and with an excess accumulation of petrodollars to recycle, First World bankers were eager to make loans on easy terms to Second and Third World governments. Thus, for example, in 1981 (the eve of the debt crisis), First World banks loaned approximately $40 billion (net) to Second and Third World countries (UNDP 1992). Debt became an important mechanism through which the contradictions of the postwar developmentalist social contracts were managed in the short run. In Poland, for example, extensive overseas borrowing allowed the Polish government to promote rapid industrialization. At the same time, borrowed funds were used by the Polish government to accommodate the periodic upsurges of labor militancy in the 1970s, making it possible for the government simultaneously to increase wages and food subsides, expand employment, and maintain high levels of capital investments. In the 1970s, the Polish government expected that industrialization would lead to a surge in exports, allowing the government not only to pay back the loans but also to increase national wealth and finally deliver on the promises of socialism to a restive working class (Silver 1992: chapter 2; Singer 1982).

Needless to say, managing the contradictions of the developmentalist social contract through debt was a highly unstable solution. To the extent that Second and Third World states used the borrowed funds to promote further industrialization and/or expand state employment in social services, the marketplace bargaining power (and potentially the workplace bargaining power) of labor was strengthened. If they attempted to accommodate this growing strength of labor, they risked losing further access to foreign investment funds and/or becoming internationally uncompetitive and thus unable to pay the accumulated debt service through exports. If they failed to accommodate the growing strength of labor, they risked a crisis of legitimacy for having failed to deliver to the masses the expected benefits of national sovereignty (or social revolution) and industrialization/modernization. The social compacts in Second and Third World countries thus faced contradictions analogous to those plaguing core social contracts.

The stepped-up demands in the 1970s for a New International Economic Order from Third World states no doubt reflected an awareness of this fragility. Moreover, in the 1970s, such demands appeared to have a reasonable chance of success. With the U.S. military defeat in Vietnam and the success of OPEC, the relative power of Third World states seemed strong. The new nationalist militancy in the Third World, in turn, re-created some aspects of the favorable political conditions that had fed labor movement strength during the period of the national liberation struggles. Labor militancy (especially actions directed against foreign corporations) once again came to enjoy a large degree of cross-class support in the 1970s as a major wave of nationalizations swept through the Third World.

Nevertheless, most of the Second and Third World labor movements that had been impressively strong in the 1970s and 1980s were in a crisis themselves in the 1990s. To some extent, the weakening was an outcome of spatial fixes. Yet, as argued throughout this book, such spatial fixes cannot explain a *general* weakening of labor movements because although labor movements would be weakened in the sites of capital emigration, new movements would be created and strengthened in the new sites to which capital flows.[32] Rather, a central part of the explanation for the severity and spread

---

[32] And as we have also argued, this line of reasoning leads us to predict major Marx-type waves of labor unrest in China in the not too distant future (see Chapter 3).

of the crisis of labor movements appears to be rooted in the enormous ballooning of the financial fix in the 1980s and 1990s, as well as a shift in its character.

The stock of international bank lending mushroomed in size from 4 percent of the total GDP of all OECD countries in 1980 to 44 percent in 1991 (The Economist 1992). At the same time, there was a major reversal in the direction of finance capital flows, with the U.S. sucking in liquidity from around the world. The net inflow of capital from North to South of approximately $40 billion in 1981 (referred to earlier) turned into a net *outflow* of almost $40 billion by 1988 (UNDP 1992). The sudden drought of loan capital precipitated the first round of the debt crisis in the early 1980s. The debt crisis, in turn, opened the door for the International Monetary Fund to enforce "structural adjustment" packages in debtor countries as a condition of refinancing. Major cutbacks on state expenditures meant massive layoffs, mushrooming unemployment, and weakened marketplace bargaining power for labor. The elimination of trade barriers contributed to deindustrialization and the collapse of large state-owned or subsidized industrial enterprises, the growth of informal sector firms, and the weakening of both marketplace and workplace bargaining power.

The shift in the character of the financial expansion in the 1980s and 1990s was linked to a radical change in U.S. government policy (Arrighi 1994: 314–24). Whereas in the 1970s the U.S. government had tried unsuccessfully to stem the flight of capital into liquid form, in the 1980s the United States actively entered the competition for this liquid capital to finance simultaneously tax cuts at home and a new escalation of the Cold War abroad. The United States won the final act of the Cold War with the USSR (the latter was unable to compete on financial as much as military grounds), while capital going to the rest of the world (including the Second World) dried up. The change in U.S. government policy was not just economic/financial; it involved, in essence, a "global counterrevolution" (i.e., the liquidation of the relatively labor- and development-friendly international regime of the postwar era in favor of an international regime reminiscent of the late-nineteenth and early-twentieth-century *belle époque*). By the 1990s, the crisis of world capitalism and U.S. world power had turned into a world-scale crisis for labor movements.

Yet, as we have seen in this chapter, the late-twentieth-century financial fix is not an unprecedented phenomenon. A major financial fix was also a central aspect of the late-*nineteenth*-century period of capitalist globalization. Moreover, the take-offs of both the late-nineteenth-century and the late-twentieth-century financial expansions were followed in short order by labor-movement crises. Although labor movements suffered a setback in the late 1890s (as the financial fix took off), within less than a decade labor unrest was once again rising, leading to growing labor movement strength and militancy on a world-scale in the first half of the twentieth century. From the vantage point of 2002, the late-twentieth-century crisis of labor movements appears to be longer and deeper than that experienced by labor movements in the late nineteenth century.

Nevertheless, given the historical analysis carried out here, should we expect this general crisis of contemporary labor movements also to be temporary? In other words, given the analogies between the late nineteenth and late twentieth centuries, are we likely to be on the eve of a period of escalating labor unrest, combining Polanyi-type and Marx-type waves of labor unrest – similar to the first half of the twentieth century? After all, Polanyi-type waves of labor unrest accompanied the collapse of the developmentalist social compact, as structural adjustment packages provoked mass protests in Third World countries in the 1980s in the form of "anti-IMF riots" (Walton and Ragin 1990). These waves of labor unrest continued into the early twenty-first century – dramatically, in Argentina in 2001. Likewise, the smashing of the iron rice bowl in China has provoked widespread Polanyi-type waves of labor unrest from workers whose established ways of life and livelihood are being overturned (Solinger 1999, 2001; Eckholm 2001; Pan 2002). At the same time, the escalation of anti-globalization protests in core countries, from Seattle to Genoa, has been in significant part fueled by Polanyi-type labor unrest.

Nevertheless, there are also good reasons to think that processes of contemporary globalization and labor unrest are not simply retracing the path followed in the late nineteenth and early twentieth centuries. In Chapter 3, we argued that the nature and degree of workers' bargaining power are transformed as leading industries rise and decline. This chapter has argued that world politics in general and wars in particular have been central in determining both the nature and degree of workers' bargaining power and the patterning of labor unrest over time. In thinking about the future of labor movements, therefore, a key question that emerges is whether the dynamics of war and world politics in the early twenty-first century are fundamentally different from those that so heavily influenced the world-scale patterning of labor unrest in the twentieth century. This is one of the central questions to which we now turn in the fifth and final chapter.

5

Contemporary Dynamics in World-Historical Perspective

Our premise at the start of this book was that, by recasting labor studies in a world-historical framework, we would be able to shed a new light on the contemporary global crisis of labor movements. The central chapters of the book sought to distinguish, from successive angles of vision, dynamics that are recurrent from those that are fundamentally new and unprecedented in the trajectory of world labor unrest. This final chapter returns to the debates highlighted in Chapter 1 about the causes, depth, and nature of the contemporary crisis of labor movements, informed now by our study of the past.

I. A Race to the Bottom?

Our analysis of the globalization of mass production in the world automobile industry in Chapter 2 concluded that the geographical relocation of production has not created a simple race to the bottom. Rather, we found a recurrent pattern in which the geographical relocation of production tended to create and strengthen new working classes in each favored new site of investment. While multinational capital was attracted by the promise of cheap and controllable labor, the transformations wrought by the expansion of the industry also transformed the balance of class forces. The strong labor movements that emerged succeeded in raising wages, improving working conditions, and strengthening workers' rights. Moreover, they often played a leading role in democracy movements, pushing onto the agenda social transformations that went well beyond those envisioned by pro-democracy elites.

To be sure, the relocation of capital from existing sites of production tended to weaken established working classes. Nevertheless, the image of Third World workers being on "a hopeless treadmill without international protection" (Greider 1999: 5) elides the contradictions for capital that consistently recurred with each spatial fix. For with the geographical diffusion of the industry, strong workplace bargaining power also diffused. Thus, workers in each new low-wage site of investment were able in no small measure to rely on their *own* structural bargaining power. Our narrative of the world automobile industry thus suggests that, had the relocation of industrial activities been the main thrust of the ongoing restructuring of world capitalism, we would not have witnessed a general structural weakening of labor. Moreover, if past patterns are any guide to the future, then we should expect major waves of industrial labor unrest (of the Marx-type) to occur in those regions that have been experiencing rapid industrialization and proletarianization. (Of greatest world-historical significance, in this regard, is the case of China.)

One alternative explanation ties the crisis of labor to the impact of transformations in the organization of production on workers' bargaining power. Yet, our analysis of the world automobile industry in Chapter 2 also suggested that such technological fixes have not had a clear-cut weakening effect on workers' bargaining power. If anything, just-in-time production systems have increased labor's workplace bargaining power by increasing the vulnerability of capital to disruptions in the flow of production.

We therefore need to look elsewhere to explain the late-twentieth-century global crisis of labor and labor movements. We turn to the impact of product fixes and financial fixes in Sections III and IV.

II. The End of the North–South Divide?

While the analysis carried out in Chapter 2 suggests that spatial fixes in established mass-production industries have not provoked a straightforward race to the bottom, it might be read as suggesting a tendency toward the homogenization of conditions for labor globally, blurring the North–South divide. For our narrative emphasized the ways in which mass production in the automobile industry tended to create similar social contradictions, including similar sources of workers' bargaining power and forms of struggle. The result was a striking sense of *déjà vu* over a half century of struggles from Detroit to Turin to Ulsan.

While our story of *déjà vu* in Chapter 2 emphasized the homogenizing impact of capital relocation, our deployment of a *critically* reformulated product-cycle model in Chapter 3 emphasized systematic countertendencies whereby the North–South divide is continually reproduced – with important implications for differentially located labor movements. Each recurrence of the *déjà vu* pattern took place in a *fundamentally different competitive environment*. In both the auto and textiles product cycles, as the epicenter of production (and workers' struggles) moved to lower-wage areas, the "monopoly windfall profits" reaped in the innovation stage were no longer available, thus diminishing the room for maneuver in establishing stable labor–capital accords.

More generally, there has been a systemic tendency for technological and product fixes to recurrently produce monopoly windfall profits in high-income countries where innovations concentrate, while low-income countries rarely share in the windfall. Moreover, protectionism has also played a prominent role in maintaining or restoring the global competitive position of high-wage sites of production. To put it differently, we found that while spatial fixes tended to erode the North–South divide, technological fixes, product fixes, and protectionism tended to reconstitute the divide continually.

From the angle of vision adopted in Chapter 3, the difficulties faced by Third World workers are not due to a lack of international pressure to maintain labor standards. Rather the roots of the problem are the systemic processes that continually reproduce the North–South divide. Spatial fixes relocated the social contradictions of mass production (including strong working classes), but they have not relocated the wealth through which high-wage countries historically accommodated those same contradictions. As a result, strong grievances and strong bargaining power go hand in hand, creating the conditions for permanent social crises in much of the post-colonial world.

III. *The Weakening of Workers' Structural Bargaining Power?*

The leading industry of twentieth-century world capitalism – the automobile industry – imparted to production workers a strong workplace bargaining power rooted in their strategic location within a capital-intensive and complex technical division of labor that is vulnerable to costly disruptions in the flow of production (see Chapter 2). Moreover, we argued that the technological/organizational fixes associated with post-Fordism have not weakened the workplace bargaining power of labor in the automobile industry. Finally, we argued (in Chapter 3) that the workplace bargaining power of labor in the automobile industry has been far stronger than that of workers in the textile industry – the leading industry of world capitalism in the nineteenth century. In sum, the twentieth century appears to have been characterized by a trend toward the overall strengthening of labor's workplace bargaining power.

Yet, the automobile industry (and more generally mass production of consumer durables) is no longer the leading industry of world capitalism in the twenty-first century, either symbolically or in terms of employment growth (especially in high-wage countries). This has led some observers to attribute the crisis of labor movements to the disappearance of the working class itself (see Chapter 1). Our focus on the continuous making and remaking of the world's working classes has brought us to a substantially different conclusion. In Chapter 3 we argued that the epicenter of labor unrest not only shifts from site to site within industries in line with successive spatial fixes, but it also shifts from industry to industry in line with successive product fixes. Historically, we saw this with the shift from textiles to automobiles. In the course of the first half of the twentieth century, labor unrest in the textile industry was first peripheralized and then withered away. At the same time, however, major new working classes were created/strengthened in the new leading industry of the twentieth century – automobiles (see Table 3.1). Likewise, although labor unrest in the automobile industry is also increasingly peripheralized (and may eventually wither away) in the twenty-first century, we should expect to see new working-class formation and emerging labor movements in the leading industry/industries of the twenty-first century. In other words, from the perspective adopted here, the late-twentieth-century crisis of labor movements is temporary and will likely be overcome with the consolidation of new working classes "in formation."

Nevertheless, the question regarding the nature and degree of workers' bargaining power in the new leading industry/industries remains. In other words, will the trend toward increased workplace bargaining power continue in the twenty-first century? To answer this question, Chapter 3 attempted to identify the new leading industries of the twenty-first century and to compare the nature and degree of workers' bargaining power therein with the nature and degree of workers' bargaining power in the textile and automobile industries. A very heterogeneous picture emerged, both in terms of potential candidates for new leading industries and in terms of the implications for the bargaining power of labor. We found that while workers in some key contemporary sectors (e.g., transportation and communication) have as much workplace bargaining power as automobile workers ever had, others have far less (hotel and restaurant workers). Some, like teachers, lack significant workplace bargaining power (i.e., they do not work within a complex technical division of labor), yet they still have a significant degree of bargaining power rooted in their strategic position within the social division of labor.

In sum, although much less straightforwardly negative than widely thought, the twentieth-century trend toward increasing workplace bargaining power, it is probably safe to say, is at least partially being reversed in the twenty-first century. The bargaining power of many of today's low-wage workers in producer and personal services is closer to that of workers in the nineteenth-century textile industry than that of workers in the twentieth-century automobile industry.

From this perspective, the contemporary decline of labor militancy might be traced to a trend toward the overall weakening of labor's workplace bargaining power. Yet, our comparison of the historical dynamics of labor unrest in the textile and automobile industries suggested that there is no correlation between strong workplace bargaining power and labor militancy. Indeed, if anything, textile workers, while less successful in achieving their immediate demands, were consistently more militant than automobile workers. A crucial difference between workers in the two industries, however, was that textile workers' successes were far more dependent on a strong (compensatory) *associational* bargaining power (trade unions, political parties, and cross-class alliances with nationalist movements). As such, we might expect the weight of associational power in the overall power strategies of labor movements to be on the increase.

Indeed, as we saw in Chapter 3, the strategies of some of the most successful recent labor movement campaigns in rapidly growing core service industries have had much in common with the campaigns of late-nineteenth- and early-twentieth-century textile workers. Textile workers, operating in a vertically disintegrated industry with multiple small firms and unstable employment, had to develop a countervailing power based on citywide or regionwide political and trade union organization. Likewise today, low-wage service workers operating in industries that are at least on the surface vertically disintegrated[1] have followed a community-based organizing model rather than a model that relies on the positional power of workers at the point of production. The Living Wage Campaign and

---

[1] Crucially, there is not a simple return to the past because vertical disintegration is often only a surface characteristic. Beneath the plethora of small firms are large corporations, governments, and universities who have subcontracted tasks to cut costs and shelter themselves from responsibility.

the Justice for Janitors campaigns in the United States have sought to base labor organization in the community, severing its dependence on stable employment in any given firm or group of firms. As for textile workers historically, victory could not be achieved by relying mainly on the workers' autonomous structural bargaining power but rather depended on alliances with (and resources from) groups and strata in the community at large.[2]

If the significance of associational bargaining power is growing, then the future trajectory of labor movements will be strongly conditioned by the broader political context of which they are a part. Our discussion of the early twentieth-century textile workers in Chapter 3 perforce brought us to an emphasis on the links between labor movements and national liberation movements. Analogous links between contemporary labor movements and other movements need to be traced.

Moreover, a full assessment of current trends in workers' bargaining power requires that we bring the world political context into sharp focus for another reason. So far, this section has emphasized the impact of changes in the organization of production on workers' bargaining power. Yet as Chapter 4 emphasized, workers' bargaining power in the twentieth century was founded at least as much on workers' centrality within the world power strategies of states as on their centrality within complex processes of production. There is every reason to expect that the trajectory of twenty-first century labor movements will continue to be intertwined with the (changing) dynamics of war and world politics – a theme to which we now turn.

IV. Whither War and Workers' Rights?

As argued in Chapter 4, twentieth-century world labor unrest has been deeply enmeshed in the dynamics of world politics and war. Several important tendencies stand out. First, the power of workers vis-à-vis their states increased dramatically beginning in the late nineteenth century as states

---

[2] It is important to note that a significant proportion of the new working classes in formation in core countries are (documented and undocumented) immigrants. This fact influences, both positively and negatively, the amount and type of resources available to build associational bargaining power. Legal constraints are among the obvious negative influences. Ethnic community ties and potential access to transnational resources are among the positive influences. As in the early twentieth century, today's internationally mobile working classes (to the extent that they can in fact move) provide a structural basis for the international diffusion of labor unrest, as carriers of ideologies and forms of struggle as well through the development of transnational forms of associational bargaining power (e.g., cross-border solidarity and transnational organizing).

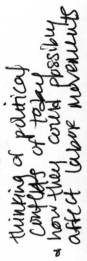
thinking of political conflicts of today & how they could possibly affect labor movements

became increasingly dependent for victory on the willingness, even enthusiasm, of worker-citizens sent to the front, as well as workers in factories supplying the front. It was in the context of the escalation of interimperialist rivalries and armed conflict in the first half of the twentieth century that workers (especially in metropolitan countries) succeeded in pushing their states toward a more rapid expansion of both workers' rights and broad democratic rights. Yet, this socialization of the state had only limited success in retaining workers' loyalties. The horrors and dislocations caused by modern industrialized warfare made such efforts at national social compacts increasingly unstable, eventually unleashing a vicious circle of war, labor unrest, and revolutionary crises. The general systemic chaos of the first half of the twentieth century was only resolved through substantial political-economic reforms *at the global level* after the Second World War. This included the successful establishment of international monetary and trade regimes whose rules implicitly recognized that labor is a fictitious commodity that needs to be protected from the harshest verdicts of an unregulated world market. These global reforms opened the space for the establishment of mass consumption and developmentalist social compacts at the national level (see Chapter 4).

From this perspective, the decline in labor unrest and the de-radicalization of labor movements in the second half of the twentieth century is a result of the transition to a situation of more controlled and limited warfare as well as a more labor-friendly international environment. Moreover, whether we might in the twenty-first century return to a situation of escalating and radicalized labor unrest on a world-scale is tied to whether we will return to a situation of growing interstate conflict and world war analogous to the first half of the twentieth century.

The war in Vietnam in this regard has a wide-ranging significance. First, the Vietnam War experience reinforces our conclusion about the radicalizing effects of costly and unpopular wars as well as the propensity of states to deal with the contradictions by further socializing the state (see Chapter 4). But the Vietnam War was also significant because it provoked a major crisis of U.S. global economic and military power, setting off a series of moves that culminated in a counterrevolution in U.S. global policy. At the heart of this counterrevolution was a major shift in U.S. global military strategy as well as a major shift in U.S. global social–economic strategy.

The counterrevolution in military strategy was tantamount to a recognition by the United States (and other metropolitan countries) that any war that risked the lives of more than a handful of their worker-citizens was a serious risk to social stability. Recognition of this fact at first paralyzed the United States in the military sphere in the 1970s. In the 1980s, in contrast, this paralysis was overcome through a sharp shift from labor-intensive to capital-intensive warfare. The advantages for countries that could afford the high-tech strategy were first made clear by the United Kingdom in the Falkland/Malvinas War. It was confirmed spectacularly in the Gulf War and again, less spectacularly, with the Kosovo War. Internal opposition to these wars within First World countries remained low because First World governments (the United States in particular) went to extreme lengths to keep casualties *among their own worker–citizen–soldiers* to a minimum (tending toward *zero*). Moreover, tremendous energies in the research and development sphere have been devoted to the automation of war (i.e., the complete removal of the First World human from both the risk of being killed and *direct* contact with the process of mass killing) (Greider 1998).

This is a very different type of war than the type that radicalized workers and created the explosive pattern of world labor unrest in the first half of the twentieth century. Recent wars have inflicted tremendous damage on the generally poor countries on whom the high-tech explosives land – destroying economic infrastructures and hence stable working classes – but they have not "violently moved the masses" in the First World. Thus, if warfare continues to insulate First World workers (and citizens more generally) from its more horrifying aspects while destroying stable working classes elsewhere, it is not likely to produce the kind of powerful and explosive labor unrest that characterized the first half of the twentieth century.[3]

At the same time, the more First World states move toward the automation of war, the more they emancipate themselves from dependence on their worker–citizens for success in war. As such, one of the most powerful processes underlying the expansion of workers' and democratic rights is being reversed, raising the question of whether this reversal is facilitating a major contraction in workers' and democratic rights. Indeed, the other side of the 1980s counterrevolution in the military sphere has been a counterrevolution in the social–economic sphere. The relatively labor-friendly and development-friendly international regime was replaced in the 1980s by a decidedly labor- and development-*unfriendly* regime. The mass consumption and developmentalist social contracts at the heart of the postwar global New Deal were abandoned from above. Social safety nets at the

---

[3] How the "war on terrorism" will affect the relationship between war and labor unrest remains to be seen. For an early assessment of the impact on U.S. labor, see Kutalik 2002.

national level were cut or dismantled worldwide along with the institutions at the international level that allowed/promoted them. Thus, the counter-revolution in the social–economic sphere can be said to have brought about a trend toward the de-socialization of the state.

So far we have argued that the contemporary global political–military context contrasts sharply with the global political–military context that pro-duced radicalized and explosive labor unrest in the late nineteenth and first half of the twentieth century. Nevertheless, with the dismantling of the labor-friendly international regime, the contemporary global social–economic context has come to share important features with the global social–economic context of the earlier period. In both periods, laissez-faire ideology was embraced, and there was a concerted move to free up capital from restrictions, thus facilitating an acceleration in the restructuring of global processes of capital accumulation (wide-ranging fixes) that destroyed noncommodified and socially protected sources of livelihood. Critically, in both periods, there was a major shift of investment out of trade and produc-tion into finance and speculation – what we have called a financial fix.[4] In both periods, these transformations, including the financialization of capi-tal, contributed to growing structural unemployment, escalating inequality, and major disruptions in established ways of life and livelihood for workers worldwide. Finally, in both periods, the take-off of the financial fix went hand in hand with major employer antilabor offensives and a decline of labor unrest. In the late nineteenth century, this decline was short-lived. In the first half of the twentieth century, growing grievances and the strength-ening structural bargaining power of workers (at the point of production and in world politics) combined to produce powerful waves of Marx-type and Polanyi-type labor unrest (see Chapters 1 and 4). These upsurges of labor unrest, in turn, played a key role in forcing the world's elites to imple-ment major political and social–economic reforms at the global level (see Chapter 4).

---

[4] The financial fix and the shift in international regimes are *critical* explanatory factors because they are the two elements that distinguish the late-nineteenth- and late-twentieth-century periods of globalization from the thirty to forty years following the Second World War. As we argued in Chapter 4, the Golden Age of Capitalism in the 1950s and 1960s was characterized by continual spatial, technological, and product fixes that weakened labor movements at specific points in time and space, but that overall produced a trend of labor movement strengthening that lasted until the 1970s. The turning point was in the 1980s, with the intertwined take-off of the financial fix and dismantling of the labor-friendly international regime.

V. A New Labor Internationalism?

The analogies between the late nineteenth century and late twentieth century raise the question of whether we can also expect the contemporary decline of labor unrest to be short-lived (or at least temporary). Indeed, many observers see signs of a mounting backlash in the anti-globalization demonstrations in Seattle and beyond. The belief in TINA ("there is no alternative") has been fundamentally shaken, and proposals for a fundamental labor-friendly transformation of the world political and social–economic regime are being forcefully put forward. What are the chances that a new labor-friendly international regime will be established? And what are the chances that such a regime will come out of (and substantively reflect) a genuine labor internationalism? These are the questions to which we turn in the next and concluding section.

V. A New Labor Internationalism?

The late-nineteenth- and early-twentieth-century period of globalization was associated not only with rising and explosive labor unrest but also with the eventual collapse of the Second International and two world wars. The collapse of labor internationalism, we argued, was closely related to imperialism and the socialization of the state, processes that tied the security of workers' livelihoods to the power of their nation-states. With the late-twentieth-century trend toward the de-socialization of the state, are the underlying conditions becoming more favorable to the flourishing of labor internationalism?

In answering this question, another parallel between the two periods of globalization is instructive. In both periods national-protectionism with racist and xenophobic overtones has been an important part of the reaction by workers (and others) to the dislocations provoked by an unregulated global labor market.[5] In Chapter 1, we suggested that there is no reason to expect that just because capital finds it profitable to treat all workers as interchangeable equivalents, workers would themselves find it in their interests to accept this. Rather, insecure human beings (including workers), have good reason to insist on the salience of nonclass boundaries and borders (e.g., race, citizenship, gender) as a way of making claims for privileged protection from the maelstrom. The de-socialization of the state thus does

---

[5] In this regard, the parallels between the U.S. labor movement's stance toward China and the Chinese in the late nineteenth and late twentieth centuries is striking (see Silver and Arrighi 2000; Saxton 1971; Cockburn 2000).

not in itself supply fertile ground for labor internationalism to take root. Indeed, one could argue that the living standards of First World workers today are less dependent on the ability of their states to fight interimperialist wars than on their ability to keep out competition from Third World labor by imposing import and immigration restrictions.

World labor unrest in the twentieth century, we argued in Chapter 4, has been embedded in a pendulum swing between crises of profitability and crises of social legitimacy. The crisis of profitability marked by the Great Depression of the late nineteenth century was resolved through a series of fixes that undermined livelihoods and established ways of life throughout the world. The outcome was a deep crisis of social legitimacy and a vicious circle of mounting labor unrest, revolutionary crises, and world war. After a half century of increasing systemic chaos, the postwar social contracts involved an explicit recognition that workers had to be protected from unregulated global market forces. Although profits were never completely subordinated to livelihood, there was a widespread recognition that unless capitalism could be shown to be capable of providing physical and economic security, it would not survive the growing revolutionary challenges from below. Workers could not be treated as simple commodities to be used or left unused according to market forces. Nevertheless, such a philosophical and policy stance by the 1970s had come to be seen as a growing fetter on profits, and in the 1980s it was abandoned by the world's elites. The world-scale dislocations of established ways of life and livelihood caused by this late-twentieth-century swing toward unregulated markets is once again producing a deep crisis of social legitimacy for world capitalism. Whether the crisis of social legitimacy is (will become) sufficiently troublesome to the world's elites so as to provoke a new swing of the pendulum back toward an emphasis on livelihood and security remains to be seen.

Nevertheless, the analysis carried forward in this book makes it clear that the global social contracts of the postwar era did not provide a stable solution, either for labor or for capital, and that, moreover, a simple return to the past is impossible. For in promising to meet the aspirations of the escalating workers' and nationalist movements of the period, the U.S.-sponsored global regime fudged several issues. The ideology of unlimited growth that underpinned the global New Deal meant that, for a time, both the capitalist limits and the environmental limits of the mass-consumption social and developmentalist contracts could be ignored. The combined profitability and environmental crises of the 1970s (loudly signaled by the oil price shocks of the decade) revealed the limits inherent in the world-hegemonic promises made. Moreover, decades of industrialization and development – the alleged prerequisite to Third World workers' entry into the Age of High Mass Consumption – had by the end of the American Century only consolidated world inequalities in income and resource use/abuse. While the overlap between the racial and wealth divides on a world-scale has been consolidated, environmental degradation has proceeded at a pace and scale unprecedented in human history. Thus the ultimate challenge faced by the workers of the world in the early twenty-first century is the struggle, not just against one's own exploitation and exclusion, but for an international regime that truly subordinates profits to the livelihood of all.

The World Labor Group Database: Conceptualization, Measurement, and Data Collection Procedures

The World Labor Group (WLG) database is one of the key empirical sources used in this book to document world-historical patterns of labor unrest. This database originates in a collective research effort by a group of graduate students and faculty (The World Labor Research Working Group) at the Fernand Braudel Center (Binghamton University) in the 1980s. The outcome of the group's work was published as a special issue of *Review* – hereafter referred to as "the special issue" (see Silver, Arrighi, and Dubofsky 1995). The present author subsequently expanded and updated the database produced in the first phase of the project.

This appendix describes the WLG data collection project including issues of conceptualization, measurement, and data collection procedures (see Silver 1995a in the special issue for a more in-depth treatment of these issues). The next section discusses the conceptualization of labor unrest used by the World Labor Group (see also Chapter 1). The second section discusses measurement issues, the third section discusses data collection procedures, and the fourth section discusses the outcome of various reliability studies. Finally, Appendix B reproduces the data collection instructions used for compiling the WLG database.

I. The Concept of World-Scale Labor Unrest

Efforts to gain an adequate picture of the long-term, world-scale patterns of labor unrest face special problems of conceptualization and measurement. Workers' resistance has taken a variety of forms over the space and time of the world economy. While it might at first seem intuitively obvious, the concept of labor unrest as a world-historical phenomenon and how one might go about measuring it are far from obvious. In Chapter 1, we discussed the broad conceptualization of labor unrest used here, taking off from Marx's and Polanyi's conceptualizations of labor power as a "fictitious commodity." Here we focus on clarifying concretely the types of actions that would be included and excluded in a collection of labor unrest events built on this conceptualization. In so doing, we focus on two distinct components of the labor unrest concept in turn – *labor* and *unrest*.

Labor Unrest

What makes *labor* unrest distinctive from other forms of social unrest is that it is rooted in the proletarian condition; that is, it is composed of the resistances and reactions by human beings to being treated as a commodity. The resistances that encompass *labor* unrest include both:

(a) struggles against being treated as a commodity at the point of production (i.e., Marx's focus on the struggle over the extraction of surplus labor); and

(b) struggles against being treated as a commodity on the labor market (i.e., Polanyi's focus on the struggles for protection against the ravages of the self-regulating market system).

Labor unrest includes resistance to commodification by:

(a) workers who have been thoroughly proletarianized and who struggle without any thought of escaping wage labor, and

(b) workers who are only recently or partially proletarianized and who struggle with the aim of escaping the proletarian condition.

In sum, the relevant actors included in the concept of *labor* unrest are all those reacting against the effects of the commodification of their labor power.

The commodification of labor power creates a wide arena of struggles:

(a) resistance to the prolongation, intensification, and degradation of work at the point of production;

(b) resistance to low or falling real wages and mass unemployment on the labor market; and

(c) resistance to forced proletarianization and the destruction of customary ways of life, whether through the direct use of violence or the destruction of alternatives to wage labor.

I. Conceptualizing World-Scale Labor Unrest

The targets of these acts of resistance to the proletarian condition are varied.

(a) *They may target the employer directly* – strikes, slowdowns, or sabotage to protest the prolongation, intensification, or degradation of work; similar actions aimed at raising wages or establishing an internal labor market that protects the firm's workers against the vicissitudes of the labor market; machine-wrecking, land occupations by landless agricultural workers, or desertions to the nonwage rural sector by workers seeking to escape the proletarian condition.

(b) *They may target the state* – seek to achieve their aims by eliciting state intervention on their behalf (or by stopping pro-capitalist state intervention). Such acts of resistance include demonstrations, general strikes and other forms of agitation on behalf of policies restricting the length of the working day or regulating other conditions of work at the point of production. They also include similar acts aimed at eliciting state action designed to lessen the impact of a "formally free" labor market such as a legal minimum wage, government spending to create employment, or basic food subsidies. Likewise included are community revolts and revolutions against states (particularly colonial states) perceived as assisting in the forced creation of a proletariat through the willful destruction of established (non-capitalist) means of livelihood through taxation, enclosures, or military campaigns.

Thus, the proletarian condition produces a wide range of resistances traceable to the negative effects of the commodification of labor power. These forms of resistance constitute, as a set of social actions, the category of *labor unrest*.

Historically, however, workers are embedded in ethnic, religious, national, and gender communities/identities, and the solidarities that bind them are often those of such communities. The "banners" raised in struggles are often those of communal identification rather than specifically those of working-class identification. In some cases, the overlap between class and ethnicity, nationality, or gender is so close that struggles taking place under a communal banner can be easily identified as *labor* unrest (i.e., as struggles against the proletarian condition). In other cases, however, workers make alliances with other classes and their struggles become merged (sometimes submerged) in cross-class struggles that receive some of their momentum from resistances to the proletarian condition but that become difficult to

183

label comfortably as *labor* unrest. In these cases, we are confronted by a practical difficulty since we do not want to ignore the proletarian component, but we do not want to include the nonproletarian component within our concept of *labor* unrest. Such movements, then, must be kept in a separate intermediate category, neither simply included nor simply excluded from the study of *labor* unrest.

Labor *Unrest*

Before we proceed with a discussion of measurement issues, we must further specify the *unrest* component of our concept. As discussed in the previous section, labor unrest is composed of acts of resistance by human beings to being turned into and/or treated as commodities. Many of these acts of resistance are easily identifiable as labor *unrest* because the actors themselves openly declare that their purpose is to challenge and/or contain exploitation. Certain kinds of open protests (e.g., strikes, boycotts, riots, demonstrations) combined with certain kinds of open demands (e.g., increased wages, decreased work loads, government subsidization of basic food and transportation, full-employment) are easily identifiable as acts of labor unrest.

However, there is a whole other sphere of hidden acts of resistance (undeclared and unacknowledged class warfare), which precisely because it remains undeclared is often not easily identifiable as unrest. These acts of resistance are what James Scott (1985) has dubbed "the weapons of the weak" or "everyday forms of resistance" (e.g., foot dragging, soldiering, shoddy workmanship, undeclared slowdowns, pilfering, false compliance, desertion, absenteeism, feigned ignorance, slander, sabotage, "accidents"). According to Scott (1985: 33):

What everyday forms of resistance share with more dramatic public confrontations is of course that they are intended to mitigate or deny any claims made by superordinate classes or to advance claims vis-à-vis those superordinate classes . . . Where everyday resistance most strikingly departs from other forms of resistance is in its implicit disavowal of public and symbolic goals. Where institutionalized politics is formal, overt, concerned with systematic, de jure change, everyday resistance is informal, often covert, and concerned largely with immediate de facto gains.

The masking of de facto resistance with apparent acquiescence and conformity often leads observers to overlook these forms of unrest. However, these forms have been found to be pervasive in situations ranging from the labor-coercive economy of the Rhodesian mines studied by Van Onselen (1976) to the Ford assembly line studied by Beynon (1973) and the Hungarian machine shop studied by Harazti (1977).

Basing himself on the African labor studies literature, Cohen (1980: 12–17) enumerated a wide range of "hidden forms of resistance." These include desertion (to the nonwage sector or systematic labor turnover within the wage sector); community withdrawal or revolt to escape proletarianization;[1] task, time, and efficiency bargaining (e.g., quota restrictions, soldiering, bamboozling the time-and-motion men); and sabotage (to give workers a break from the machine-driven pace of work or to forestall the introduction of labor-saving and job-eliminating new machinery). We also include all these acts of resistance within our concept of labor unrest when they are widespread, collective practices.

However, Cohen included in his concept of hidden forms of resistance actions by workers that are not consciously intended to be acts of resistance. Thus, he argued that sickness and accidents, even when *not* acts of volition, "do indeed constitute forms of resistance" because they are responses to unacceptable working and living conditions (1980: 18–19). Here we must depart. Our concept of labor unrest only includes *purposeful* (although not necessarily openly declared) acts of resistance by workers to the commodification of their labor power.

Finally, among his hidden forms of resistance, Cohen also included the creation of a contraculture by workers, drug use, and belief in otherworldly solutions. Here we must say "it all depends on the context." That is, in some contexts, these are indeed forms of labor *unrest* or resistance; in other contexts, they are merely forms of adaptation to the commodification of labor. It depends on whether these acts function as part of efforts to resist exploitation or as part of efforts to forget about exploitation.[2] Thus, religion may be the "opium of the masses" (e.g., exploitation at work can be tolerated because the meek will be rewarded in an afterlife), or it may provide community networks and a counterideology of justice and struggle for the oppressed (e.g., the active church role in the workers' struggles in Poland and Brazil). Likewise, alcohol and drugs may be the "opium of the masses" (making hard labor and authoritarian relations at work easier to withstand), or it may be part of a general resistance to giving employers the effective use

---

[1] This is hidden only in the sense that it is often interpreted as wars of pacification or proto-nationalism, with its labor component ignored.

[2] Cohen himself is ambiguous about whether these always constitute resistance.

of the commodity labor-power (as absenteeism and shoddy workmanship take their toll). Similar distinctions apply to contracultures.

Hirschman's (1970) categories of exit, voice, and loyalty are helpful in further clarifying our concept of labor *unrest*. Hirschman (1970: 30) defined "voice" as any "attempt to change, rather than escape from an objectionable state of affairs." Our concept of labor *unrest* includes all acts that can be classified as voice. Hirschman (1970: 4–5) argued that both voice and certain forms of "exit" play a "recuperative role": They make capitalists aware that changes in the way of doing business are necessary if they are to survive. Our concept of labor *unrest* includes all those forms of resistance that play a recuperative or transformatory role. Apart from voice, these include certain types of exit and everyday forms of resistance. These are discussed next, in turn.

The types of exit included are: (1) attempts to escape proletarianization through collective revolt or desertion (noisy exit); and (2) attempts to improve wages or working conditions through systematic turnover in situations of labor shortage (voiceless exit). Systematic turnover in a situation of labor shortage is often recognized by capitalists as a form of worker resistance and as a problem that requires an active and transformatory response. Examples range from Ford's Five Dollar Day to the elimination of racial restrictions on residence in South Africa. Conversely, exit/migration out of labor-surplus firms or regions is not included in our concept of labor unrest. The workers' exit is not experienced *relationally* as resistance to exploitation. There is no significant "recuperative" (or transformatory) impact on the firms or areas from which the surplus workers depart.

The everyday forms of resistance discussed earlier can be categorized as *feigned* loyalty. These acts involve the purposeful muting of one's critical opinions and a roundabout resistance to exploitation. This roundaboutness and muting of open protest is a result of the weakness of the subordinate groups and the ability of the dominant groups to impose severe sanctions on those who do not obey. According to Hirschman (1970: 96–7), when organizations make the price of both exit and voice (protest) too high through the threat of severe sanctions (e.g., loss of livelihood, loss of life), "they also largely deprive themselves of both recuperative mechanisms." In other words, the resistances of the weak, given that they are masked by feigned loyalty, do not send signals about the need for change to capitalists; that is, they do not set off the processes of restructuring of social and economic relations that characterize the impact of more overt forms of protest.

I. Conceptualizing World-Scale Labor Unrest

Hirschman's argument probably holds true when hidden forms of labor unrest are scattered and sporadic individual acts; however, when they reach a widespread and pathological level, we would argue that unmistakable signals are indeed sent to employers about the need for restructuring. One relevant example would be the widespread drunkenness, absenteeism, and shoddy workmanship that plagued Soviet enterprises in the 1970s and 1980s. It could be argued that these forms of labor unrest, rather than more overt protests, were critical in prompting the initial revolution from above (*perestroika*). Thus, our concept of labor unrest includes the "weapons of the weak" *when these forms of resistance are widespread, collective practices*, but it excludes these same acts if they are deemed to be isolated and sporadic individual acts.

Finally, acts of labor *unrest* are generally acts of *inter-class* (labor–capital) struggle (i.e., unrest directed against capitalists or against the state as an intermediary or as an agent of capital). However, as was discussed earlier, workers are embedded in ethnic, religious, national, and gender communities/identities. These identities may be incorporated into mobilizing slogans, or they may be used to build cross-class alliances. However, they may also be used to mobilize one group of workers (e.g., whites, men) against competition from another group of workers (e.g., Blacks, women). In these cases, workers' struggles are directed against other workers (e.g., job demarcation strikes by white/male workers protesting the employment of Black/women workers). However, these struggles are also directed against the capitalists. They seek to restrict the ability of the capitalist to treat all workers as equal commodities. Thus, however unsympathetic, they will be counted as forms of labor unrest.

What then about movements that produce racist cross-class alliances (e.g., apartheid) or, for that matter, alliances between workers and capitalists such as those between the U.S. textile or autoworkers and their respective bosses agitating for restrictions on foreign competition for their industry? Like the cross-class movements discussed in the previous section (e.g., national liberation movements), these movements are impossible to label simply as labor unrest, but at the same time we do not want to ignore their proletarian component. Thus, they must also be treated as part of an "intermediate" category of multiclass movements that can be neither simply included nor simply excluded from our analyses.

To sum up, the concept of labor unrest that we aim to measure is composed of all the (observable) resistances and reactions by human beings to being treated as a commodity, both at the point of production and in the labor market. It includes all consciously intended, open acts of resistance. It also includes hidden forms of resistance when these are widespread, collective practices. Finally, the concept of labor unrest includes acts by workers who organize themselves under communal banners other than labor, when there is a clear overlap between class and community, and when the struggle is directed at resisting the proletarian condition.

II. The Measurement of World-Scale Labor Unrest

This section first discusses the limits of previously existing data sources on labor unrest before moving on to a discussion of the advantages and disadvantages of using newspapers as a source on world labor unrest.

The Uses and Abuses of Official Strike Statistics

Government-collected strike statistics are the most commonly used indicator of labor unrest or labor militancy. Strike statistics have much to recommend them, but there are several major difficulties involved in relying solely (or even mainly) on strike statistics in a study of labor unrest – especially one that seeks to analyze labor unrest as integral to the processes of long-term, world-historical social change.

The meaning of a strike is considerably different at different points in time and space. Strikes that occur in a time and place where they are illegal cannot be easily equated with a strike in a time and place where they have become legal, routine, and routinized. Yet, strike statistics necessarily make this equation. The following example illustrates the problem. There was a historically high level of strike activity in the United States in the 1950s and 1960s; most observers, however, attributed this fact to the institutionalization of labor–capital conflict after the Second World War. The official strike became accepted as a normal bargaining tool in contract negotiations. Thus, a large volume of strikes is not necessarily an indication of a correspondingly large volume of labor unrest. Treating a strike in Franco's Spain as indicative of roughly the same "amount" of labor unrest as a strike in the 1960s United States (or 1990s Spain for that matter) is a dubious equation and procedure.[3]

---

[3] Along these same lines, Piven and Cloward (1992) have complained of a widespread tendency to conflate such routine and nonnormative collective action in the social science literature on protest.

Moreover, as discussed in Section I, the strike is far from the only or even main form in which labor unrest is expressed. Labor unrest may manifest itself primarily in nonstrike forms of struggle ranging from slowdowns and sabotage to riots and demonstrations. The prevalence of nonstrike forms of struggle may be especially significant at two ends of a spectrum: that is, they may be especially prevalent where strikes are illegal and open confrontation impossible or where strikes have become routinized and generally meaningless as a significant form of struggle against the proletarian condition. Thus, the assumption (frequently made) that strikes can serve as a proxy indicator for all forms of labor unrest is unacceptable and potentially quite misleading.

Finally, strike statistics are often collected according to criteria that exclude what may be very relevant strikes from the point of view of measuring labor unrest. For example, most countries at one time or another have excluded "political strikes" from their official count of strike activity. Yet, as was discussed in Section I, workers frequently make demands on the state (e.g., through political strikes) as part of their efforts to resist the proletarian condition.

Beyond the question of whether strike counts are good indicators of labor unrest, there is perhaps a more obvious problem in using strike statistics in studies of long-term, world-historical social change. This limitation is the insufficient temporal and geographical scope of existing strike series data. Only a handful of countries have data series that date back to the beginning of the twentieth century. For most countries, there are no strike statistics at all, or they begin only after the Second World War. Furthermore, with the exception of the United Kingdom, all countries' series contain major gaps (e.g., during the period of fascism and world war for Germany, France, and Italy or for a period in the early twentieth century when the U.S. government decided to discontinue strike data collection). Moreover, data collections covering nonstrike forms of unrest are even more rare.[4]

Some studies attempt to skirt the difficulties involved in the limited geographical scope of strike statistics by (implicitly or explicitly) assuming that it is possible to generalize from national cases (for which data are available) to other countries or even the world. Many studies have raised questions about the wisdom of making generalizations about so-called advanced

---

[4] For works that discuss the methodological problems involved in the collection and use of official strike statistics, see Edwards (1981), Hyman (1972), Jackson (1987), Knowles (1952), Shalev (1978), and Franzosi (1995), among others.

industrial countries (e.g., Korpi and Shalev 1979). Generalizing from this group of countries to rest of the world would seem to be an even more dubious practice.

Moreover, as discussed in Chapter 1, proceeding on the basis of national case studies forces us to assume that each case evolves in isolation from the other cases. If, as we assume, a single set of world-level processes link workers in different parts of the globe, then the only acceptable way of proceeding is by building up a picture of the functioning of the system as a whole in order to understand (or forecast) the trajectory of each case. We need to build up a picture of the patterning of labor unrest over time for the world-economy as a whole to be able to proceed with our work.

Thus, we find ourselves without a readily available indicator of labor unrest, which would be acceptable for the study of long-term, world-historical social change.

Newspapers as a Source of Reliable Information

Faced with these difficulties, the World Labor Research Working Group at the Fernand Braudel Center decided to create a new database on world labor unrest. This database has been compiled from reports of labor unrest in *The Times* (London) and the *New York Times* – the major newspapers of the two world hegemonic powers of the nineteenth and twentieth centuries.

Tapping major newspapers as a source to construct indexes of protest has become a fairly widespread and developed practice in the social sciences.[5] As Burstein (1985: 202) wrote: "In recent years ... a small but growing group of social scientists has concluded that valid time-series data on many of the more visible aspects of politics could be collected by drawing on an obvious but hitherto untapped data source – major newspapers." Burstein collected data on civil rights demonstrations and other protest activities from the *New York Times* and concluded that the data from this source "convey a generally accurate picture of the events and time trends analyzed ... and are far better than any other actual or potentially available data." Likewise, the Tillys (1975: 315) concluded from their study of collective violence in

---

[5] Burstein (1985), Danzger (1975), Jenkins and Perrow (1977), Koopmans (1993), Korzeniewicz (1989), Kowalewski (1993), McAdam (1982), Paige (1975), Snyder and Kelly (1977), Snyder and Tilly (1972), Sugimoto (1978a, 1978b), Tarrow (1989), Tilly (1978, 1981), and Tilly et al. (1975) are among those who have used the newspapers to construct indexes of protest. On methodological issues, see Franzosi (1987, 1990).

II. Measuring World-Scale Labor Unrest

France that "the newspaper scanning provides a more comprehensive and uniform sample of events than any alternative source available to us."

These studies use information gleaned from national newspapers to measure occurrences of protest within that state. What is innovative about the World Labor Group's project is that we attempted to create reliable indicators of *world-level* labor unrest from newspaper reports. We rejected the route of aggregating information from national newspapers. The amount of work involved in reading and recording all reports of labor unrest over the last century from a major national newspaper for *each* country of the world was simply beyond reason. Moreover, even if the data collection effort were feasible, intractable problems of comparability of data sources would arise in attempting to combine the information retrieved from many different national sources into a single world indicator. Our solution has been to rely on the major newspapers of the world's hegemonic powers. Our reasoning was as follows:

1. *The Times* (London) and the *New York Times* have had world-level information-collecting capabilities throughout the twentieth century. As a result, geographical bias rooted in the technological limits of newspaper reporting during the period of our research is not a major problem, especially with regard to *The Times* (London) (see Dangler 1995 in the special issue).
2. Our choice of *The Times* (London) and the *New York Times* was also intended to minimize the problem of geographical bias in reporting due to editorial policies (as opposed to technological constraints). World hegemonic powers, by definition, take the entire world as their sphere of interest or influence. The reporting of both sources is global (see Dangler 1995 and Appendix B in the special issue).
3. While the reporting of both newspapers is global, both also show regional biases, apparently in favor of areas that have historically been considered spheres of influence or interest, for example, South Asia and Australia for *The Times* (London) and Latin America for the *New York Times* (see Appendix B in the special issue). By combining the two sources into a single indicator of world labor unrest, we may counterbalance the regional biases of each source taken separately.[6]

---

[6] Moreover, the regional biases appear to be less significant when it comes to reporting labor unrest waves. Both sources tend to report on waves of unrest, even for countries where their routine coverage is not extensive.

In sum, the World Labor Research Working Group began with the premise that reliable indicators of world-scale patterning of labor unrest could be constructed from *The Times* (London) and the *New York Times*. Section IV summarizes the results of reliability studies carried out on the World Labor Group database in order to either validate or invalidate this claim. First, however, we will describe the steps taken to create the World Labor Research Working Group Database on Labor Unrest.

III. Data Collection Procedures

Individual members of the research group read the indexes of *The Times* (London) and the *New York Times* to identify reports of labor unrest.[7] A first round of data collection covered the *New York Times* from 1870 to 1990 and *The Times* (London) from 1906 to 1990. In a second phase of the project, the database was updated in the same manner through 1996. In addition, during this second round, the Palmer's Index (on-line) was used as a source of reports on labor unrest in *The Times* (London) from 1870 to 1905, since the official index to *The Times* only begins in 1906.[8]

For each report of labor unrest found in the newspapers' indexes, we recorded onto a specially designed standard recording form the month, day,

---

[7] Several measures were taken to ensure that the collection of labor unrest mentions from the indexes was as complete and accurate as possible. The central difficulty was in achieving completeness: relevant mentions of labor unrest might be buried throughout the index (under country, industry, or other subject headings). Moreover, the organization of the indexes varied for each newspaper source across time. A first stage in the data collection process, thus, involved a series of tests and revisions of coding procedures; the data recording instructions were successively refined so as to maximize inter-coder reproducibility of results. Inter-coder reliability assessments were also used as part of the training procedure for coders.

Second, despite our very limited resources, we decided to assign two data collectors, working independently, to each year of the *New York Times* index to maximize the thoroughness of the search for labor unrest mentions. When the collection of data from the newspaper index for a given year was completed by both coders, coding sheets were compared and combined so that all the citations identified by either or both coders were included in the database. A measure similar to Burstein's (1985: 211–12) "inclusion reliability" was used to assess both the performance of individual coders and the reliability of individual years. We used the ongoing assessments of individual coder performance in making coding assignments. That is, we tried to ensure that at least one "high-confidence" coder was assigned to each year. Because of our limited resources, this complete duplication of the data collection work was not possible for *The Times* (London) index. Nevertheless, the present author was responsible for almost the entire London *Times* series, thus strengthening our confidence in the relative completeness and consistency of *The Times* database.

[8] The data-recording instructions used in the project are reproduced as Appendix B. In addition a prepackaged training kit was developed and used to both train and evaluate coders.

III. Data Collection Procedures

year, page and column of the article, the location of the action (country, city), the action-type (e.g., strike, riot), and the industry or industries involved.[9]

Reports on labor unrest in all countries of the world were recorded, with one exception. Because of the totally disproportionate criteria for reporting on domestic news, incidents of labor unrest in the United States and the United Kingdom were not recorded from the *New York Times* and *The Times*, respectively. Instead, we relied on the U.S. coverage of *The Times* (London) and the U.K. coverage of the *New York Times*, for our U.S. and U.K. data.

The end result of the first two phases of the project was a complete census of all mentions of labor unrest around the world in the indexes. Specifically, the database covers from 1870 to 1996 for both the *New York Times* and *The Times* (London).[10] To put it concretely, we have recorded onto our standard form a total of 91,947 mentions of labor unrest around the world, with information on the year, action-type, country, city, and industry for each, as well as the article, page, date, and column number.[11]

---

[9] The recording unit used is the "mention" of labor unrest by the index. Thus, for example, the same strike may be mentioned several times because it is reported on in several articles. Each mention (corresponding to a different article) was recorded and counted separately. Likewise, a single article may report on a number of different acts of labor unrest (e.g., several strikes in different locations, a strike *plus* a riot in the same location). Each action, even if reported on in the same article, is recorded and counted separately. If, on the other hand, the index repeated the same exact information twice at two different spots in the index, the duplicate was eliminated from the database. The assumption underlying this data-recording procedure is that more intense acts of labor unrest will be reported on more frequently than less intense acts. Our procedure, thus, gives more weight to an action that is mentioned in two or more articles than an action that is only mentioned once. It would be possible at some future date to aggregate mentions into separate events; however, this would be a very labor-intensive project. Since, for this book, the data are only being used to identify major waves of labor unrest, rather than study specific event sequences in depth, there would be no particular payoff to such an effort.

[10] The *New York Times* is based entirely on the official index, while *The Times* (London) is based on a combination of Palmer's Index (on-line) for 1870–1905 and the official index from 1906 to 1996.

[11] For this stage of the project, we relied on the newspapers' indexes as the source. The assumption is that the newspapers' indexes accurately reflect the contents of the newspaper, or that errors are sufficiently random so as not to have any significant effect on our overall results. Comparisons of sample years coded from the indexes and from the newspapers on microfilm and through the Nexis electronic archive indicate: (1) recording information from the indexes results in a slight undercounting of the number of articles with mentions of labor unrest; (2) this undercounting seems to be consistent across time and space, thus having no significant effect on the types of indicators we are constructing from the data at this point; (3) the time-savings involved in identifying labor unrest mentions from the indexes rather than from the newspapers on microfilm is significant (cutting the time by at least one-half); (4) at this point, the lost information is not sufficient to warrant the

This information was then entered into two computer files, one file for the mentions from the *New York Times* and one for those from *The Times* (London). Two time series of mentions were created for each country[12] – one based on each newspaper. For the analyses in this book, these two series were then combined into a single series for each country – the number of mentions of labor unrest being the sum of the two sources for each year. Figures 4.1, 4.2 and 4.3 as well as Table 4.1 are based on the resulting 1870–1996 time series.

Figures 2.1, 3.3, and 3.4 as well as Tables 2.1, 3.1, and 3.2 disaggregate the combined time series by country and/or industry. Country and industry codes were assigned to each of the 91,947 mentions of labor unrest and disaggregated country and industry time series were created. For Tables 2.1, 3.1, and 3.2, industry- and country-specific high points of labor unrest were identified using the criteria spelled out in Chapter 2 (footnotes 1 and 3) and Chapter 3 (footnote 5).

IV. Assessing the Reliability of the World Labor Group Database

It is necessary to emphasize that the data collection project was not designed to produce a count of *all or even most incidents* of labor unrest that have taken place in the world over the last century. The newspapers report on only a small fraction of the labor unrest that occurs. Instead, the procedure is intended to produce a measure that reliably indicates *the changing levels* of labor unrest – when the incidence of labor unrest is rising or falling, when it is high or low – *relative to* other points in time or locations in space.[13] In

increased time commitment necessary to collect the data from the newspapers on microfilm. Finally, although the Nexis and microfilm searches yield more information, the index search nevertheless often uncovered important citations that eluded multiple attempts with complex Nexis search-strings.

12 Names and boundaries of countries as they existed in 1990 are used throughout. In the cases where names and/or borders were different at some time in the past, an effort was made to identify the exact location (e.g., city, region) of the labor unrest and to group those mentions together with the "country" of which that area is now a part. Thus, for example, strikes that were indexed under the heading "Austro-Hungarian Empire" were counted as part of Hungary if they took place in Budapest and as part of Austria if they took place in Vienna. Likewise, 1990 borders have so far been retained for post 1990 data, despite the recent major wave of border changes.

13 The number of incidents of labor unrest recorded in the database in any given year has no absolute meaning; rather its meaning (high/low, rising/falling) is relative to the number of reported incidents in other years.

particular we are interested in being able to identify *waves* or high points of labor unrest across the time and space of the world economy.

Reliability studies for seven countries are reported on in the special issue. Wave years of labor unrest for each country were identified using two different criteria, which are modified versions of the method used to calculate strike waves by Shorter and Tilly (1974).[14] To qualify as a wave year:

1. The number of mentions of labor unrest in that year had to be at least 50 percent greater than the average of the preceding five years and
2. The number of mentions of labor unrest in that year had to be greater than the mean number of mentions for that country over the entire eighty-five-year period. (At the time these studies were carried out the series stopped in 1990.)

Reliability studies were carried out by members of the research team on the basis of the key years identified. The picture of labor unrest derived from the World Labor Group database was compared with the picture derived from other existing sources (the labor history literature and any available statistical series) for seven countries (Argentina, China, Egypt, Germany, Italy, South Africa, and the United States). These reliability studies are presented in Part II of the special issue. They provide strong support for the contention that the newspapers of the world's hegemonic powers can be used to create reliable indicators of the actual incidence of labor unrest waves across the time and space of the world economy.

More specifically, the central strength of the World Labor Group database appears to be its fairly consistent ability to identify labor unrest waves within individual countries – and in particular those waves of labor unrest that represent turning points in the history of labor–capital relations. This reliability in identifying turning-point waves of unrest is tied to the particular characteristics of newspapers as a source for sociohistorical data: that is, the newspapers' bias against reporting routine events (such as institutionalized strike activity) and their bias in favor of reporting labor unrest that is not routine – "not just from a quantitative point of view, but

---

[14] The procedures used to identify major waves (high points) of labor unrest and to aggregate the time series of the two newspaper sources are slightly different in the special issue (see Silver 1995a) and this book. The procedures used in this book do not produce significant differences in the years singled out as major waves (high points) of labor unrest (and have the added advantage of being far less cumbersome). The results of the reliability studies thus apply to the data elaborations in both the special issue and this book.

as watersheds in labor–capital relations" (Arrighi 1995 in the special issue). Thus, the World Labor Group indicator correctly identifies as waves virtually all those years that are generally agreed to have been major quantitative or qualitative turning points in labor unrest for the countries examined in Part II of the special issue.

One systematic bias that requires caution does emerge from the country studies in Part II of the special issue. The World Labor Group indicator underestimates the severity of labor unrest in the immediate post–Second World War years for several of the countries studied. For China, Egypt and the United States, the immediate postwar years qualify as labor unrest waves, but the relative number of labor unrest mentions is smaller than expected in relation to other wave years in the century. And for South Africa, the World Labor Group does not identify 1946 as a wave year, although it is generally acknowledged to be a wave year based on other sources. The explanation is fairly straightforward: *The Times* (London) experienced a severe paper shortage in the immediate postwar years and cut back on the number of pages (and therefore the extensiveness of its reporting). Fortunately, the *New York Times* did not experience any similar constraints.

Another major strength of the World Labor Group database is the fact that it includes all the diverse forms of labor unrest. This means that our indicator is able to identify correctly the years of the major waves of labor unrest that are sometimes excluded or undervalued by official strike statistics. Nevertheless, it seems reasonable to expect (intuitively and from the experience of other researchers) that the newspapers will exhibit a systematic bias in favor of reporting incidents of labor unrest that are more openly confrontational (as opposed to hidden), use more violent (as opposed to nonviolent) tactics, and/or have larger (as opposed to smaller) numbers of participants (see, e.g., Snyder and Kelly 1977). Thus, although we have not yet done a study of the distribution of unrest by types of action, it is likely that many of the forms of labor unrest that we discussed under the category of weapons of the weak or hidden forms of resistance will be systematically underreported by our newspaper sources relative to the reporting of more open forms of resistance. As Scott (1985: 33–6) noted:

It is reasonably clear that the success of de facto resistance is often directly proportional to the symbolic conformity with which it is masked . . . The nature of the acts themselves and the self-interested muteness of the antagonists thus conspire to create a complicitous silence that all but expunges everyday forms of resistance from the historical record.

IV. Reliability of WLG Database

Our database cannot be used for a detailed study of hidden forms of resistance, but our experience has shown that when hidden acts of resistance reach pathological levels, they are indeed reported on by the newspapers. For example, employer complaints of widespread absenteeism, drunkenness on the job, and shoddy workmanship in the Soviet Union were in fact reported on by our two newspaper sources during the 1970s and 1980s.

In sum, while the WLG database, like all data sources, should be used with due caution, it has nevertheless proven to be a broadly reliable source for identifying world-scale patterns of labor unrest. It is unique in its geographical and temporal scope, opening up previously unavailable options for the empirical study of labor unrest as a world-historical phenomenon.

Instructions for Recording Data from Indexes

This appendix contains the instructions used by persons recording data from newspaper indexes. Examples of how to classify events, the introductory statement, and the lists of index headings to use as a guide in searching the index are not included here. The latter is a several-pages-long list of industries, countries, and other subject headings.

A. What Types of Reported Actions to Record

1. Record any action indicative of labor unrest (see definition).
2. "Labor" includes wage workers and the unemployed (it does not include peasants, students, soldiers, communists, etc., but it does include agricultural wage laborers). In the case of actions by the unemployed, write "unemployed" in the industry column of the coding sheet.
3. Record actions even if they are only rumored, threatened, or planned, or if the report is that the action is completed and over. Also record actions that have been cancelled.
4. Record even if the act is referred to in an editorial, is a report of persons commenting on the action, or an analysis of the impact of the action (e.g., on the nation's economy).
5. Reports of state action against labor should be recorded in the following way:
   (a) If the index clause mentions a government action *only*, record it if it is indicative of labor unrest (e.g., anti-strike legislation, arbitration);
   (b) If an index clause mentions *both* a labor action and a government action, do not record the government action unless:
       (i) The government action indicates a state of siege, coup d'état, or martial law in response to labor unrest (government sending

        in troops can be interpreted as martial law; arrests should not be);

   (ii) The government action involves violence (e.g., police clash with strikers).

     The intent of the foregoing rules is to record the government action on a separate line only if it is indicative of an escalation of a conflict involving labor. If you are unsure about how to code a government action, play it safe by recording it and writing out the exact words used in the index.

6. Do not record actions in the United States from the *New York Times* or ones in Great Britain from *The Times* (London).
7. Record acts in Puerto Rico, Ireland, and Northern Ireland from both indexes. Record on sheets separate from the United States and Great Britain, respectively.

B. Categories to Check in Newspaper Indexes

The entire index should be skimmed. Relevant entries can be found throughout. The following are the most likely categories under which relevant entries are found:

1. Labor
2. Labor unions
3. Strikes
4. Countries (read through index using attached list as advisory guide)
5. Industries (read through index using attached list as advisory guide)
6. Follow up all cross-references encountered

C. How to Use Data Recording Sheet

1. Use one coding sheet for each year for each country (unless there are more than thirty-five events for that country in a given year; if so, you will have to use more than one sheet).
2. Write your initials on top of sheet – after "coder."
3. Use one line of the coding sheet for each mention of an act of labor unrest. Thus, if there are two events reported in a single article (e.g., strike *and* riot; strike in auto *and* strike in mines) use two lines of the coding sheet.

4. Record an event *each* time there is a report on it, even if there is more than one article on that event in a given day, or if there are successive reports on the same event over a number of days, weeks, and so on.

5. The index page number should be recorded in the first column of the coding sheet; the date, page, and column number of the article should be recorded in the second column. The action type should be recorded in the third column, the location of the act in the fourth column, and the industry (if known) in the fifth column.

6. Record the country and year in the space provided at the top of the page.

D. Guidelines for the Recording of Action Types

1. General Strikes
   (a) Record as general strike whenever (and only when) the index uses the words "general strike."
   (b) If it is a general strike in a particular industry, be sure to record the industry under "industry/occupation."
   (c) One exception: if the index does not use the words "general strike," you may infer it is a general strike only with reasonably strong evidence. The following two cases constitute reasonably strong evidence:
      (i) The sandwich principle: report 1 – general strike called; report 2 – workers out; report 3 – general strike over. One may infer that report 2 is about a general strike.
      (ii) Immediate follow-up report: report 1 – general strike called in Bari; report 2 – workers out in Bari.
      Otherwise, record as a "strike," not as a "general strike."

2. Strikes. Record as strikes if the index refers to "strikes" without specifying what they are. However, if the index entry for the article specifies more than one specific strike (e.g., "auto, textile, and tramway workers strike,") record this on three separate lines, each as a "strike," and specify the industry for each of the three cases (i.e., 1 auto, 2 textile, 3 tramway).

3. Strike Wave. Record as "strike wave" if the index uses the words "wave of strikes" or "strike wave."

4. Strike
   (a) Strikes that do not fall into the above categories should be coded as "strike."

(b) If a single article mentions strikes in more than one industry, be sure to give a separate line on the coding sheet to each strike and specify each industry.

5. Riot
   (a) Record as a riot if the index specifies "riot."
   (b) Only record riots that are listed under labor or involve workers.
   (c) Exception: record bread riots, food riots, housing riots, and anti-IMF riots even if workers are not mentioned, *but* write out the words "bread riot," "housing riot," and so on. Do not just write "riot" or the abbreviation "R."
   (d) When the index reports an event where there is violence, do not code as "Riot" unless the word "riot" is used. Instead, use the index's exact wording (e.g., "strikers clash with police" or "violence at strike scene"). In addition, be sure to code two separate entries in such instances, i.e., on one line of the coding sheet record the "strike" and on the next line record the "violence" or "clash with police."

6. Unemployed Protest
   (a) Under action, record the action engaged in by the unemployed (e.g., demonstrate, riot).
   (b) Under industry, be sure to write "unemployed."

7. Protest, Dispute. Record as Protest or Dispute if the index uses the words "protest" or "dispute," respectively.

8. Demonstration. Record as demonstration if the index uses the word "demonstration." If the index uses the word "rally," you may record it as either rally or demonstration.

9. Lockout. Record lockout if the index uses the word "lockout."

10. "Weapons of the Weak." Record hidden forms of resistance such as absenteeism, shoddy workmanship, drunkenness or laziness *on the job*, using the abbreviation "WW" *and* then write out the action reported by the index.

11. Other Actions. Record any other relevant action not listed here by using the words used by the index.

12. Action-Type Abbreviations
    (a) Ten standard abbreviations for action types are listed at the bottom of the coding sheet.
    (b) If an action does not have a standard abbreviation, write out the action, taking from the index's wording.

(c) You may create your own abbreviations, but you *must* note what your abbreviations mean at the bottom of the coding sheet in the space provided for notes.

E. Guidelines for Recording Location

1. Country
   (a) Record country location of act in space provided at the top of the recording sheet.
   (b) Record under the geographical entity given by the index (give separate sheets to, for example, Alsace-Lorraine or Silesia when these are distinct entities in the index). Do not attempt to use your own judgment and knowledge in assigning these to particular countries.
2. Sub-national Location. Record the city or region in which the action takes place (using the wording of the index) in the fourth column.

F. Guidelines for Recording Industry

1. If the act is industry-specific and is indicated in the index, record this in column six using the wording of the index.
2. If it is an act by the unemployed, write "unemployed" in the industry column.

G. Inferences

There are situations where you should infer a specific action type from the context of the index citations surrounding it. For example, it is common to find a clause referring to a specific action (e.g., general strike) followed by clauses that obviously refer to the same general strike, but that do not use the words "general strike." In such cases, code the subsequent clauses as "general strike." The following is a relevant example.

These entries appear on successive days:

Entry 1 – general strike called.
Entry 2 – gov't–labor talks fail.
Entry 3 – state of emergency called after governor fails to end strike.
Entry 4 – strike is in 4th day.
Entry 5 – general strike continues.

Appendix B: Instructions for Recording Data

It is clear that each of these entries refers to the same general strike, particularly because they report on articles that appeared in the newspaper on successive days. Each entry should be recorded as "general strike." And, by the rule of government action given in foregoing Section A5, entry 3 should be given two lines: (1) GS and (2) state of emergency. Likewise, entry 2 should be given one line and recorded as GS.

APPENDIX C

Country Classifications

For Figures 4.2 and 4.3, a very broad rough classification of countries was used. Countries in North America (except Mexico), Europe (both east and west), and Australia and New Zealand were included in the metropolitan aggregate (Figure 4.2). Countries in Asia (east and south), North Africa and the Middle East, Latin America, and Africa were included in the colonial and semi-colonial aggregate (Figure 4.3).

Countries included in the metropolitan aggregate (Figure 4.2) (1990 names; countries with fewer than 100 labor unrest mentions in the WLG database not included in this list): North America (Canada, United States); Europe (Albania, Austria, Belgium, Bulgaria, Cyprus, Czechoslovakia, Denmark, Finland, France, Germany, Greece, Hungary, Iceland, Ireland, Italy, Malta, Netherlands, Norway, Poland, Portugal, Romania, Spain, Sweden, Switzerland, United Kingdom, USSR/Russia, Yugoslavia); Oceania (Australia, New Zealand).

Countries included in the colonial and semi-colonial aggregate (Figure 4.3) (1990 names; countries with fewer than 100 labor unrest mentions in the WLG database not included in this list): Middle East and North Africa (Algeria, Egypt, Iran, Israel, Lebanon, Morocco, Sudan, Tunisia, Turkey); Latin America (Argentina, Bolivia, Brazil, Chile, Colombia, Cuba, Dominican Republic, Ecuador, El Salvador, Guyana, Jamaica, Mexico, Nicaragua, Panama, Peru, Puerto Rico, Trinidad & Tobago, Uruguay, Venezuela); Africa (Ghana, Kenya, Nigeria, South Africa, Zambia, Zimbabwe); Asia (Bangladesh, Burma, China, Hong Kong, India, Japan, Korea, Malaysia, Pakistan, Philippines, Singapore, Sri Lanka).

Countries included in the world aggregate: Figure 4.1 includes all countries with mentions of labor unrest in the WLG database.

References

AAMA. 1995. *World Motor Vehicle Data, 1996 Edition*. Detroit: American Automobile Manufacturers Association.

Abbott, Andrew, and Stanley DeViney. 1992. "The Welfare State as Transnational Event: Evidence from Sequences of Policy Adoption." *Social Science History*, 16 (2), 245–74.

Abendroth, Wolfgang. 1972. *A Short History of the European Working Class*. New York: Monthly Review Press.

Abo, Tetsuo, ed. 1994. *Hybrid Factory: The Japanese Production System in the United States*. London: Oxford University Press.

Abrahamian, Ervand. 1982. *Iran: Between Two Revolutions*. Princeton, NJ: Princeton University Press.

Adler, Glenn, and Eddie Webster. 2000. *Trade Unions and Democratization in South Africa, 1985–1997*. New York: St. Martin's Press.

Agence France-Presse. 2000. "International Unions at Odds on Need for Stricter Labour Standards," *Agence France-Presse*, April 6.

Aglietta, Michel. 1979. *A Theory of Capitalist Regulation: The U.S. Experience*. London: New Left Books.

Altshuler, Alan, et al., 1984. *The Future of the Automobile: The Report of MIT's International Automobile Program*. Cambridge, MA: MIT Press.

Apple, Nixon. 1980. "The Rise and Fall of Full Employment Capitalism," *Studies in Political Economy*, 4, Autumn, 5–39.

Arrighi, Giovanni. 1990a. "Marxist-Century, American-Century: The Making and Remaking of the World Labor Movement," *New Left Review*, 179, Jan–Feb, 29–63.

1990b. "The Developmentalist Illusion: A Reconceptualization of the Semiperiphery." In William G. Martin, ed., *Semiperipheral States in the World-Economy*, pp. 11–42. New York: Greenwood Press.

1994. *The Long Twentieth Century: Money, Power and the Origins of Our Times*. London: Verso.

1995. "Labor Unrest in Italy, 1880–1990." *Review* (Fernand Braudel Center), 18 (1), 51–68.

Arrighi, Giovanni and Beverly Silver. 1984. "Labor Movements and Capital Migration: The US and Western Europe in World-Historical Perspective." In C. Bergquist ed., *Labor in the Capitalist World-Economy*, pp. 183–216. Beverly Hills, CA: Sage.

Arrighi, Giovanni, Satoshi Ikeda, and Alexander Irwan. 1993. "The Rise of East Asia: One Miracle or Many?" In Ravi A. Palat, ed., *Pacific-Asia and the Future of the World-System*, pp. 41–65. Westport, CT: Greenwood Press.

Arrighi, Giovanni and Beverly J. Silver with I. Ahmad, K. Barr, S. Hisaeda, P. K. Hui, K. Ray, R. E. Reifer, M. Shih, and E. Slater. 1999. *Chaos and Governance in the Modern World System*. Minneapolis: University of Minnesota Press.

Arrighi, Giovanni, Beverly J. Silver, and Benjamin D. Brewer. 2003. "Industrial Convergence and the Persistence of the North-South Divide." *Studies in Comparative International Development*, 38 (1), 3–31.

Automotive News. 1996. "Automakers Stampede to Build Plants in Brazil," *Automotive News*, November 25, p. 9.

Ball, Stephen J. 1993. "Education Markets, Choice and Social Class: The Market as a Class Strategy in the UK and USA." *British Journal of Sociology of Education*, 14, (1), 3–19.

Barraclough, Geoffrey. 1967. *An Introduction to Contemporary History*. Harmondsworth: Penguin.

Barton, Ava. 1989. "Questions of Gender: Deskilling and Demasculinization in France, 1830–1871." *Gender and History*, 1, 178–99.

Bataille, Georges. 1988. *The Accursed Share: An Essay on General Economy*. New York: Zone Books.

Beinin, Joel, and Zachary Lockman. 1987. *Workers on the Nile: Nationalism, Communism, Islam, and the Egyptian Working Class, 1882–1954*. Princeton, NJ: Princeton University Press.

Beittel, Mark. 1989. "Labor Unrest in South Africa" (unpublished manuscript), SUNY, Binghamton, NY.

Bell, Daniel. 1973. *The Coming of Post-Industrial Society*. New York: Basic Books.

Benería, Lourdes. 1995. "Response: The Dynamics of Globalization." *International Labor and Working-Class History*, 47, Spring, 45–52.

Berghahn, V. R. 1973. *Germany and the Approach of War in 1914*. New York: St. Martin's.

Bergquist, Charles. 1986. *Labor in Latin America: Comparative Essays on Chile, Argentina, Venezuela, and Colombia*. Stanford, CA: Stanford University Press.

Berlanstein, Lenard R. 1993. "Introduction." In Lenard R. Berlanstein, ed., *Rethinking Labor History: Essays on Discourse and Class Analysis*. Urbana: University of Illinois Press.

Beynon, Huw. 1973. *Working for Ford*. Harmondsworth: Penguin.

Biernacki, Richard. 1995. *The Fabrication of Labor: Germany and Britain, 1640–1914*. Berkeley: University of California Press.

Blashill, J. 1972. "The Proper Role of US Corporations in South Africa," *Fortune*, July.

References

Block, Fred L. 1977. *The Origins of International Economic Disorder: A Study of the United States International Monetary Policy from World War II to the Present.* Berkeley: University of California Press.

1990. *Postindustrial Possibilities: A Critique of Economic Discourse.* Berkeley: University of California Press.

1996. *The Vampire State: And Other Myths and Fallacies about the U.S. Economy.* New York: The New Press.

2001. "Introduction." Karl Polanyi, *The Great Transformation: The Political and Economic Origins of Our Times* (second edition), pp. xviii–xxxviii. Boston: Beacon Press.

Bloomfield, Gerald T. 1991. "The World Automobile Industry in Transition." In C. M. Law, ed., *Restructuring the Global Automobile Industry*, pp. 19–60. London: Routledge.

Bluestone, Barry, and Bennett Harrison. 1982. *The Deindustrialization of America: Plant Closings, Community Abandonment, and the Dismantling of Basic Industry.* New York: Basic.

Bonacich, Edna, and Richard P. Appelbaum. 2000. *Behind the Label: Inequality in the Los Angeles Apparel Industry.* Berkeley, CA: University of California Press.

Borden, William S. 1984. *The Pacific Alliance: United States Foreign Economic Policy and Japanese Trade Recovery, 1947–1955.* Madison: University of Wisconsin Press.

Boyer, Robert. 1979. "Wage Formation in Historical Perspective: The French Experience." *Cambridge Journal of Economics* 3 (2), 99–118.

Bradsher, Keith. 1997. "In South America, Auto Makers See One Big Showroom," *New York Times*, April 25, D1.

Brecher, Jeremy. 1972. *Strike!* Boston: South End Press.

1994/95. "Global Unemployment at Seven Hundred Million." In *Global Issues 94/95*, pp. 32–35. Guilford, CT: Dushkin Publishing.

Brennan, James P. 1994. *Labor Wars in Cordoba, 1955–1976. Ideology, Work and Politics in an Argentine Industrial City.* Cambridge, MA: Harvard University Press.

Bridges, Amy. 1986. "Becoming American: The Working Classes in the United States before the Civil War." In I. Katznelson and A. R. Zolberg, eds., *Working-Class Formation*, pp. 157–96. Princeton, NJ: Princeton University Press.

Brody, David. 1980. *Workers in Industrial America.* New York: Oxford University Press.

Bronfenbrenner, Kate. 1996. *The Effects of Plant Closing or Threat of Plant Closing on the Right of Workers to Organize.* Final Report Submitted to the Labor Secretariat of the North American Commission for Labor Cooperation, September 30.

Bronfenbrenner, Kate, Sheldon Friedman, Richard W. Hurd, Rudolph A. Oswald, and Ronald L. Seeber, eds. 1998. *Organizing to Win: New Research on Union Strategies.* Ithaca, NY: Cornell University Press.

Brooke, James. 1994. "Inland Region of Brazil Grows Like Few Others." *New York Times*, August 11.

Brown, Carolyn A. 1988. "The Dialectics of Colonial Labour Control: Class Struggles in the Nigerian Coal Industry, 1914–1949." *Journal of Asian and African Studies* 23 (1–2), 32–59.

Burawoy, Michael. 1982. "The Hidden Abode of Underdevelopment: Labor Process and the State in Zambia." *Politics and Society* 11 (4), 123–66.

1983. "Factory Regimes Under Advanced Capitalism." *American Sociological Review*, 48 (5), October, 587–605.

1985. *The Politics of Production: Factory Regimes Under Capitalism and Socialism.* London: Verso.

Burbach, Roger, and William I. Robinson. 1999. "The Fin de Siècle Debate: Globalization as Global Shift." *Science and Society*, 63 (1), 10–39.

Burley, Anne-Marie. 1993. "Regulating the World: Multilateralism, International Law, and the Projection of the New Deal Regulatory State." In J. G. Ruggie, ed., *Multilateralism Matters: The Theory and Praxis of an Institutional Form*, pp. 125–56. New York: Columbia University Press.

Burstein, Paul. 1985. *Discrimination, Jobs and Politics.* Chicago: University of Chicago Press.

Camuffo, Arnaldo, and Giuseppe Volpato. 1997. "Italy: Changing the Workplace in the Automobile Industry." In Thomas A. Kochan et al., eds., *After Lean Production*. Ithaca, NY: Cornell University Press, 155–76.

Cargo Info. 1997. "Motor industry turnaround impacts on Durban port," *Cargo Info: Freight and Trading Weekly* (South Africa), January 31 [http://cargoinfo.co.za/ftw/97/97ja31j.html].

Carr, Edward H. 1945. *Nationalism and After.* London: Macmillan.

Castells, Manuel. 1997. *The Information Age, vol. 2: The Power of Identity.* Oxford: Blackwell.

Castells, Manuel and Yukio Aoyama. 1994. "Paths Toward the Informational Society: Employment Structure in G-7 Countries, 1920–1990." *International Labour Review*, 133 (1), 5–33.

Chalmers, Norma J. 1989. *Industrial Relations in Japan: The Peripheral Workforce.* London: Routledge.

Chandavarkar, Rajnarayan. 1994. *The Origins of Industrial Capitalism in India: Business Strategies and the Working Classes in Bombay, 1900–1940.* Cambridge: Cambridge University Press.

Chandler, Alfred D., Jr. 1977. *The Visible Hand: The Managerial Revolution in American Business.* Cambridge, MA: Harvard University Press.

Chapman, Sidney J. 1904. *The Lancashire Cotton Industry: A Study in Economic Development.* Manchester: Manchester University Press.

Chase-Dunn, Christopher. 1989. *Global Formation: Structures of the World-Economy.* Cambridge, MA: Basil Blackwell.

Chatterjee, Partha. 1986. *Nationalist Thought and the Colonial World: A Derivative Discourse?* London: Zed Press.

Chesneaux, Jean. 1968. *The Chinese Labor Movement, 1919–1927.* Stanford, CA: Stanford University Press.

China Automotive Technology and Research Center. 1998. *Automotive Industry of China.* Tianjin: Nankai University Press.

Chossudovsky, Michel. 1997. *The Globalisation of Poverty: Impacts of IMF and World Bank Reforms.* Penang: Third World Network.

References

Ciccantell, Paul S., and Stephen G. Bunker, eds. 1998. *Space and Transport in the World-System*. Westport, CT: Greenwood Press.

Claude, Jr., Inis. 1956. *Swords into Plowshares: The Problems and Progress of International Organization* (second edition). New York: Random House.

Cockburn, Alexander. 2000. "Short History of the Twentieth Century," *The Nation*, January 3, p. 9.

Cockburn, Cynthia. 1983. *Brothers: Male Dominance and Technological Change*. London: Pluto.

Cohen, Isaac. 1990. *American Management and British Labor: A Comparative Study of the Cotton Spinning Industry*. New York: Greenwood Press.

Cohen, Robin. 1980. "Resistance and Hidden Forms of Consciousness Amongst African Workers." *Review of African Political Economy*, 19, September-December, 8–22.

Cole, Stephen. 1969. *The Unionization of Teachers: A Case Study of the UFT*. New York: Praeger.

Collier, Ruth Berins. 1999. *Paths Toward Democracy: The Working Class and Elites in Western Europe and South America*. Cambridge: Cambridge University Press.

Collier, Ruth Berins and David Collier. 1991. *Shaping the Political Arena: Critical Junctures, the Labor Movement, and Regime Dynamics in Latin America*. Princeton, NJ: Princeton University Press.

Cooper, Frederick. 1996. *Decolonization and African Society: The Labor Question in French and British Africa*. Cambridge: Cambridge University Press.

2000. "Farewell to the Category-Producing Class?" *International Labor and Working-Class History*, 57, Spring, 60–68.

Cowie, Jefferson. 1999. *Capital Moves: RCA's Seventy-Year Search for Cheap Labor*. Ithaca, NY: Cornell University Press.

Cronin, James E. 1983. "Labor Insurgency and Class Formation: Comparative Perspectives on the Crisis of 1917–1920 in Europe." In C. Siriani and J. Cronin, eds., *Work, Community, and Power: The Experience of Labor in Europe and America, 1900–1925*, pp. 20–48. Philadelphia: Temple University Press.

1996. *The World the Cold War Made*. New York: Routledge.

Crouch, Colin, and Alessandro Pizzorno, eds. 1978. *The Resurgence of Class Conflict in Western Europe Since 1968* (2 volumes). New York: Holmes & Meier.

Cuban, Larry. 1984. *How Teachers Taught: Constancy and Change in American Classrooms, 1890–1990*. New York: Longman.

Cusumano, Michael A. 1985. *The Japanese Automobile Industry: Technology and Management at Nissan and Toyota*. Cambridge, MA: Harvard University Press.

Dangler, Jamie Faricellia. 1995. "The *Times* (London) and the *New York Times* as Sources on World Labor Unrest." *Review* (Fernand Braudel Center), 18, 1, 35–47.

Danto, Arthur C. 1965. *Analytical Philosophy of History*. Cambridge: Cambridge University Press.

Danylewycz, Marta, and Alison Prentice.1988. "Teachers' Work: Changing Patterns and Perspectives in the Emerging School Systems of Nineteenth- and Early Twentieth-Century Central Canada." In Jenny Ozga, ed., *Schoolwork:*

Interpreting the Labour Process of Teaching, pp. 61–80. Philadelphia: Open University Press.

Danzger, Herbert M. 1975. "Validating Conflict Data." *American Sociological Review*, XL (5), 570–84.

Dassbach, Carl. 1988. *Global Enterprises and the World Economy: Ford, General Motors and IBM, The Emergence of the Transnational Enterprise.* PhD Dissertation, SUNY-Binghamton.

Davis, Mike. 1986. *Prisoners of the American Dream.* London: Verso.

Deyo, Frederic C. 1989. *Beneath the Miracle: Labor Subordination in the New Asian Industrialism.* Berkeley: University of California Press.

1996a. "Introduction: Social Reconstructions of the World Automobile Industry." In F. C. Deyo, ed., *Social Reconstructions of the World Automobile Industry,* pp. 1–17. New York: St. Martin's Press.

1996b. "Competition, Flexibility and Industrial Ascent: The Thai Auto Industry." In F. C. Deyo, ed. *Social Reconstructions of the World Automobile Industry,* pp. 136–56. New York: St. Martin's Press.

Dicken, Peter. 1998. *Global Shift: Transformation the World Economy.* New York: Guilford Press.

Dickerson, Kitty, G. 1991. *Textiles and Apparel in the International Economy.* New York: Macmillan.

DIEESE. 1995. *Rumos do ABC: A Economia do Grande ABC na Visa~o dos Metalurgicos.* Sao Bernardo do Campo: DIEESE (subsection of Sindicato dos Metalurgicos).

Drucker, Peter. 1993. *Post-Capitalist Society.* New York: Harper.

Dubofsky, Melvyn. 1983. "Abortive Reform: The Wilson Administration and Organized Labor". In C. Siriani and J. Cronin, eds., *Work, Community and Power: The Emergence of Labor in Europe and America, 1900–1925,* pp. 197–220. Philadelphia: Temple University Press.

Dubofsky, Melvyn and W. Van Tine. 1977. *John L. Lewis: A Biography.* Chicago: Quadrangle.

Dubois, Pierre. 1978. "New Forms of Industrial Conflict 1960–1974." In C. Crouch and A. Pizzorno, eds. *The Resurgence of Class Conflict in Western Europe Since 1968, Vol. 2,* pp. 1–34. New York: Holmes & Meier.

Dugger, Celia W. 1999. "Poor Nations United to Fight Clinton's Labor-Trade Linkage", *International Herald Tribune,* December 18, p. 9.

Eckholm, Erik. 2001. "Chinese Warn of Civil Unrest Across Country: Communist Party Document Paints Picture of Discontent," *International Herald Tribune,* June 2–3, pp. 1, 4.

Economist, The. 1992. "World Economic Survey," *The Economist,* September 19.

Economist Intelligence Unit. 1990. *Country Profile: Brazil,* # 1.

Edwards, P. K. 1981. *Strikes in the United States, 1881–1974.* New York: St. Martin's Press.

Edwards, Richard. 1979. *Contested Terrain: The Transformation of the Workplace in the Twentieth Century.* New York: Basic Books.

Elson, Diane, and Ruth Pearson. 1981. "Nimble Fingers Make Cheap Workers: An Analysis of Women's Employment in Third World Manufacturing." *Feminist Review,* 7, 87–107.

References

Escobar, Arturo. 1995. *Encountering Development: States and Industrial Transformation*. Princeton, NJ: Princeton University Press.

Esteva, Gustavo. 1992. "Development." In Wolfgang Sachs, ed., *The Development Dictionary*, pp. 6–25. London: Zed Books.

Evans, Peter. 1995. *Embedded Autonomy: States and Industrial Transformation*. Princeton, NJ: Princeton University Press.

Fantasia, Rick. 1988. *Cultures of Solidarity: Consciousness, Action and Contemporary American Workers*. Berkeley; CA: University of California Press.

Farley, Miriam S. 1950. *Aspects of Japan's Labor Problems*. New York: The John Day Company.

Feldman, Gerald. 1966. *Army, Industry and Labor in Germany, 1914–1918*. Princeton, NJ: Princeton University Press.

Fernandez-Kelly, Maria Patricia. 1983. *For We Are Sold, I and My People: Women and Industry in Mexico's Frontier*. Albany, NY: SUNY Press.

Filkins, Dexter. 2000. "Punching in the Future: Technology Puts India to Work from Afar," *International Herald Tribune*, April 8–9, pp. 1, 8.

Fischer, F. 1975. *Germany's Aims in the First World War*. New York: W. W. Norton.

Fishman, Robert M. 1990. *Working-Class Organization and the Return of Democracy in Spain*. Ithaca: Cornell University Press.

Florida, Richard, and Martin Kenney. 1991. "Transplanted Organizations: The Transfer of Japanese Industrial Organization in the U.S." *American Sociological Review*, 56, 381–98.

Foweraker, Joe. 1989. *Making Democracy in Spain*. Cambridge: Cambridge University Press.

Franzosi, Roberto. 1987. "The Press as a Source of Socio-Historical Data", *Historical Methods*, 20, 1, Winter, 5–16.

 1990. "Strategies for the Prevention, Detection, and Correction of Measurement Error in Data Collected from Textual Sources." *Sociological Methods and Research*, 28 (4), May, 442–72.

 1995. *The Puzzle of Strikes: Class and State Strategies in Postwar Italy*. Cambridge: Cambridge University Press.

Frieden, Jeffry. 1987. *Banking on the World*. New York: Harper and Row.

Fröbel, Folker, Jürgen Heinrich, and Otto Kreye. 1980. *The New International Division of Labour: Structural Employment and Industrialization in Developing Countries*. Cambridge: Cambridge University Press.

Gereffi, Gary. 1994. "The Organization of Buyer-Driven Global Commodity Chains." In Gary Gereffi and Miguel Korzeniewicz, eds., *Commodity Chains and Global Capitalism*, pp. 95–122. Westport, CT: Praeger.

Giddens, Anthony. 1987. *The Nation-State and Violence*. Berkeley: University of California Press.

Giddy, Ian. 1978. "The Demise of the Product Cycle in International Business Theory." *Columbia Journal of World Business*, Spring, 90–97.

Gill, Stephen, and James H. Mittleman, eds., 1997. *Innovation and Transformation in International Studies*. Cambridge: Cambridge University Press.

Gills, Barry, and Andre G. Frank. 1992. "World System Cycles, Crises, and Hegemonic Shifts, 1700 BC to 1700 AD." *Review* (Fernand Braudel Center), 15 (4),
621–87.

Godfrey, Walter. 1986. *Global Unemployment: The New Challenge to Economic Theory.*
Sussex: Harvester Press.

Goldfield, Michael. 1987. *The Decline of Organized Labor in the United States.*
Chicago: University of Chicago Press.

Goldstone, Jack A. 1991. *Revolution and Rebellion in the Early Modern World.*
Berkeley: University of California Press.

Gordon, David M. 1996. *Fat and Mean: The Corporate Squeeze of Working
Americans and the Myth of Managerial "Downsizing."* New York: Martin Kessler
Books.

Gordon, David M, Richard Edwards, and Michael Reich. 1982. *Segmented Work,
Divided Workers: The Historical Transformation of Labor in the United States.*
Cambridge: Cambridge University Press.

Greenhouse, Stephen. 2000. "Low-Paid Jobs Lead Advance in Employment," *New
York Times*, October 1.

Greider, William. 1998. *Fortress America: The American Military and the Consequences
of Peace.* New York: Public Affairs.

1999. "The Battle Beyond Seattle," *The Nation*, December 27, pp. 5–6.

2001. "It's Time to Ask 'Borderless' Corporations: Which Side Are You On?" *The
Nation*, October 26.

Griffin, Larry. 1992. "Temporality, Events, and Explanation in Historical Sociology:
An Introduction." *Sociological Methods and Research*, 20 (4), May, 403–27.

Griffin, Larry J., Holly J. McCammon, and Christopher Botsko. 1990. "The
'Unmaking' of a Movement? The Crisis of US Trade Unions in Compara-
tive Perspective." In Maureen Hallinan, David Klein, and Jennifer Glass, eds.,
Change in Societal Institutions, pp. 169–94. New York: Plenum Press.

Grosfoguel, Ramón. 1996. "From Cepalismo to Neoliberalism: A World-System
Approach to Conceptual Shifts in Latin America." *Review* (Fernand Braudel
Center) 19 (2), 131–54.

Gwynne, Robert. 1991. "New Horizons? The Third World Motor Vehicle Industry
in an International Framework." In C. M. Law, ed., *Restructuring the Global
Automobile Industry*, pp. 61–87. London: Routledge.

Hammel, E. A. 1980. "The Comparative Method in Anthropological Perspective."
Comparative Studies in Society and History, 22 (2), April, 145–55.

Harazti, Miklos. 1977. *Workers in a Workers' State.* Harmondsworth: Penguin.

Hardt, Michael, and Antonio Negri. 2000. *Empire.* Cambridge, MA: Harvard
University Press.

Harris, Nigel. 1987. *The End of the Third World. Newly Industrializing Countries and
the Decline of an Ideology.* Harmondsworth, Middlesex: Penguin Books.

Harrison, Bennett. 1997. *Lean and Mean: Why Large Corporations Will Continue to
Dominate the Global Economy.* New York: Guilford Press.

Hartwell, R. M. 1973. "The Service Revolution: The Growth of Services in Modern
Economy." In C. M. Cipolla, ed., *The Fontana Economic History of Europe: The
Industrial Revolution*, pp. 359–96. London: Collins Clear-Type Press.

References

Harvey, David. 1989. *The Condition of Postmodernity: An Enquiry into the Origins of Cultural Change*. Oxford: Basil Blackwell.

1999. *The Limits of Capital*. London: Verso.

2000. *Spaces of Hope*. Edinburgh: Edinburgh University Press.

Harwit, Eric. 1995. *China's Automobile Industry: Policies, Problems and Prospects*. Armonk, NY: M. E. Sharpe.

Haupt, Georges. 1972. *Socialism and the Great War: The Collapse of the Second International*. Oxford: Clarendon Press.

Held, David, Anthony McGrew, David Goldblatt, and Jonathan Perraton. 1999. *Global Transformations. Politics, Economics and Culture*. Stanford, CA: Stanford University Press.

Hexter, J. H. 1979. *On Historians*. Cambridge, MA: Harvard University Press.

Hibbs, Douglas A., Jr. 1978. "On the Political Economy of Long-Run Trends in Strike Activity." *British Journal of Political Science*, 8: (2), April, 153–75.

Hirschman, Albert O. 1970. *Exit, Voice, Loyalty: Responses to Decline in Firms, Organizations and States*. Cambridge, MA: Harvard University Press.

1979. *Essays in Trespassing: Economics to Politics and Beyond*. Cambridge: Cambridge University Press.

1989. "How the Keynesian Revolution was Exported from the United States, and other Comments." In Peter A. Hall, ed., *The Political Power of Economic Ideas: Keynesianism Across Nations*, pp. 347–59. Princeton, NJ: Princeton University Press.

Hirschsohn, Philip. 1997. "South Africa: The Struggle for Human Resource Development." In Thomas A. Kochan et al., eds., *After Lean Production*, pp. 231–54. Ithaca, NY: Cornell University Press.

Hobsbawm, Eric. 1987. *The Age of Empire, 1875–1914*. New York: Pantheon Books.

1994. *The Age of Extremes: A History of the World, 1914–1991*. New York: Vintage.

Honig, Emily. 1986. *Sisters and Strangers: Women in the Shanghai Cotton Mills, 1919–1949*. Stanford, CA: Stanford University Press.

Hoogvelt, Ankie. 1997. *Globalization and the Postcolonial World: The New Political Economy of Development*. Baltimore, MD: Johns Hopkins University Press.

Hopkins, Terence K. 1982a. "World-Systems Analysis: Methodological Issues". In Terence K. Hopkins, Immanuel Wallerstein and Associates. *World Systems Analysis: Theory and Methodology*, pp. 145–58. Beverly Hills, CA: Sage.

1982b. "The Study of the Capitalist World-Economy." In T. K. Hopkins, I. Wallerstein and Associates, *World-Systems Analysis: Theory and Methodology*, pp. 9–38. Beverly Hills: Sage.

Humphrey, John. 1982. *Capitalist Control and Workers' Struggle in the Brazilian Auto Industry*. Princeton, NJ: Princeton University Press.

1987. "Economic Crisis and Stability of Employment in the Brazilian Motor Industry." In W. Brierley, ed., *Trade Unions and the Economic Crisis of the 1980's*, pp. 119–31. Gower: Aldershot.

1993. "Japanese Production Management and Labour Relations in Brazil." *The Journal of Development Studies*, 30 (1), October, 92–114.

Huntington, Samuel P. 1968. *Political Order in Changing Societies*. New Haven, CT: Yale University Press.

Hyman, Richard. 1972. *Strikes*. London: Fontana/Collins.

1992. "Trade Unions and the Disaggregation of the Working Class." In M. Regini, ed., *The Future of Labour Movements*, pp. 150–68. Newbury Park, CA: Sage.

Ikenberry, John G. 1989. "Rethinking the Origins of American Hegemony." *Political Science Quarterly*, 104 (3), 375–400.

Imig, Doug, and Sidney Tarrow. 2000. "Political Contention in a Europeanising Polity", *West European Politics*, 23 (4), 73–93.

Ingham, Geoffrey. 1994. "States and Markets in the Production of World Money: Sterling and the Dollar." In S. Corbridge, R. Martin, and N. Thrift, eds., *Money, Power, and Space*, 29–48. Oxford: Blackwell.

Irons, Janet. 2000. *Testing the New Deal: The General Textile Strike of 1934 in the American South*. Urbana: University of Illinois Press.

Ishida, Mitsuo 1997. "Japan: Beyond the Model for Lean Production." In T. A. Kochan, R. D. Lansbury and J. P. MacDuffie, eds., *Beyond Lean Production*, pp. 45–60. Ithaca: Cornell University Press.

Jackson, Michael. 1987. *Strikes*. New York: St. Martin's Press.

James, Daniel. 1981. "Rationalisation and Working Class Response: The Context and Limits of Factory Floor Activity in Argentina." *Journal of Latin American Studies*, 13 (2), 375–402.

Jelin, Elisabeth. 1979. "Labour Conflicts under the Second Peronist Regime, Argentina, 1973–76." *Development and Change*, 10 (2), 233–57.

Jenkins, J. Craig, and Kevin Leicht. 1997. "Class Analysis and Social Movements: A Critique and Reformulation." In John R. Hall, ed., *Reworking Class*, pp. 369–97. Ithaca: Cornell University Press.

Jenkins, J. Craig and Charles Perrow. 1977. "Insurgency of the Powerless: Farm Workers Movements." *American Sociological Review*, XLII (2), 249–67.

Johnson, Richard. 1997. "GM and Korea Dance a Two-Step in World's Automotive Ballroom," *Automotive News*, June 9, p. 14.

Kaiser, D. E. 1983. "Germany and the Origins of the First World War." *Journal of Modern History* 55: 442–74.

Kalb, Don, 2000. "Class (in Place) Without Capitalism (in Space)? " *International Labor and Working-Class History*, 57, Spring, 31–9.

Kane, N. F. 1988. *Textiles in Transition: Technology, Wages and Industry Relocation in the U.S. Textile Industry, 1880–1930*. New York: Greenwood Press.

Kapstein, Ethan B. 1996. "Workers and the World Economy." *Foreign Affairs*, 75 (3), May/June, 16–37.

1999. *Sharing the Wealth: Workers and the World Economy*. New York: W. W. Norton.

Katznelson, Ira, and Aristide Zolberg. 1986. *Working-Class Formation: Nineteenth-Century Patterns in Western Europe and the United States*. Princeton, NJ: Princeton University Press.

Keck, Margaret. 1989. "The New Unionism in the Brazilian Transition." In Alfred Stepan, ed., *Democratizing Brazil: Problems of Transition and Consolidation*, Chapter 8, pp. 252–96. New York: Oxford University Press.

References

Keck, Margaret E. and Kathryn Sikkink.1998. *Activists Beyond Borders: Advocacy Networks in International Politics*. Ithaca, NY: Cornell University Press.

Kendall, W. 1975. *The Labour Movement in Europe*. London: Allen Lane.

Kerr, Clark, and Abraham Siegel. 1964. "The Interindustry Propensity to Strike – An International Comparison." In Clark Kerr, *Labor and Management in Industrial Society*, pp. 105–47. Garden City, NY: Anchor Books.

Keynes, John Maynard. [1920] 1971. *The Economic Consequences of the Peace*. New York: Harper & Row.

Khor, Martin. 1999. "Take Care, the WTO Majority Is Tired of Being Manipulated," *International Herald Tribune*, December 21, p. 4.

Kirk, Donald. 1994. *Korean Dynasty: Hyundai and Chung Ju Yung*. New York: M. E. Sharpe.

Knowles, K. G. J. C. 1952. *Strikes: A Study of Industrial Conflict*. Oxford: Basil Blackwell.

Kochan, Thomas A., Russell D. Lansbury, and John Paul MacDuffie. 1997. *After Lean Production: Evolving Employment Practices in the World Auto Industry*. Ithaca, NY: Cornell University Press.

Kocka, Jürgen. 1986. "Problems of Working-Class Formation in Germany: The Early Years, 1800–1875." In Ira Katznelson and Aristide R. Zolberg, eds., *Working-Class Formation*, pp. 279–351. Princeton, NJ: Princeton University Press.

Koo, Hagen. 1993. "The State, *Minjung*, and the Working Class in South Korea." In H. Koo, ed., *State and Society in Contemporary Korea*, pp. 131–62. Ithaca, NY: Cornell University Press.

2001. *Korean Workers: The Culture and Politics of Class Formation*. Ithaca: Cornell University Press.

Koopmans, Ruud. 1993. "The Dynamics of Protest Waves: West Germany, 1965 to 1989." *American Sociological Review*, LVIII (5), October, 637–58.

Korpi, Walter, and Michael Shalev. 1979. "Strikes, Industrial Relations, and Class Conflict in Capitalist Societies." *British Journal of Sociology*, 30 (2), June, 164–87.

Korzeniewicz, Roberto P. 1989. "Labor Unrest in Argentina, 1887–1907." *Latin American Research Review*, 24 (3), 71–98.

Korzeniewicz, Roberto P., and Timothy P. Moran. 1997. "World Economic Trends in the Distribution of Income, 1965–1992." *American Journal of Sociology*, 102 (4), 1000–39.

Kowalewski, David. 1993. "Ballots and Bullets: Election Riots in the Periphery, 1874–1985." *Journal of Development Studies*, 24 (3), April, 518–40.

Krishnan, R. 1996. "December 1995: The First Revolt Against Globalization." *Monthly Review*, 48 (1), May, 1–22.

Kutalik, Chris. 2002. "September 11: One Year Later, U.S. Workers Still Feel Fallout," *Labor Notes* (Detroit), #282, September, pp. 1, 14.

Kutscher, R. E., and J. A. Mark. 1983. "The Service Producing Sector: Some Common Perceptions Reviewed," *Monthly Labor Review*, April, pp. 21–24.

Labor Notes. 2001. "AFL-CIO Pulls Out of Mobilization for Global Justice." *Labor Notes*, 271, October, p. 3.

215

LaFeber, Walter. 1963. *The New Empire: An Interpretation of American Expansion, 1860–1898*. Ithaca, NY: Cornell University Press.

Landes, David. 1969. *The Unbound Prometheus*. Cambridge: Cambridge University Press.

Laqueur, Walter. 1968. "Revolution." *International Encyclopedia of the Social Sciences*, XIII, 501–7.

Laux, James M. 1992. *The European Automobile Industry*. New York: Twayne Publishers.

Lawn, Martin. 1987. "What Is the Teacher's Job." In Martin Lawn and Gerald Grace, eds., *Teachers: The Culture and Politics of Work*, pp. 50–64. New York: The Falmer Press.

Lawn, Martin and Jenny Ozga. 1988. "The Educational Worker? A Reassessment of Teachers." In Jenny Ozga, ed., *Schoolwork: Interpreting the Labour Process of Teaching*, pp. 81–98. Philadelphia: Open University Press.

Lazonick, William. 1990. *Competitive Advantage on the Shop Floor*. Cambridge, MA: Harvard University Press.

Lebow, R. N. 1981. *Between Peace and War*. Baltimore: Johns Hopkins University Press.

Legters, Nettie. 1993. "Teachers as Workers in the World System." Paper presented at the Social Science History Association Annual Meeting, Baltimore, November 4–7.

Lenin, Vladimir. [1916] 1971. "Imperialism, the Highest Stage of Capitalism." In *V. I. Lenin Selected Works*, pp. 169–263. New York: International Publishers.

Levi, Margaret, and David Olson. 2000. "The Battles of Seattle." *Politics and Society*, 28 (3), September, 309–29.

Levine, S. B. 1958. *Industrial Relations in Postwar Japan*. Urbana: University of Illinois Press.

Levy, Jack. 1989. "The Diversionary Theory of War: A Critique." In M. I. Midlarsky, ed., *Handbook of War Studies*, pp. 258–88. London: Allen and Unwin.

  1998. "The Causes of War and the Conditions of Peace." *Annual Review of Political Science*, 1, 139–65.

Lewis, Jon, and Estelle Randall. 1986. "The State of the Unions." *Review of African Political Economy*, 35, May, 68–77.

Lim, Linda Y. C. 1990. "Women's Work in Export Factories: The Politics of a Cause." In Irene Tinker, ed., *Persistent Inequalities: Women and Development*, pp. 101–19. New York: Oxford University Press.

Litvak, Lawrence, Robert De Grasse, and Kathleen McTigue. 1978. *South Africa: Foreign Investment and Apartheid*. Washington, DC: Institute for Policy Studies.

Lohr, Steve. 2002. "I. B. M. Opening a $2.5 Billion Specialized Chip Plant," *New York Times*, August 1, C1.

Loth, Wilfried. 1988. *The Division of the World, 1941–1955*. London: Routledge.

MacEwan, Arthur, and William K. Tabb. eds. 1989. *Instability and Change in the World Economy*. New York: Monthly Review Press.

Machado, Kit G. 1992. "ASEAN State Industrial Policies and Japanese Regional Production Strategies: The Case of Malaysia's Motor Vehicle Industry." In

References

C. Clark and S. Chan, eds., *The Evolving Pacific Basin in the Global Political Economy*, pp. 169–202. Boulder, CO: Lynne Rienner Publishers.

Maier, Charles. 1978. "The Politics of Productivity: Foundations of American Economic Policy after World War II." In P. Katzenstein, ed., *Between Power and Plenty: Foreign Economic Policies of Advanced Industrial States*, pp. 23–49. Madison: University of Wisconsin Press.

1981. "The Two Postwar Eras and the Conditions for Stability in Twentieth Century Europe." *American History Review*, 86, 327–52.

1987. *In Search of Stability: Explorations in Historical Political Economy.* Cambridge: Cambridge University Press.

Mamdani, Mahmood. 1996. *Citizen and Subject: Contemporary Africa and the Legacy of Late Colonialism.* Princeton, NJ: Princeton University Press.

Mann, Michael. 1988. *States, War and Capitalism.* Oxford: Blackwell.

1993. *The Sources of Social Power, Vol. 2, The Rise of Classes and Nation-States, 1760–1914.* Cambridge: Cambridge University Press.

Maree, Johann. 1985. "The Emergence, Struggles and Achievements of Black Trade Unions in South Africa from 1973 to 1984." *Labour, Capital and Society* 18 (2), November 278–303.

Markoff, John. 1996. *Waves of Democracy: Social Movements and Political Change.* Thousand Oaks, CA: Pine Forge Press.

Marshall, Neill, and Peter Wood. 1995. *Services and Space: Key Aspects of Urban and Regional Development.* New York: John Wiley & Sons.

Martin, Benjamin, 1990. *The Agony of Modernization: Labor and Industrialization in Spain.* Ithaca, NY: Cornell University Press.

Marx, Karl. 1959. *Capital, Vol. 1.* Moscow: Foreign Languages Publishing House.

Marx, Karl and Friedrich Engels. 1967. *The Communist Manifesto.* Harmondsworth: Penguin.

Mayer, Arno J. 1967. "Domestic Causes and Purposes of War in Europe, 1870–1956." In L. Krieger and F. Stern, eds., *The Responsibility of Power*, pp. 286–300. New York: Doubleday.

1977. "Internal Crisis and War Since 1870." In C. L. Bertrand, ed., *Revolutionary Situations in Europe, 1917–1922*, pp. 201–33. Montreal: Inter-university Centre for European Studies.

1981. *The Persistence of the Old Regime: Europe and the Great War.* New York: Pantheon.

Mazur, Jay. 2000. "Labor's New Internationalism," *Foreign Affairs*, January/February, 79–93.

McAdam, Doug. 1982. *Political Process and the Development of Black Insurgency, 1930–1970.* Chicago: University of Chicago Press.

and Dieter Rucht. 1993. "The Cross-National Diffusion of Movement Ideas." *The Annals of the American Academy of Political and Social Science*, 528, July, 56–74.

McAdam, Doug, John D. McCarthy, and Mayer N. Zald. 1996. "Introduction: Opportunities, Mobilizing Structures, and Framing Processes – Toward a Synthetic, Comparative Perspective on Social Movements." In D. McAdam, J. D. McCarthy, and M. N. Zald, eds., *Comparative Perspectives on Social*

Movements: Political Opportunities, Mobilizing Structures, and Cultural Framings, pp. 1–20. Cambridge: Cambridge University Press.

McAdam, Doug, Sidney Tarrow, and Charles Tilly. 2001. *Dynamics of Contention.* Cambridge: Cambridge University Press.

McCormick, Thomas J. 1989. *America's Half-Century: United States Foreign Policy in the Cold War.* Baltimore: Johns Hopkins University Press.

McMichael, Philip.1990. "Incorporating Comparison within a World-Historical Perspective: An Alternative Comparative Method." *American Sociological Review,* 55, 385–97.

⎯⎯ 1996. *Development and Social Change: A Global Perspective.* Thousand Oaks, CA: Pine Forge Press.

McNeill, William. 1982. *The Pursuit of Power: Technology, Armed Force and Society since A.D. 1000.* Chicago: University of Chicago Press.

Meyer, John W., John Boli, George M. Thomas, and Francisco Ramirez. 1997. "World Society and the Nation-State." *American Journal of Sociology,* 103 (1), July, 144–81.

Michaels, Daniel. 2001. "Pilot Alliances Spook Airlines: Union Solidarity Isn't the Synergy the Carriers Had in Mind," *The Wall Street Journal Europe,* June 1–2, pp. 23, 28.

Midlarsky, Manus I., ed. 1990. "Big Wars, Little Wars – A Single Theory?" Special Issue of *International Interactions,* 16 (3), 157–224.

Milanovic, Branko.1999. "True World Income Distribution, 1988 and 1993." *Policy Research Working Paper 2244.* Washington, DC: The World Bank.

Milkman, Ruth. 1991. *Japan's California Factories: Labor Relations and Economic Globalization.* Los Angeles: Institute of Industrial Relations, UCLA.

Mittleman, James H. 1996. *Globalization: Critical Reflections.* Boulder, CO: Lynne Rienner.

Mjöset, Lars. 1990. "The Turn of Two Centuries: A Comparison of British and U.S. Hegemonies." In D. P. Rapkin, ed., *World Leadership and Hegemony,* pp. 21–47. Boulder, CO: Lynne Rienner.

Montgomery, David. 1979. *Workers' Control in America.* Cambridge: Cambridge University Press.

⎯⎯ 1987. *The Fall of the House of Labor: The Workplace, the State, and American Labor Activism, 1865–1925.* Cambridge: Cambridge University Press.

Moody, Kim. 1988. *An Injury to All: The Decline of American Unionism.* London: Verso.

⎯⎯ 1997. *Workers in a Lean World.* London: Verso.

⎯⎯ 1999. "On the Eve of Seattle Trade Protests, Sweeney Endorses Clinton's Trade Agenda," *Labor Notes* (Detroit), #249, December, pp. 1, 14.

Moreira Alves, Maria Helena. 1989. "Trade Unions in Brazil: A Search for Autonomy and Organization." In E. C. Epstein, ed., *Labor Autonomy and the State in Latin America,* pp. 39–72. Boston: Unwin Hyman.

Morris, Morris David. 1965. *The Emergence of an Industrial Labor Force in India: A Study of the Bombay Cotton Mills, 1854–1947.* Berkeley: University of California Press.

References

Muto, Ichiyo. 1997. "The Birth of the Women's Liberation Movement in the 1970s." In Joe Moore, ed., *The Other Japan: Conflict, Compromise and Resistance Since 1945*, pp. 147–71. Armonk, NY: M. E. Sharpe.

Myers III, Desaix. 1980. *US Business in South Africa: The Economic, Political and Moral Issues.* Bloomington: Indiana University Press.

Naroll, Raoul. 1970. "Galton's Problem." In Raoul Naroll and Ronald Cohen, eds., *A Handbook of Method in Cultural Anthropology*, Chapter 47, pp. 974–89. Garden City, NY: The Natural History Press.

Nation, The. 1999. "Democracy Bites the WTO" (Editorial), *The Nation*, December 27, pp. 3–4.

Needleman, Ruth. 1998. "Building Relationships for the Long Haul: Unions and Community-Based Groups Working Together to Organize Low-Wage Workers." In K. Bronfenbrenner, S. Friedman, R. W. Hurd, R. A. Oswald, and R. L. Seeber, eds., *Organizing to Win*, Chapter 4, pp. 71–86.

Ness, Immanuel. 1998. "Organizing Immigrant Communities: UNITE's Workers Center Strategy." In K. Bronfenbrenner et al., eds., *Organizing to Win*, Chapter 5, pp. 87–101.

Neumann, Franz. 1942. *Behemoth: The Structure and Practice of National Socialism.* London: Victor Gollancz.

New York Times. 1995. "Layoffs at G.M. in Brazil," *New York Times*, August 23, p. D-8.

——— 1997. "Strike at G.M. Factory Halts Work at 3 Plants." *New York Times*, July 25.

Nkrumah, Kwame. 1965. *Autobiography.* New York: Nelson.

Obrery, Ingrid. 1989. "COSATU Congress: Unity in Diversity." *Work in Progress* (South Africa), 60, August/September, 34–9.

Obrery, Ingrid and Sharren Singh. 1988. "A Review of 1988: Labour." *Work in Progress* (South Africa), 56/57, November–December, 36–42.

O'Brien, Robert. 2000. "The World Trade Organization and Labour." In R. O'Brien, A. M. Goetz, J. A. Scholte, and M. Williams, *Contesting Global Governance: Multilateral Economic Institutions and Global Social Movements*, Chapter 3, pp. 67–108. Cambridge: Cambridge University Press.

OECD. 1981. *International Investment and Multinational Enterprises: Recent International Direct Investment Trends.* Paris: OECD.

Offer, A. 1985. "The Working Classes, British Naval Plans, and the Coming of the Great War." *Past and Present*, 107, 204–26.

Okayama, Reiko. 1987. "Industrial Relations in the Japanese Automobile Industry 1945–70: The Case of Toyota." In S. Tolliday and J. Zeitlin, eds., *The Automobile Industry and Its Workers: Between Fordism and Flexibility*, pp. 168–89. New York: St. Martin's Press.

Ong, Aihwa. 1987. *Spirits of Resistance and Capitalist Discipline: Factory Women in Malaysia.* Albany: State University of New York Press.

O'Rourke Kevin H., and Jeffrey G. Williamson. 1999. *Globalization and History: The Evolution of a Nineteenth Century Atlantic Economy.* Cambridge, MA: MIT Press.

Ozawa, Terutomo. 1979. *Multinationalism, Japanese Style.* Princeton, NJ: Princeton University Press.

Ozga, Jenny. 1988a. "Introduction: Teaching, Professionalism and Work." In Jenny Ozga, ed., *Schoolwork: Interpreting the Labour Process of Teaching*, pp. ix–xv. Philadelphia: Open University Press.

Ozga, Jenny, ed., 1988b. *Schoolwork: Interpreting the Labour Process of Teaching*. Philadelphia: Open University Press.

Paige, Jeffery M. 1975. *Agrarian Revolution: Social Movements and Export Agriculture in the Underdeveloped World*. New York: Macmillan.

Pan, Philip P. 2002. "'High Tide' of Labor Unrest in China," *Washington Post*, January 21, p. A1.

Panitch, Leo. 1977. "The Development of Corporatism in Liberal Democracies." *Comparative Political Studies*, 10 (1), April, 61–90.

1980. "Recent theorizations of corporatism: reflections on a growth industry." *British Journal of Sociology*, 31 (2), June, 159–87.

1981. "Trade Unions and the Capitalist State." *New Left Review*, 125, January/February, 21–43.

2000. "Reflections on Strategy for Labour." In Leo Panitch and Colin Leys, eds., *Socialist Register 2001* (Working Classes, Global Realities), pp. 367–92. London: Merlin Press.

Park, Y., and K. Anderson. 1992. "The Experience of Japan in Historical and International Perspective." In Kym Anderson, ed., *New Silk Roads: East Asia and World Textile Markets*, pp. 15–29. Cambridge: Cambridge University Press.

Perlmutter, Ted. 1991. "Comparing Fordist Cities: The Logic of Urban Crisis and Union Response in Turin 1950–1975, and Detroit 1915–1945." Center for European Studies Working Paper Series, no. 31. Cambridge, MA: Harvard University.

Perrone, Luca. 1984. "Positional Power, Strikes and Wages." *American Sociological Review*, XLIX (3), June, 412–26.

Phelps Brown, Henry, and M. H. Browne. 1968. *A Century of Pay*. New York: Macmillan.

Phillips, Anne, and Barbara Taylor. 1980. "Sex and Skill: Notes towards a Feminist Economics." *Feminist Review*, 6, 57–79.

Piore, Michael J. 1979. *Birds of Passage: Migrant Labor and Industrial Societies*. Cambridge: Cambridge University Press.

Pitcher, Brian L., Robert L. Hamblin, and Jerry L. L. Miller.1978. "The Diffusion of Collective Violence." *American Sociological Review*, 43 (1), February, 23–35.

Piven, Frances Fox, ed., 1992. *Labor Parties in Postindustrial Societies*. New York: Oxford.

1995. "Is It Global Economics or Neo-Laissez-Faire?" *New Left Review*, 213, 107–14.

Piven, Frances Fox and Richard A. Cloward. 1977. *Poor Peoples Movements*. New York: Vintage Books.

1992. "Normalizing Collective Protest." In Aldon D. Morris and Carol McClurg Mueller, eds., *Frontiers in Social Movement Theory*, pp. 301–25. New Haven, CT: Yale University Press.

2000. "Power Repertoires and Globalization." *Politics and Society*, 28 (3), September, 413–30.

References

2001. "Disrupting Cyberspace: A New Frontier for Labor Activism?" *New Labor Forum*, 8, Spring–Summer, 91–4.

Podobnik, Bruce. 2000. *Global Energy Shifts: Future Possibilities in Historical Perspective*. PhD Thesis, The Johns Hopkins University, Baltimore.

Polanyi, Karl. [1944] 1957. *The Great Transformation*. Boston: Beacon.

Pollack, Andrew. 1993. "Japanese Starting to Link Pay to Performance, Not Tenure," *New York Times*, October 2, p. A1.

Post, Ken. 1988. "The Working Class in North Viet Nam and the Launching of the Building of Socialism." *Journal of Asian and African Studies*, 23 (1–2), 141–55.

Quadagno, Jill, and Stan J. Knapp. 1992. "Have Historical Sociologists Forsaken Theory: Thoughts on the History/Theory Relationship." *Sociological Methods and Research*, 20 (4), May, 481–507.

Radosh, Ronald. 1969. *American Labor and United States Foreign Policy*. New York: Random House.

Reyes, Teófilo. 2001. "Will the Drive to War Kill International Labor Solidarity?" *Labor Notes*, 271, October, 1–2.

Riddle, Dorothy I. 1986. *Service-Led Growth: The Role of the Service Sector in World Development*. New York: Praeger.

Ritter, G. 1970. *The Sword and the Scepter: The Problems of Militarism in Germany, Vol. 2*. Coral Gables, FL: University of Miami Press.

Roberts, Bryan R. 1995. *The Making of Citizens: Cities of Peasants Revisited*. London: Arnold.

Robinson, William I., and Jerry Harris. 2000. "Towards a Global Ruling Class? Globalization and the Transnational Capitalist Class." *Science and Society*, 64 (1), 11–54.

Rodgers, Ronald A. 1996. "Industrial Relations in the Korean Auto Industry: The Implications of Industrial Sector Requirements and Societal Effects for International Competitiveness." In F. C. Deyo, ed., *Social Reconstructions of the World Automobile Industry*, pp. 87–135. New York: St. Martin's Press.

Rodríguez-Pose, Andrés, and Glauco Arbix. 2001. "Strategies of Waste: Bidding Wars in the Brazilian Automobile Sector." *International Journal of Urban and Regional Research*, 25 (1), 134–54.

Rodrik, Dani. 1997. *Has Globalization Gone Too Far?* Washington, DC: Institute for International Economics.

Roediger, David R. 1991. *The Wages of Whiteness: Race and the Making of the American Working Class*. London: Verso.

Rollier, Matteo. 1986. "Changes in Industrial Relations at Fiat." In O. Jacobi et al., eds., *Technological Change, Rationalisation and Industrial Relations*, pp. 116–33. London: Croom Helm.

Rose, Sonya O. 1992. *Limited Livelihoods: Gender and Class in Nineteenth-Century England*. Berkeley: University of California Press.

1997. "Class Formation and the Quintessential Worker." Chapter 4 in John R. Hall, ed., *Reworking Class*. Pp. 133–66. Ithaca, NY: Cornell University Press.

Rosecrance, R. 1963. *Action and Reaction in World Politics*. Boston: Little, Brown.

Rosenberg, Hans. 1943. "Political and Social Consequences of the Great Depression of 1873–1896 in Central Europe." *Economic History Review* 13, 58–73.

Ross, Arthur M., and Paul T. Hartman. 1960. *Changing Patterns of Industrial Conflict.* New York: Wiley.

Ross, Robert J. S. 1982. "Capital Mobility, Branch Plant Location and Class Power." Paper presented at the Annual Meeting of the Society for the Study of Social Problems, San Francisco, September.

Ross, Robert J. S., and Kent Trachte. 1990. *Global Capitalism: The New Leviathan.* Albany: State University of New York Press.

Rostow, Walter W. 1960. *The Stages of Economic Growth: A Non-Communist Manifesto.* Cambridge: Cambridge University Press.

Rubenstein, James M. 1992. *The Changing US Auto Industry: A Geographical Analysis.* London: Routledge.

Ruggie, John G. 1982. "International Regimes, Transactions and Change: Embedded Liberalism in the Postwar Economic Order." *International Organization* 36 (2), 379–415.

Rupert, Mark. 1995. *Producing Hegemony: The Politics of Mass Production and American Global Power.* Cambridge: Cambridge University Press.

Sachiko, Takahashi. 1986. "Weary Wives – A Glance into Japanese Homes." *AMPO Japan-Asia Quarterly Review*, 18 (2–3), 65–9.

Sako, Mari. 1997. "Introduction: Forces for Homogeneity and Diversity in the Japanese Industrial Relations System." In M. Sako and H. Sato, eds., *Japanese Labour and Management in Transition*, pp. 1–24. London: Routledge.

Sarkar, Mahua. 1993. "Labor Protest and Capital Relocation in a Labor-Intensive Industry: Textiles in the 19th and 20th Century World Economy." Paper presented at the Social Science History Association Meeting, Baltimore, November.

Sassen, Saskia. 1988. *The Mobility of Labor and Capital.* Cambridge: Cambridge University Press.

  1999a. "Embedding the Global in the National: Implications for the Role of the State." In David A. Smith, Dorothy J. Solinger, and Steven C. Topik, eds., *States and Sovereignty in the Global Economy*, pp. 158–171. London: Routledge.

  1999b. "A New Emergent Hegemonic Structure?" *Political Power and Social Theory*, 13, 277–289.

  2000. *Cities in the World Economy* (second edition). Thousand Oaks, CA: Pine Forge Press.

  2001. *The Global City: New York, London, Tokyo,* (second edition). Princeton, NJ: Princeton University Press.

Saxton, Alexander. 1971. *The Indispensable Enemy: Labor and the Anti-Chinese Movement in California.* Berkeley: University of California Press.

Schoenberger, Erica. 1997. *The Cultural Crisis of the Firm.* Cambridge, MA: Blackwell Publishers.

Schumpeter, Joseph. 1954. *Capitalism, Socialism and Democracy.* London: Allen & Unwin.

Schurmann, Franz. 1974. *The Logic of World Power: An Inquiry into the Origins, Currents and Contradictions of World Politics.* New York: Pantheon.

Scott, James. 1985. *Weapons of the Weak.* New Haven, CT: Yale University Press.

References

Screpanti, Ernesto. 1987. "Long Cycles of Strike Activity: An Empirical Investigation." *British Journal of Industrial Relations*, XXV (1), March, 99–124.

Sedgwick, David. 1997. "VW, Suppliers Work Side by Side, Seek Big Gains in Productivity, at 'Factory of the Future' in Brazil," *Automotive News*, June 9, p. 3.

Seidman, Ann, and Neva Seidman. 1977. *South Africa and US Multinational Corporations*. Westport, CT: Lawrence Hill.

Seidman, Gay W. 1994. *Manufacturing Militance: Workers' Movements in Brazil and South Africa, 1970–1985*. Berkeley: University of California Press.

Semmel, Bernard.1960. *Imperialism and Social Reform*. Cambridge, MA: Harvard University Press.

Sewell, Jr., William H. 1986. "Artisans, Factory Workers, and the Formation of the French Working Class, 1789–1848." In Ira Katznelson and Aristide R. Zolberg, eds., *Working Class Formation*, pp. 45–70. Princeton, NJ: Princeton University Press.

1993. "Toward a Post-materialist Rhetoric for Labor History". In Lenard R. Berlanstein, ed., *Rethinking Labor History*, pp. 15–38. Urbana: University of Illinois Press.

Shaiken, Harley. 1995. "Lean Production in a Mexican Context." In S. Babson, ed., *Lean Work: Empowerment and Exploitation in the Global Automobile Industry*, pp. 247–59. Detroit: Wayne State University Press.

Shalev, Michael. 1978. "Lies, Damned Lies and Strike Statistics: The Measurement of Trends in Industrial Conflict." In C. Crouch and A. Pizzorno, eds., *The Resurgence of Class Conflict in Western Europe Since 1968*, vol. 1, pp.1–19. New York: Holmes & Meier.

1992. "The Resurgence of Labor Quiescence." In Marino Regini, ed., *The Future of Labour Movements*, pp. 102–32. London: Sage.

Shefter, Martin. 1986. "Trade Unions and Political Machines: The Organization and Disorganization of the American Working Class in the Late Nineteenth Century." In Ira Katznelson and Aristide R. Zolberg, eds., *Working-Class Formation*, pp. 197–276. Princeton, NJ: Princeton University Press.

Shorter, Edward, and Charles Tilly. 1974. *Strikes in France, 1830–1968*. Cambridge: Cambridge University Press.

Silver, Beverly J. 1990. "The Contradictions of Semiperipheral Success: The Case of Israel." In William G. Martin, ed., *Semiperipheral States in the World-Economy*, pp. 161–181. New York: Greenwood.

1992. *Labor Unrest and Capital Accumulation on a World Scale*. PhD Dissertation, SUNY-Binghamton.

1995a. "Labor Unrest and World-Systems Analysis: Premises, Concepts and Measurement." *Review* (Fernand Braudel Center), 18 (1), Winter, 7–34.

1995b. "World-Scale Patterns of Labor-Capital Conflict: Labor Unrest, Long Waves, and Cycles of World Hegemony." *Review* (Fernand Braudel Center), 18 (1), Winter, 155–92.

1997. "Turning Points of Workers' Militancy in the World Automobile Industry, 1930s–1990s". *Research in the Sociology of Work*, 6, 43–71.

Silver, Beverly J. and Giovanni Arrighi. 2000. "Workers North and South." In Leo Panitch and Colin Leys, eds., *Socialist Register* 2001 (Theme: Working Classes: Global Realities), pp. 53–76. London: Merlin Press.

Silver, Beverly J. and Eric Slater. 1999. "The Social Origins of World Hegemonies." In G. Arrighi and B. J. Silver, *Chaos and Governance in the Modern World System*, Chapter 3, pp. 151–216. Minneapolis: University of Minnesota Press.

Silver, Beverly J., Giovanni Arrighi, and Melvyn Dubofsky, eds., 1995. "Labor Unrest in the World Economy, 1870–1990." A special issue of *Review* (Fernand Braudel Center), 18 (1), Winter.

Singer, Daniel. 1982. *The Road to Gdansk.* New York: Monthly Review Press.

Singleton, John. 1990. "Showing the White Flag: The Lancashire Cotton Industry." *Business History*, 32 (4), 129–49.

1997. *The World Textile Industry.* London: Routledge.

Skocpol, Theda. 1979. *States and Social Revolutions.* Cambridge: Cambridge University Press.

Slaughter, Jane, and Kim Moody. 2001. "American History 101: War Fever Allows Government to Clamp Down on Unions," *Labor Notes*, 271, October, 3.

Smith, William C., and Roberto Patricio Korzeniewicz. 1997. "Latin America and the Second Great Transformation." In W. C. Smith and R. P. Korzeniewicz, eds., *Politics, Social Change and Economic Restructuring in Latin America*, pp. 1–20. Boulder, CO: Lynne Rienner.

Smitka, Michael J. 1991. *Competitive Ties: Subcontracting in the Japanese Automotive Industry.* New York: Columbia University Press.

Snyder, David, and William R. Kelly. 1977. "Conflict Intensity, Media Sensitivity, and the Validity of Newspaper Data." *American Sociological Review*, XLII (1), February, 104–23.

Snyder, David, and Charles Tilly. 1972. "Collective Violence in France." *American Sociological Review*, XXXVII (5), October, 520–32.

Solinger, Dorothy J. 1999. *Contesting Citizenship in Urban China: Peasant Migrants, the State and the Logic of the Market.* Berkeley: University of California Press.

2001. "WTO and China's Workers." Paper presented at the Woodrow Wilson Center, Washington, DC, December 12.

Somers, Margaret. 1995. "The 'Misteries' of Property: Relationality, Rural-Industrialization, and Community in Chartist Narratives of Political Rights." In John Brewer and Susan Staves, eds., *Early Modern Conceptions of Property*, pp. 62–92. London: Routledge.

Sonn, Hochul. 1997. "The 'Late Blooming' of the South Korean Labor Movement." *Monthly Review*, 49 (3), 117–29.

Southall, Roger. 1985. "Monopoly Capitalism and Industrial Unionism in the South African Motor Industry." *Labour, Capital and Society* 18 (2), November, 304–42.

Standard and Poor's. 2002. *Industry Surveys: Auto & Auto Parts*, June 13.

Stark, David. 1986. "Rethinking Internal Labor Markets: New Insights from a Comparative Perspective." *American Sociological Review*, 51 (4), August, 492–504.

Stavrianos, L. S. 1981. *Global Rift: The Third World Comes of Age.* New York: William Morrow and Company.

References

Steven, Rob. 1997. "Japanese Investments in Thailand, Indonesia and Malaysia: A Decade of JASEAN." In Joe Moore, ed., *The Other Japan: Conflict, Compromise, and Resistance Since 1945*, pp. 199–245. Armonk, NY: M. E. Sharpe. New edition.

Stiglitz, Joseph E. 2001. "Foreword." Karl Polanyi, *The Great Transformation: The Political and Economic Origins of Our Time* (second edition), pp. vii–xvii. Boston: Beacon Press.

Stohl, Michael. 1980. "The Nexus of Civil and International Conflict." In Ted Robert Gurr, ed., *Handbook of Political Conflict: Theory and Research*, pp. 297–330. New York: The Free Press.

Sugimoto, Yoshio. 1978a. "Measurement of Popular Disturbance." *Social Science Research*, VII (3), September, 284–97.

1978b. "Quantitative Characteristics of Popular Disturbances in Post-Occupation Japan (1952–1960)." *Journal of Asian Studies*, XXXVII (2), February, 273–91.

Sumiko, Takagi. 1986. "Women on the Labor Front." *AMPO: Japan-Asia Quarterly Review*, 18 (2–3), 48–54.

Tabb, William. 1997. "Globalization Is *an* Issue, the Power of Capital Is *the* Issue." *Monthly Review*, 49 (2), 20–30.

Tabili, Laura. 1994. *"We Ask for British Justice": Workers and Racial Difference in Late Imperial Britain*. Ithaca, NY: Cornell University Press.

Tarrow, Sidney. 1989. *Democracy and Disorder: Protest and Politics in Italy, 1965–1975*. Oxford: Oxford University Press.

1998. "Fishnets, Internets and Catnets: Globalization and Social Movements." In Michael P. Hanagan, Leslie P. Moch, and Wayne te Brake, eds., *Challenging Authority*, pp. 228–44. Minneapolis: University of Minnesota Press.

Taylor, A. J. P. 1954. *The Struggle for Mastery in Europe, 1848–1918*. London: Oxford University Press.

Taylor, M. 1986. "The product-cycle model: a critique." *Environment and Planning A*, 18, 751–61.

Therborn, Goran. 1977. "The Rule of Capital and the Rise of Democracy." *New Left Review* 103, 3–41.

Thompson, E. P. 1966. *The Making of the English Working Class*. New York: Vintage Books.

1978. "Eighteenth-Century English Society: Class Struggle without Class?" *Social History*, 3/2, May, 146–64.

Tilly, Charles. 1978. *From Mobilization to Revolution*. Reading, MA: Addison-Wesley.

1981. "Computing History." In C. Tilly, ed., *As History Meets Sociology*, pp. 53–83. New York: Academic Press.

1984. *Big Structures, Large Processes, Huge Comparisons*. New York: Russell Sage Foundation.

1989. "Introduction: The Effects of Short-Term Variation." In L. Haimson and C. Tilly, eds., *Strikes, Wars, and Revolutions in International Perspective*, pp. 433–48. Cambridge: Cambridge University Press.

1990. *Coercion, Capital, and European States, A.D. 990–1990*. Cambridge, MA: Basil Blackwell.

1995. "Globalization Threatens Labor's Rights." *International Labor and Working-Class History* 47, 1–23.

Tilly, Charles, Louise Tilly, and Richard Tilly. 1975. *The Rebellious Century, 1830–1930*. Cambridge, MA: Harvard University Press.

Tolliday, Steven. 1987. "Management and Labour in Britain, 1896–1939." In S. Tolliday and J. Zeitlin, eds., *The Automobile Industry and Its Workers: Between Fordism and Flexibility*, pp. 29–56. New York: St. Martin's Press.

Torigian, Michael. 1999. "The Occupation of the Factories: Paris 1936, Flint 1937." *Comparative Studies in Society and History*, 41 (2), 324–47.

Traub, James. 2000. "This Campus Is Being Simulated." *New York Times Magazine*, November 19, 88–93 ff.

Treece, James B. 1997a. "GM Kicks Off Major Push in China," *Automotive News*, June 16, pp. 1 & 34.

1997b. "Warning on Overcapacity Has Korean Industry in an Uproar," *Automotive News*, June 30, p. 4.

1997c. "China Takes Hard Road to a Market Economy," *Automotive News*, July 14, p. 1.

Tronti, Mario. 1971. *Operai e Capitale*. Turin: Einaudi.

Truchil, Barry E. 1988. *Capital-Labor Relations in the U.S. Textile Industry*. New York: Praeger.

Tsurumi, Patricia E. 1990. *Factory Girls: Women in the Thread Mills of Meiji Japan*. Princeton, NJ: Princeton University Press.

Uchitelle, Louis, and N. R. Kleinfeld. 1996. "The Downsizing of America: On the Battlefields of Business, Millions of Casualties," *The New York Times*, March 3, p. A1.

UNCTAD. 2000. *World Investment Report 2000*. New York: United Nations.

UNDP. 1992. *Human Development Report 1992*. New York: Oxford University Press.

UNESCO (various). *Statistical Yearbook*. Paris: UNESCO.

Van Onselen, Charles. 1976. *Chibaro: African Mine Labour in Southern Rhodesia, 1900–1933*. London: Pluto Press.

Vernon, Raymond. 1966. "International Investment and International Trade in the Product Cycle." *Quarterly Journal of Economics*, 80 (2), 190–207.

Vogel, Ezra F., and David L. Lindauer. 1997. "Toward a Social Compact for South Korean Labor." In D. L. Lindauer, J. Kim, J. Lee, H. Kim, J. Son, and E. Vogel, eds., *The Strains of Economic Growth: Labor Unrest and Social Dissatisfaction in Korea*, pp. 93–121. Cambridge, MA: Harvard University Press.

Volpato, Giuseppe. 1987. "The Automobile Industry in Transition: Product Market Changes and Firm Strategies in the 1970s and 1980s." In S. Tolliday and J. Zeitlin, eds., *The Automobile Industry and Its Workers: Between Fordism and Flexibility*, pp. 193–223. New York: St. Martin's Press.

Wade, Robert. 1990. *Governing the Market: Economic Theory and the Role of Government in East Asian Industrialization*. Princeton, NJ: Princeton University Press.

Walder, Andrew G. 1986. *Communist Neo-Traditionalism: Work and Authority in Chinese Industry*. Berkeley: University of California Press.

Waldinger, Roger, Chris Erickson, Ruth Milkman, Daniel J. B. Mitchell, Abel Valenzuela, Kent Wong, and Maurice Zeitlin. 1998. "Helots No More:

References

A Case Study of the Justice for Janitors Campaign in Los Angeles." In K. Bronfenbrenner, S. Friedman, R. W. Hurd, R. A. Oswald, and R. L. Seeber, eds., *Organizing to Win*, Chapter 6, pp. 102–19.

Wall Street Journal. 2000. "Work Week: A Special News Report About Life on the Job and Trends Taking Shape There," *Wall Street Journal*, October 17, p. 1.

Wallace, Michael, Larry Griffin, and Beth Rubin. 1989. "The Positional Power of American Labor, 1963–1977." *American Sociological Review*, 54 (2), 197–214.

Wallerstein, Immanuel. 1974. *The Modern World System I. Capitalist Agriculture and the Origins of the European World-Economy in the Sixteenth Century*. New York: Academic Press.

1979. *The Capitalist World-Economy*. Cambridge: Cambridge University Press.

1995. "Response: Declining States, Declining Rights?" *International Labor and Working Class History*, 47, 24–7.

Walton, John. 1984. *Reluctant Rebels: Comparative Studies of Revolution and Underdevelopment*. New York: Columbia University Press.

Walton, John and Ragin, Charles. 1990. "Global and National Sources of Political Protest: Third World Responses to the Debt Crisis." *American Sociological Review*, 55, December, 876–90.

Weinraub, Bernard. 2000. "Strike Fears Grip Hollywood as Unions Flex New Muscle," *New York Times*, October 1, pp. A1, A25.

Western, Bruce. 1995. "A Comparative Study of Working-Class Disorganization: Union Decline in Eighteen Advanced Capitalist Countries." *American Sociological Review*, 60 (2), April, 179–201.

Williams, William A. 1969. *The Roots of the Modern American Empire: A Study of the Growth and Shaping of Social Consciousness in a Marketplace Society*. New York: Random House.

Wolf, Eric. 1969. *Peasant Wars of the Twentieth Century*. New York: Harper and Row.

Wood, Phillip J. 1991. "Determinants of Industrialization on the North American Periphery." In Jerry Leiter, Michael D. Schulman and Rhonda Zingraff, eds., *Hanging by a Thread: Social Change in Southern Textiles*, pp. 58–78. Ithaca, NY: ILR Press.

Woods, Ellen Meiksens, Peter Meiksens, and Michael Yates, eds., 1998. *Rising from the Ashes? Labor in the Age of Global Capitalism*. New York: Monthly Review Press.

World Bank. 1984. *World Tables*. Vols. 1 & 2. Washington, DC: World Bank.

2001. *World Development Indicators*. CD-ROM, Washington, DC: World Bank.

Wright, Erik O. 1997. *Class Counts: Comparative Studies in Class Analysis*. Cambridge: Cambridge University Press.

2000. "Working-Class Power, Capitalist-Class Interests, and Class Compromise." *American Journal of Sociology*, 105 (4), January, 957–1002.

Zhang, Jikang. 1999. "Multinational Corporations' Investment in China and Its Effects on the Chinese Market – The Case of the Automobile Industry". *Chinese Industrial Economy* (Beijing), vol. 4 (in Chinese).

Zolberg, Aristide. 1995. "Response: Working-Class Dissolution." *International Labor and Working Class History*, 47, 28–38.

227

Index

Abbott, Andrew, 136
Abendroth, Wolfgang, 134, 139.
Abo, Tetsuo, 67
Abrahamian, Ervand, 164
Adler, Glenn, 60
Africa, 5, 23–4, 27, 33, 115, 126, 144,
  145, 148, 156, 185, 204; *see also*
  under names of individual countries
Agence France-Presse, 11
Aglietta, Michel, 153
Albania, 204
Algeria, 145, 204
Altshuler, Alan, 50–1
American Automobile Manufacturers
  Association (AAMA), 61, 64, 65, 67
Anderson, K., 88
anti-globalization protests, 2, 9, 11,
  17–18, 117–18, 167, 177
Aoyama, Yukio, 107
Appelbaum, Richard P., 111
Apple, Nixon, 125, 154
Arbix, Glauco, 57
Argentina, 43, 44, 45, 54, 82, 116, 167,
  195, 204
armaments industry, 132–3, 141, 146–7
Arrighi, Giovanni, 6, 10, 13, 22–3, 36,
  38, 40, 48, 50, 71, 79, 106, 132, 133,
  136, 150, 153, 154, 157, 159, 160,
  166, 177, 181, 196
Asia, 5, 36, 66–7, 71–2, 95, 105–6, 126,
  137, 144, 145, 148, 157, 191, 204;

see also under names of individual
  countries
associational bargaining power, 13–16,
  19, 47, 49–50, 60, 84, 90–1, 93–4,
  110–3, 120–1, 123, 172–3; *see also*
  bargaining power of labor
Australia, 36, 82, 116, 191, 204
Austria, 143, 204
automobile industry, 32, 38–9, 41–74,
  75–85, 89–97, 103–6, 114–15, 117,
  119–20, 122–3, 159, 163–4, 168–72
Automotive News, 57
aviation, 15, 99–103, 115, 123, 163

Ball, Stephen J., 119
Bangladesh, 204
bargaining power of labor, 4–6, 12–16,
  18–19, 33, 41–2, 53, 71, 83–4, 92,
  103, 108–9, 138, 146–7, 150,
  159–60, 167; relationship with labor
  militancy, 15–16, 81, 89–90, 92,
  96–7, 172; *see also* associational
  bargaining power; marketplace
  bargaining power; workplace
  bargaining power
Barraclough, Geoffrey, 135, 147, 148
Barton, Ava, 22
Bataille, Georges, 158
Beinin, Joe, 158
Beittel, Mark, 58–9
Belgium, 82, 116, 140, 143, 204

229

Index

Index

Index